THE THEOLOGY OF CHRIST:
SOURCES

CONTEMPORARY COLLEGE THEOLOGY SERIES

GENERAL EDITORS: J. FRANK DEVINE, S.J.
BOSTON COLLEGE
RICHARD W. ROUSSEAU, S.J.
FAIRFIELD UNIVERSITY

THE THEOLOGY OF CHRIST: SOURCES is one of the volumes in the
Historical Theology Section of the Series

The Theology of Christ: Sources

EDITED BY

VINCENT ZAMOYTA, Ph.D.
ASSOCIATE PROFESSOR OF THEOLOGY
ST. JOHN'S UNIVERSITY, JAMAICA, NEW YORK

THE BRUCE PUBLISHING COMPANY / Milwaukee

Library of Congress Catalog Card Number: 67–24540

© 1967 THE BRUCE PUBLISHING COMPANY
MADE IN THE UNITED STATES OF AMERICA

To four friends
whose friendship has taught me more of Christ than multitudes
of books

Dennis Ahearn, Sr.
Roseanna Beary
Raymond Brustman
Henry Ford Moore

EDITORS' INTRODUCTION

THE CONTEMPORARY CATHOLIC COLLEGE THEOLOGY SERIES

This series begins with the presupposition that theology is necessary. It is necessary if Christian intelligence is to search for meaning in its dialogue with God, man and the world. Since Christian intelligence is not the exclusive possession of the theological specialist or the cleric, the search must be carried out in all those areas of life, secular as well as religious, including the college situation, where meaning is to be found.

This search is a peaceful one for in some mysterious way it has already achieved its goal: the vision of faith and the fullness of love. Still it remains a relentless and universal search. Its inner certainty must radiate out not only to the edges of the mind but also into the farthest recesses of the world. We could call it "lay" theology but this word seems too pale a description for such an exciting enterprise of the Christian life.

In view of this the editors of this series are convinced that new questions had to be asked, new structures created and new books written. These books would be neither catechetical nor apologetic. They would be purely and simply theological. The primary audience would be believers but all thinking men would find them useful. In scope they would be broad enough to insure perspective. They would be scholarly enough to be intellectually relevant. They would avoid pedantry. In short, they would try to present a rich and deep understanding of Christian revelation in such a way that to-day's college students would be able to respond with a Christian faith and life that are both culturally mature and scientifically precise. Finally the authors of these books would be, for the most part, teachers in colleges and universities where much of the contemporary theological dialogue is now going on.

The series falls into four parts: biblical, historical, ecclesial and ethical. The divisions were not predetermined by the editors. They follow the shape of the most vigorous theological work now being done.

The books in the biblical section are intended to go beyond the traditional treatment of bible history and the now familiar perspectives of salvation history. They concentrate on various books of the Bible. Their method has been especially designed for college work. Tentatively, it might be called "exegetical theology." Every verse is not considered after the fashion of a commentary, nor are narratives developed as a biography, nor is there any attempt to create large theological syntheses. Rather the individual books are studied in chronological sequence; key passages are treated in detail and the rest are summarized. At the same time some attention is paid to the growing theological synthesis.

Since scholastic theology is already represented by individual works and sets of textbooks, the books in our historical section study dogmatic questions from a developmental point of view. In this way the editors hope to make the college students more aware of the great wealth of theological thinking that recent historico-theological studies have uncovered. This method which is more inductive than deductive should happily coincide with the thought processes of the college students. The three basic poles for synthesis are: God, Christ, and Man. In each area the historical development will be studied and a significant number of basic source texts presented. The problems raised in these studies will range all the way from Augustinian pessimism to Teilhardian optimism.

The textbooks for the third part of the series will deal with issues of great contemporary importance. They will examine questions discussed by the Second Vatican Council. As the name implies, ecclesial theology must first concern itself with the Church, what the Church knows herself to be as expressed in the insights of the new Constitution of the Church and with the more significant of the Church's allied concerns: other world religions, American Protestantism, its history, its motivating forces and spirit, and finally, the new sacramental theology so enriched by the many magnificent liturgical advances. All of this growth has brought a wider and deeper appreciation of the nature of the Roman Catholic Church and her relationship rooted in understanding and love with the whole world.

The fourth and final section of the series is devoted explicitly to Christian moral response. The editors subscribe to the position that the proper place for the Catholic college or university to examine ethical questions is in a revelational rather than in a purely philosophical context. In addition to the "virtue" divisions of the *Summa* or the classic moral theology text, designed primarily for confessors, there is a need and a place for a "Christian ethics" that reflects the new insights which both biblical and dogmatic theology can provide. These books will strive to be openly Christian in spirit, eclectic in approach, up-to-date in scholarship and they will address themselves to those ethical problems which are most real to the modern American mind.

Finally, the editors would like to express their thanks to all those whose interest, advice and cooperation have made this series possible. They are especially grateful to Mr. William May of The Bruce Publishing Company, who not only initiated the project and sustained it through the inevitable disappointments and complications, but contributed so much of his editorial skill to its final shape. To the individual authors who so graciously added to their heavy burden of academic responsibility by undertaking these books, we can only express the hope that their share in the shaping and influencing of the American Catholic community of today and of tomorrow will be far more meaningful to them than any meager thanks of ours.

The Editors,
   REV. J. FRANK DEVINE, S.J.,
   Boston College
   REV. RICHARD W. ROUSSEAU, S.J.,
   Fairfield University

GENERAL INTRODUCTION

Theology is a sacred science embodying the methods and the results of the man of faith's continued and devoted effort both to analyze and to synthesize all that is given in the divine revelation entrusted to the Church by the mediator between God and man, Jesus Christ. It is his attempt to see God's revealed truth both as a whole, in the true wisdom of a total vision, and also in terms of true distinctions which relate the various parts to the whole and to each other. It is, furthermore, an effort to integrate the data of revelation and to show its implications in all fields of human knowledge. The data of theology derive from Holy Scripture and Tradition interpreted by the living *magisterium* of the Church.

Theology became a possibility the moment God first spoke to man. And the moment man first heard God speak, theology became a reality and a necessity. The words and deeds of God are received by man only in a way that is in harmony with his being, only in a totally human way. Once God confronted man with his word and man listened with responsiveness, it was inevitable that the mind of man would seek evermore to penetrate that word, that his heart might follow safely and his spirit rejoice truly.

Once confronted with his object, the theologian becomes a true scientist, impelled by the desire of knowing, yet proceeding from an advantaged position as a man of faith connaturally enlightened[1] to comprehend in a real, though limited, way what belongs to him as his own yet is from above. Fascinated by its attraction, frustrated by his limitations, the theologian is compelled in faith to pursue the "power to comprehend . . . what is the breadth and length and height and depth, and to know the love of Christ which surpasses knowledge . . ." (Eph 3:18–19).

This volume of source texts in Christology is intended to help the undergraduate student reach some understanding and evaluation of the body of doctrine and major theological conclusions concerning the principal mysteries of the incarnation of Jesus Christ and his work of redemption.

CHRISTOLOGY — WHO IS JESUS OF NAZARETH?

Christology is the study of the person of Jesus, the carpenter and rabbi from Nazareth, whom "God has made

---

[1] "Not merely learning about divine things but also experiencing them — that does not come from mere intellectual acquaintance with the terms of scientific theology, but from loving the things of God and cleaving to them by affection. Fellow-feeling comes from fondness rather than from cognizance, for things understood are in the mind in the mind's own fashion, whereas desire goes out to things as they are in themselves; love would transform us into the very condition of their being. . . . so also the lover of divine matters divinely catches their gist." St. Thomas Aquinas, *de Divinis Nominibus*, ii, 4. T. Gilby, tr., from *St. Thomas Aquinas: Philosophical Texts* (New York: Oxford University Press, 1960), p. 33.

both Lord and Christ" (Acts 2:36).
The Gospel gives us the facts about
Jesus of Nazareth, but does not go
into any explanations of the facts.
Christology is concerned with meaningful explanations and determinations
about the God-man in regard to his
possession of divinity, of humanity,
and of the union of these in his one
being. The texts presented here com-
prise an account of what the Church
has taught about Jesus and what conclusions theologians have reached in
regard to Jesus from the data of the
New Testament and the living Tradition of the Church.

Soteriology, that part of theology
which deals with the redemption and
salvation wrought by Jesus, Messiah
and Lord, is so closely allied to Christology that the two form a unitary
study. There cannot be an authentic
Christology without an accompanying
soteriology; i.e., the full reality of who
Jesus is can be studied only in terms
of what he did and why he did it.
Just as the Israelites came in their
limited way to know who God is and
discovered their relationship to him
only in virtue of the acts of God — in
his revelation of himself as Lord of
creation and Lord of history — so also
the Word of God is revealed to us for
who he is in terms of those mighty
acts by which he accomplished the
redemption of all mankind. Jesus of
Nazareth re-created humanity through
his obedient immolation as the Suffering Servant of Yahweh and redirected
human history as the second Adam.

CHRISTOLOGICAL DEVELOPMENT — TILL
THE WHOLE TRUTH BE "SELF-BAL-
ANCED ON ITS CENTER HUNG"

The initial attempts to clarify the
meaning and implications of Word-

made-flesh as presented to us in the
Gospel resulted from the need to defend the reality of who Jesus is from
grossly falsifying misconceptions. At
the root of the question *Who is Jesus
of Nazareth?* lies an impenetrable mystery. Jesus, son of Mary, is God existing in another way. Man can neither
conceive nor imagine what is involved
in the terms of such a mystery. It is
a mystery concerning existence, of
"being" in act. With regard to the
redemption, what can man understand
of the desire of God to restore man by
dying for him? Yet man will seek to explain these things for himself, impelled
by a faith seeking understanding.

In the early Church the first implications which developed concerning
the nature of the mystery of the God-
man, Jesus of Nazareth, revolved
around the poles of the divine and the
human in him and took up solid
positions of affirmation and denial.
The Ebionites, "the poor ones," an
early and extremely ascetical group
of Jewish Christians, conceived of
Jesus as the human Messiah, denying
any personal aspect of divinity in him.
On the other hand, the Gnostics, "the
spiritualized ones," sought to preserve
the divine reality in Jesus at the expense of his humanity, maintaining
that the body of Jesus was merely
phantasmal, or that, in Jesus, God
temporarily inhabited a human being
by a sort of divine possession.

Later, theological thought shifted
from a predominantly either/or position to a more basic both/and standpoint, with varieties of emphasis
toward the polarity of the divine or
that of the human in Jesus. A diversity
of approaches evolved from the traditions derived from the two schools of
Antioch and of Alexandria, the former

emphasizing the human aspects of the Incarnate Word and the latter stressing his divinity. In the third and fourth centuries we find Arius asserting the unity of the Godhead to the loss of divinity in the human Son. Nestorius acknowledges both natures in Jesus but in a manner of existence which is so mutually exclusive that Jesus almost becomes two persons. The great difficulty of this age was to formulate with precision the nature of the union of the divine and the human in Jesus. The Council of Chalcedon (451) courageously combatted these heresies and their variants by laying down the terms of the Christological mystery: "one Christ in two natures, without confusion, without change, without division, without separation."

The basic determinations of the Councils of Nicea, Ephesus, Chalcedon, and Constantinople went through a period of assimilation and development up to and throughout the period of scholastic philosophy in the Middle Ages. Further conclusions developed within the framework of the expression of belief determined at the previous councils: having two natures meant that there are two wills in Jesus; since in the effects produced *ad extra* the Trinity acts as a whole, the Incarnation was not the independent act of the Second Person alone but rather of the complete Godhead. Christology of the person of Christ had developed apace with soteriology in the Fathers and early Doctors of the Church. Relating the Incarnation to the fall of man, St. Thomas Aquinas now stated that the former was contingent upon the latter, thus essentially linking Incarnation and Redemption. On the other hand, the Scotists held the view that the Word would have become flesh whether the fall had occurred or not. The great synthesis of Aquinas, his *Summa Theologiae,* integrated and related the great truths of faith, using the mystery of the Incarnation to form a firm dogmatic basis for his theology of grace and of the sacraments.

The Reformation theology of the sixteenth century accepted in general the traditional credal beliefs concerning the person of Christ and the mystery of the Redemption. However, in terms of emphasis the humanity of the Redeemer came to the fore, especially in aspects of the humility and sufferings of Christ. Christ is abject as he condescends to take on the conditions of humanity. His "emptying" of himself of his divinity in order to become man allows only intermittent use of his divine attributes. Jesus, the Man of Sorrows, becomes too human at the expense of his divinity. Later, in Lutheranism, for example, the effects of eighteenth-century rationalism tended increasingly to dilute all of its supernatural elements. This has been offset by a revival of Lutheran orthodoxy under the influence of Karl Barth and the soul-searching effects of the persecution of the Jews and the response of Christians in Hitler's Germany.

Reformed theologians in the nineteenth century reached an extreme in maintaining that in becoming man the Word abandoned altogether his divine attributes. For Schleiermacher the divinity of Christ consists only in his consciousness of his unique relation to God. For Albert Ritschl the judgment that Jesus of Nazareth is God is not a fact-judgment but rather a value-judgment. Some Protestant theologians of today hold that the subconscious mind of Jesus held the truth of his divine characteristics and that only by the normal and natural processes of the development of human consciousness did he become aware of them.[2]

Current Catholic Christology is breaking away from the repetition of ancient and well-used formulas. It is reexamining in a challenging way the thought of St. Thomas Aquinas. In the lead is Karl Rahner, whose stimulating viewpoints are presented in the introduction to the modern Catholic theologians in the last section of this book. To sum up both his efforts and those of Karl Adam, Jean Daniélou, and the others, we quote from the Jesuit Thomas Clarke: There is in current Catholic Christological thought:

First, an effort at integration, an attempt to integrate the conciliar with the scriptural, the ontological and objective with the psychological, subjective and personal, the sphere of being with the sphere of function, the strictly Christological with the soteriological, ecclesiological, sacramental, and eschatological. Secondly, an effort at balance, on every level, between the legitimate exigencies of Alexandria and Antioch, the descending and ascending Christologies. Thirdly, an effort at translation, at showing the relevance of the theology of the God-man to modern man's life, and especially

---

[2] In reading selections in this book taken from Protestant sources, it is of utmost importance to determine both the definition and the sense of the terms used. In most cases the selections are of such length that meanings can be inferred from the context in which the terms are used. In other cases the use of such a basic reference tool as *The Oxford Dictionary of the Christian Church* (New York: Oxford University Press, 1963) is indispensable. Traditional terms with a set meaning have, under the influence of various interpretations, no longer the same connotation as in Catholic orthodoxy.

at finding in the mystery of the Incarnation the solid basis of that integral Incarnationalism that Christians are seeking today.[3]

As with source material in modern Protestant Christology so also in regard to current Catholic Christology, it is difficult if not impossible to determine which material will be significant and of lasting worth theologically. One cannot tell what the frictions and attritions of time will allow to survive as having worthwhile value. Hence the attempt here is to point in the several directions in which current Christological thought is tending. With the rise of modern psychology, of theories of biological and of cosmic evolution, of historical process, of investigation into interpersonal relationships and the subjective factors which affect the apprehension of truth, man is progressively enlarging and deepening his knowledge of himself. As man gets to know more comprehensively what it is to be a human being, what constitutes human nature, the theologian energetically reapplies himself to the study of that man who is Jesus of Nazareth. His understanding of the divine pole in Christological study will always be deepened by further application to the sources of belief, by contemplation, and by that connaturality to the divine which is the fruit of living "the truth in charity," that faith by which the just man lives. And likewise the human pole of Christological study will always be the object of a reapplication to the Gospel of what man continues to learn about human nature from his continuing experience and accomplishments through the course of human history.

---

[3] *The Encounter with God* (New York: The Macmillan Company, 1962), pp. 55–56.

ACKNOWLEDGMENTS

We are grateful to the following publishers for permission to reprint copyrighted material:

Basil Blackwell, Oxford, for material from J. R. McCallom's *Abelard's Christian Theology;*
Burns, Oates, Ltd. (London), for material from Karl Adam's *The Christ of Faith;*
The Catholic University of America Press, for material from *St. Basil: Letters,* Vol. II; from *St. Augustine: Letters,* Vol. III; from St. Augustine's *City of God,* and from R. Arbesmann *et al., Tertullian: Apologetical Works;*
The Christian Heritage Press, for material from Thomas B. Falls, *St. Justin Martyr;*
Cima Publishers, for material from Glimm and others, *The Apostolic Fathers;*
T. and T. Clark, Ltd., Edinburgh, for material from Friedrich Schleiermacher's *The Christian Faith;*
Concordia Publishing House, for material from *What Luther Says,* used by permission;
Wm. Eerdmans Publishing Company, for material from the *Nicene and Post-Nicene Fathers of the Christian Church,* used by permission;
Harper and Row, Inc., and Wm. Collins and Sons, for material from *The Divine Milieu* and *The Future of Man* by Pierre Teilhard de Chardin;
Harper and Row, Inc., for material from A. C. McGiffert's *Protestant Thought Before Kant* and from Rudolph Bultmann's *Kerygma and Myth;*
Harvard University Press and the Loeb Classical Library, for material from *Boethius: The Theological Tractates,* translated by H. F. Stewart and E. I. Rand;
Helicon Press, for material from Volume I of Karl Rahner's *Theological Investigations;*
B. Herder Book Company, for material from St. Bonaventure's *Breviloquium;*
The John Knox Press, for material from Karl Barth's *The Humanity of God;*
The Macmillan Company, for material from St. Athanasius' *The Incarnation of the Word of God;*
McGraw-Hill Book Company, Inc., for material from St. Thomas Aquinas' *Summa Theologiae,* Vol. 50, © Blackfriars, 1965 and used by permission of McGraw-Hill Book Company;
The Newman-Paulist Press, for material from Carmody and Clarke's *Word and Redeemer* and from St. Irenaeus' *Proof of the Apostolic Preaching;*
The Open Court Publishing Co., La Salle, Illinois, for material from *Saint Anselm: Basic Writings;*
Random House (Pantheon), New York, for material from Karl Adam's *The Christ of Faith* and from Romano Guardini's *The Humanity of Christ;*
Henry Regnery Co., for material from *The Sunday Sermons of the Great Fathers* and from Jean Daniélou's *The Lord of History;*
S.C.M. Press, London, for material from *The Christology of the Later Fathers;* from *Cyril of Jerusalem and Nemesius of Emesa;* from Emil Brunner's *Truth as Encounter,* © 1943 by the Westminster Press and 1967 by W. L. Jenkins; from *Calvin: Institutes of the Christian Religion,* I, LCC, Vol. XX, edited by John T. McNeill and translated by Ford Lewis Battles, © 1960 by W. L. Jenkins; and from John A. T. Robinson's *Honest to God,* © S.C.M. Press Limited, 1963;
Sheed and Ward, Inc., for material from *Christ the Sacrament of the Encounter With God,* © Sheed and Ward, Ltd., 1963, published by Sheed and Ward, Inc., New York;
S.P.C.K., London, for material from *Irenaeus: Against Heretics;* from *Tertullian's Treatise Against Praxeas;*

The Westminster Press, Philadelphia, for excerpts from the following books: From *Truth as Being* by Emil Brunner. © 1943 by the Westminster Press and 1967 by W. L. Jenkins. Used by permission; from *Calvin: Institutes of the Christian Religion*, I, LCC, Vol. XX, edited by John T. McNeill and translated by Ford Lewis Battles. The Westminster Press. © 1960, W. L. Jenkins. Used by permission; from *Honest to God*, by John A. T. Robinson, published in the U. S. A. by The Westminister Press, 1963. © SCM Press Limited, 1963. Used by permission; from *Zwingli and Bullinger*. LCC, Vol. XXIV, edited by G. W. Bromily. Published in the U.S.A. by The Westminister Press, 1953. Used by permission; from *Alexandrian Christianity*. LCC, Vol. II, edited by John E. L. Oulton and Henry Chadwick. Published in the U.S.A. by The Westminister Press, 1954. Used by Permission.

The University of Chicago Press, for material from Paul Tillich's *Systematic Theology*, Vol. 2.

Vatican II: Decree on the Missionary Activity of the Church, I, 3

In order to establish peace or communion between sinful human beings and Himself, as well as to fashion them into a fraternal community, God determined to intervene in human history in a way both new and definitive. For He sent His Son, clothed in our flesh, in order that through this Son He might snatch men from the power of darkness and of Satan (cf. Col 1:13; Acts 10:38) and that in this Son He might reconcile the world to Himself (cf. 2 Cor 5:19). Through Him, God made all orders of existence. God further appointed Him heir of all things, so that in the Son He might restore them all (cf. Eph 1:10).

For Jesus Christ was sent into the world as a real Mediator between God and men. Since he is God, all divine fullness dwells bodily in Him (Col 2:9). According to His human nature, He is the new Adam, made head of a renewed humanity, and full of grace and of truth (Jn 1:14). Therefore the Son of God walked the ways of a true Incarnation that He might make men sharers in the divine nature. He became poor for our sakes, though He had been rich, in order that His poverty might enrich us (2 Cor 8:9). The Son of Man came not that He might be served, but that He might be a servant, and give His life as a ransom for the many — that is, for all (cf. Mk 10:45).

The sainted Fathers of the Church firmly proclaim that what was not taken up by Christ was not healed. Now, what He took up was our entire human nature such as it is found among us in our misery and poverty, though without our sin (cf. Heb 4:15; 9:28). For Christ said concerning Himself, whom the Father made holy and sent into the world (cf. Jn 10:36): "The Spirit of the Lord is upon me because he anointed me; to bring good news to the poor he sent me, to heal the broken-hearted, to proclaim to the captives release, and sight to the blind" (Lk 4:18). And again: "The Son of Man came to seek and to save what was lost" (Lk 19:10).

But what was once preached by the Lord, or what was once wrought in Him for the saving of the human race, must be proclaimed and spread abroad to the ends of the earth (Acts 1:8), beginning from Jerusalem (cf. Lk 24:47). Thus, what He once accomplished for the salvation of all may in the course of time come to achieve its effect in all.

CONTENTS

PART ONE: CHRISTOLOGICAL THOUGHT AND CONTROVERSY IN THE EARLY CHURCH

Chapter I. Christology of the Fathers and Apologists: Judaism, Gnosticism, Docetism

INTRODUCTION

The Development of Church Doctrine in the Light of the Christological Disputes[1]

by Karl Adam*

---

* Karl Adam (1876–1966) studied philosophy and theology in Regensburg, taught moral theology at the University of Strasbourg, then in 1919 assumed the chair of dogmatic theology at Tübingen where he taught for thirty years. For Karl Adam, theology is a science rooted in a faith seeking understanding. Its goal is "the scientific investigation into the faith held by all the Church in its essence, its growth, and its effects." He has written *The Spirit of Catholicism, Son of God, Christ our Brother.*

What is the relationship between the divinity in Jesus and his humanity? the humanity in Jesus and the divine Logos? This was not only an ontological but also a psychological question: What is the relationship between Jesus' consciousness of his divinity and his purely human consciousness, his awareness of hunger, anxiety, thought, will, suffering, and death?

The simplest, crudest solution was to deny absolutely this purely human consciousness. According to the view of the Docetae, Jesus' entire human nature is mere outward appearance: his body is appearance, his suffering is appearance. All that is real in him is his divinity. It is exceedingly instruc-

[1] *The Christ of Faith: The Christology of the Church* (New York: Pantheon, 1957; London: Burns & Oates, 1957), pp. 27–30.

3

tive to follow the philosophical roots of this Docetism, insofar as we can speak of such. Once again we realize that the real root of every heresy is to be found not in the sphere of revelation, but in the pagan philosophies. Tertullian had already understood this and called the philosopher the father of all heresies. The heresy of Docetism went back to Greek thought, in particular to Neo-Platonism. But the system was made still cruder by clumsy thinking. To Plato, true spiritual being, the Logos, is to be found in the ideal image of things, in which all spiritual essences have their reality. Ultimately, true being is the divine itself, whose image and expression is the Logos. Everything existent is constructed according to this pattern. Thus Plato regarded the empirical existence perceived by the senses as a secondary order of being, which, insofar as it can be perceived only by the senses, is transient and mutable. Only what is spiritual does not pass away, and is thus the true reality and source of reality. This sharp distinction between divine spiritual being and empirical sensuous being was intensified by Oriental influence into an antithesis between spirit and matter. Oriental thought is essentially dualistic. It is based upon a system of antagonistic opposites: heaven and earth, spirit and matter, soul and body. Apart from Brahmanism and its offspring, this dualistic thinking was established and propagated in particular by the religion of the Parsees. When Alexander the Great conquered Persia, Greek thought too was penetrated by this Persian dualism, giving rise to Hellenistic thought, which was characterized by this very tension between spirit and matter. It held that the sensuous world has no real existence.

To the crude-thinking it was just one further step to regarding what has no existence as something that *should* have no existence (the οὐκ ὄν as the μὴ ὄν). So now God and the world, soul and body were not merely distinct, they were opposites, indeed contradictory. Neo-Platonism, which was more a religion than a philosophy, added the further interpretation that the aim of all spiritual education and effort was absolute release from the world of the senses, especially in ecstatic mysticism, in order to emphasize the purely spiritual in man. A strong anti-sensuous tendency, which we know as Encratism, spread, particularly in those circles that were repelled by the advance of uncontrolled sensuality. As Christianity made its way into these circles, its ethics were understood primarily in Encratic terms, and its metaphysics primarily in Docetic terms. We may say that the first misinterpretation of the Christian teaching took place on Hellenistic ground in the sense that it contested the Lord's corporeality and sensuous existence. Even the writings of St. John (1 Jn 1:1; 4:1; 2 Jn 7) already had to do with Docetism. That is why the Evangelist is eager to emphasize that the Word became flesh. This Docetic Gnosticism regarded the body as something unworthy of man. With this as its starting point the Gospel according to the Egyptians did not hesitate to call woman, the symbol of closeness to nature, "a garment of shame." These Gnostics emphasized the Docetic view of Christ all the more in the hope of countering the pagan objection that the idea of God crucified was folly.

The Docetic Gnosis was decisively rejected, even in the very beginnings of Christianity, not least in the *ver-*

bum caro factum est of St. John. All the symbols of our faith emphasize that Jesus was truly born of Mary, and that his suffering and death were real. The soteriology of the early Church, as first formulated by St. Paul, is based upon the assumption of the reality of Christ's incarnation, and the reality of his death on the cross. Among the Apostolic Fathers, Ignatius of Antioch in particular countered the Gnostics of Judaic tendency by stressing the corporeality of the Lord. Docetism was furthest advanced by Marcion, who had come from Sinope to Rome about A.D. 140 and was soon excommunicated there. On the one hand his dualism made him reject the entire Old Testament as the work of the evil Demiurge; on the other hand he tried to support his Docetism by exegesis from a Gospel according to St. Luke and ten Epistles of St. Paul which he had himself cut and arranged to fit his views. For him, Christ is the manifestation of the good God. His body is mere outward appearance, and he first came forward before the world in the fifteenth year of Tiberius' reign. Only this illusory body was crucified. These fantastic ideas were passionately rejected primarily by Irenaeus and Tertullian. When Docetism emerged again in the Middle Ages among the Albigensians and Bogomilians it was refuted afresh at the Council of Lyons (1245) and the Council of Vienne (1311–1312).

The first attempt to reconcile Jesus' divinity with his low human estate by regarding the latter as mere outward appearance was rejected at the very beginning of Christianity. The Church's consciousness of faith clung just as firmly to the Lord's true humanity as it did to his true divinity. This alone withdraws the image of Christ from the oppressive realm of the pagan mythologies and theogonies. The pagan gods that had come down to earth had absorbed all their human quality into their divinity. They were not God become flesh, but gods upon earth whose human form was mere outward appearance. In contrast to this, the Christian faith firmly maintained that Christ was not a god upon earth, but God become flesh.

I. IGNATIUS OF ANTIOCH*

Letter to the Smyrneans[2]

* Ignatius (c35–c107) was a pagan and persecutor of Christians. According to Origen he became, after his conversion, the second bishop of Antioch, as successor of St. Peter. He wrote his *Letters* while under Roman guard, traveling from Antioch to Rome where martyrdom awaited him. Ardently devoted to Christ, he looks forward expectantly to a glorious death. In his epistles he warns against Judaizing heretical elements with tendencies toward Docetism. He insists repeatedly on the full reality both of the divinity and the humanity of our Lord.

I give glory to Jesus Christ, the

2 Glimm *et al.*, *The Apostolic Fathers* (New York: Cima Publishing Co., 1947), p. 95 ff.

God who has imbued you with such wisdom. I am well aware that you have been made perfect in unwavering faith, like men nailed, in body and spirit, to the Cross of our Lord, Jesus Christ, and confirmed in love by the blood of Christ.

In regard to our Lord, you are thoroughly convinced that He was of the race of David according to the flesh, and the Son of God by His will and power; that He was truly born of the Virgin and baptized by John in order that all due observance might be fulfilled by Him; that in His body He was truly nailed to the Cross for our sake under Pontius Pilate and Herod, the tetrarch — of His most blessed passion we are the fruit — so that, through His resurrection, He might raise, for all ages, in the one body of His Church, a standard for the saints and the faithful, whether among Jews or Gentiles.

For He suffered all these things for us, that we might be saved. And He suffered truly, and just as truly raised Himself from the dead. He did not suffer merely in appearance, as some of the unbelievers say — they themselves being merely in appearance; for it will be their fate, in accordance with their faith, to be bodiless and ghostlike.

As for me, I know that even after His resurrection He was in the flesh, and I believe this to be true. For, when He came to those who were with Peter, He said to them: "Take hold on me and handle me and see that I am not a spirit without a body" (cf. Lk 24:39). And, as soon as they touched Him and felt His flesh and pulse, they believed. It is for this reason that they despised death and even showed themselves superior to death. After His resurrection He ate and drank with them like any one else with a body, although in His spirit He was one with the Father.

To the Ephesians[3]

There are some who, in guile and wickedness, have a way of bearing the Name about while behaving in a way unworthy of God. Such men you must shun as you would wild beasts; for they are mad dogs that bite when you are not on your guard. Of these you must beware, for these men are hard to heal. There is one Doctor active in both body and soul, begotten and yet unbegotten, God in man, true life in death, son of Mary and Son of God, first able to suffer and then unable to suffer, Jesus Christ, our Lord. . . .

I offer up my life as a poor substitute for the Cross, which is a stumbling block to those who have no faith, but to us salvation and eternal life.

[3] *Ibid.*, pp. 95–96.

Where is the wise man? Where is the philosopher? Where is the boasting of the so-called men of prudence? For our God Jesus Christ was, according to God's dispensation, the fruit of Mary's womb, of the seed of David; He was born and baptized in order that He might make the water holy by His passion.

The maidenhood of Mary and her child-bearing and also the death of the Lord were hidden from the prince of this world — three resounding mysteries wrought in the silence of God. How, then, did He appear in time? A star, brighter than all other stars, shone in the sky, and its brightness was ineffable and the novelty of it caused astonishment. And the rest of the stars, along with the sun and moon, formed a choir about the star; but the light of the star by itself outshone all the rest. It was a puzzle to know the origin of this novelty unlike anything else. Thereupon all magic was dissolved, every bond of malice disappeared, ignorance was destroyed, the ancient kingdom was ruined, when God appeared in the form of man to give us newness of eternal life. What had been prepared in God now had a beginning. And, because of the plan for the abolition of death, all things were disturbed.

If, through your prayers, Jesus Christ should make me worthy and if it should be His will, and still more if the Lord should reveal it to me, in a second letter which I intend to write to you, I shall explain more fully what I have merely touched upon — the dispensation of becoming the new man Jesus Christ, who is of the race of David according to the passion and resurrection. Come together in common, one and all without exception in charity, in one faith and in one Jesus Christ, who is of the race of David according to the flesh, the son of man and Son of God, so that with undivided mind you may obey the bishop and the priests, and break one Bread which is the medicine of immortality and the antidote against death, enabling us to live for ever in Jesus Christ.

To the Trallians[4]

I exhort you, then, to leave alone the foreign fodder of heresy and keep entirely to Christian food. It is not I, but the love of Jesus Christ, that speaks. For the heretics mingle poison with Jesus Christ, as men might administer a deadly drug in sweet wine, without giving a hint of their wickedness, so that without thought or fear of the fatal sweetness a man drinks his own death.

Against such men be on your guard. This will be possible if you are not proud and if you keep close to Jesus Christ and the bishop and the ordinances of the Apostles. Anyone who is within the sanctuary is pure and anyone who is outside is impure, that is to say, no one who acts apart from the bishop and the priests and the deacons has a clear conscience.

Not that I have heard of anything of this sort among you; but I keep watch over you as ones I love, fore-

seeing, as I do, the snares of the devil. And so, put on the armor of forbearance and refresh yourselves in faith, that is, in the body of the Lord, and in love, that is, in the blood of Jesus Christ. Let no one be down on his neighbor. Let not the folly of a few give occasion to the pagans to calumniate your pious community. "Woe unto him through whom my name is calumniated before others without cause."

And so be deaf when anyone speaks to you apart from Jesus Christ, who was of the race of David, the son of Mary, who was truly born and ate and drank, who was truly persecuted under Pontius Pilate and was really crucified and died in the sight of those "in heaven and on earth and under the earth." Moreover, He was truly raised from the dead by the power of His Father; in like manner His Father, through Jesus Christ, will raise up those of us who believe in

[4] *Ibid.*, pp. 103–105.

Him. Apart from Him we have no true life.

If, as some say who are godless in the sense that they are without faith, He merely seemed to suffer — it is they themselves who merely seem to exist — why am I in chains? And why do I pray that I may be thrown to the wild beasts? I die, then, to no purpose. I do but bear false witness against the Lord.

Avoid, therefore, the evil sprouts that bring forth deadly fruit. Merely to taste this fruit is to meet a sudden death. Such are not the plants of the Father. If they were they would appear as branches of the Cross and their fruit would be immortal. It is by the Cross, by His passion that He invites you who are His members. The Head cannot be born without the members since it was God, that is, He Himself, who promised to keep them together.

II. ST. JUSTIN MARTYR*

The First Apology[5]

---

* Justin (c100–165), an early Christian apologist, embraced Christianity at thirty years of age after an ardent search for truth in the pagan philosophies of Aristotle, the Stoics, Plato, and the Pythagoreans. He taught at Ephesus where he disputed with Trypho the Jew (c135) and subsequently opened a school for Christians at Rome, where he published his *Dialogue with Trypho* and his *Apologies* addressed to the Emperor and to the Roman Senate. Denounced as a Christian, he was scourged and beheaded after refusing to sacrifice to the gods. Justin's theology focused on the conception of the Word, an idea current to the philosophers of his day, especially the Stoics. With Clement of Alexandria he stresses the soteriological value of the mystery of the Incarnation.

Furthermore, the Son of God who is called Jesus, even if he were only a man by common generation, is because of his wisdom worthy to be called the Son of God, for all your writers call God the Father of men and gods. And if we declare that the Word of God was begotten of God not in the ordinary, but in an extraordinary manner . . . this may be compared to your claim that Mercury is the announcing word of God. And should any one object that He [Christ] was crucified, this indignity may be compared to that of Jupiter's sons . . . [whose] sufferings at death are said to have been, not all similar, but different, so that not even His unusual manner of suffering was inferior to theirs. But, as we have promised and will prove as our discourse progresses (or rather, as we have already proved), He is their superior also in this regard, for one is proved superior by his actions. If we state that He was born of a Virgin, this may be comparable to what you admit of Perseus.[6] When we say that He cured the lame, the

5 Thomas B. Falls, *St. Justin Martyr* (New York: Christian Heritage Press, 1948), pp. 58–59, 67 ff., 220 ff.

6 In Greek mythology it is related that King Acrisius was warned by the oracle that he would perish at the hand of his daughter's son. Accordingly, he imprisoned his only daughter, the virgin Danaë, in an underground vault. But Zeus visited her in a shower of gold, and thereafter Perseus was born to Danaë.

paralytics, and those blind from birth, and raised the dead to life, we seem to attribute to Him actions similar to those said to have been performed by Aesculapius.

To make this clear to you, we shall present the following arguments to prove: [first] that whatever statements we make, because we learned them from Christ and the Prophets who preceded Him, are alone true, and are older than all writers, and that we should be believed, not because we speak the same things as the writers, but because we speak the truth; [second] that Jesus Christ alone is properly the Son of God, since He is His Word, First-begotten, and Power, and that, having become man by His will, He taught us these doctrines for the conversion and restoration of mankind; [third] that, before He assumed human nature and dwelt among men, some . . . foretold through the poets as if already accomplished those things which they invented, just as they caused to be imputed to us slanderous and impious actions, of which they can produce neither witness nor proof.

Lest anyone should object and ask, "What prevents us from supposing that He whom we call Christ was a man born of men, and has worked what we term miracles through the art of magic, and thus appeared to be the Son of God," we now present proof that such was not the case. We shall do so not by trusting in mere statements [without proof], but by necessarily believing those who predicted these things before they happened, for we are actual eyewitnesses of events that have happened and are happening in the very manner in which they were foretold. This, we are sure, will appear even to you the greatest and truest proof.

Indeed, there were certain men among the Jews who were Prophets of God, through whom the Prophetic Spirit predicted events that were to happen before they actually took place. The successive kings of Judea carefully kept their prophetic sayings in their possession, as they were worded at the time of their utterance in their Hebrew language, and as they were arranged in books by the Prophets themselves. When Ptolemy,[7] King of Egypt, was forming a library, and attempting to collect the writings of every nation, he heard about these prophetic writings and he sent to Herod, then King of the Jews, asking that he send the prophetic books to him. King Herod did send them, written, as we said, in the Hebrew language. But when the Egyptians could not understand these writings, he again sent and asked for some persons to translate them into the Greek tongue. After this was accomplished, the books remained in the possession of the Egyptians from that day to this, as they are also in the possession of every Jew, wherever he be. But these Jews, though they read the books, fail to grasp their meaning, and they consider us as their enemies and adversaries, killing and punishing us, just as you do, whenever they are able to do so, as you can readily imagine. In the recent Jewish war, Bar Kocheba, the leader of the Jewish uprising, ordered that only the Christians should be subjected to dreadful torments, unless they renounced and blasphemed Jesus Christ. In the books of the Prophets, indeed, we found

---

[7] I.e., Ptolemy Philadelphus, who in the third century before Christ had the Hebrew Scriptures translated into Greek at the Museum in Alexandria. This is the famous Septuagint version.

Jesus our Christ foretold as coming to us born of a virgin, reaching manhood, curing every disease and ailment, raising the dead to life, being hated, unrecognized, and crucified, dying, rising from the dead, ascending into Heaven, and being called and actually being the Son of God. And [we found predicted also] that He would send certain persons to every nation to make known these things, and that the former Gentiles rather [than Jews] would believe in Him. He was foretold, in truth, before He actually appeared. . . .

. . . We have been taught that Christ was First-begotten of God [the Father] and . . . that He is the Word of whom all mankind partakes. Those who lived by reason are Christians, even though they have been considered atheists: such as, among the Greeks, Socrates, Heraclitus, and others like them; and among the foreigners, Abraham, Elias, Ananias, Azarias, Misael, and many others whose deeds or names we now forbear to enumerate, for we think it would be too long. So, also, they who lived before Christ and did not live by reason were useless men, enemies of Christ, and murderers of those who did live by reason. But those who have lived reasonably, and still do, are Christians, and are fearless and untroubled. From all that has been said an intelligent man can understand why, through the power of the Word, in accordance with the will of God, the Father and Lord of all, He was born as a man of a virgin, was named Jesus, was crucified, died, rose again, and ascended into Heaven.

The Second Apology[8]

No proper name has been bestowed upon God, the Father of all, since He is unbegotten. For whoever has a proper name received it from a person older than himself. The words Father, and God, and Creator, and Lord, and Master are not real names, but rather terms of address derived from His beneficent deeds. But His Son, who alone is properly called Son, the Word, who was with Him [God, the Father] and was begotten before all things, when in the beginning He [God the Father] created and arranged all things through Him [the Son], is called Christ, because He was anointed and because God the Father arranged all the things of creation through Him. This name also has an unknown meaning, just as the term "God," which is not a real name, but the expression of man's innate opinion of a thing that can scarcely be defined. But "Jesus," which is His name both as Man and Savior, has a meaning. For He also became man . . . and was born in accordance with the will of God the Father for the benefit of believers, and for the defeat of the demons. Even now, your own eyes will teach you the truth of this last statement. For many demoniacs throughout the entire world, and even in your own city, were exorcised by many of our Christians in the name of Jesus Christ, who was crucified under Pontius Pilate; and our men cured them, and they still cure others by rendering helpless and dispelling the demons who had taken possession of these men, even when they could not be cured by all

8 *Ibid.*, p. 129 ff.

the other exorcists, and exploiters of incantations and drugs. . . .

Beyond doubt, therefore, our teachings are more noble than all human teaching, because Christ, who appeared on earth for our sakes, became the whole Logos, namely, Logos and body and soul. Everything that the philosophers and legislators discovered and expressed well, they accomplished through their discovery and contemplation of some part of the Logos. But, since they did not have a full knowledge of the Logos, which is Christ, they often contradicted themselves. And those who were born before Christ assumed human nature were dragged into law courts as irreligious and meddling persons, when they tried in human narrowness to think out and prove things by reason. Socrates, the most ardent of all in this regard, was accused of the very crimes that are imputed to us. They claimed that he introduced new deities and rejected the state-sponsored gods. But what he did was to ostracize Homer and the other poets, and to instruct men to expel the evil demons and those who perpetrated the deeds narrated by the poets; and to exhort men by meditation to learn more about God who was unknown to them, saying: "It is not an easy matter to find the Father and Creator of all things, nor, when He is found, is it safe to announce Him to all men." Yet, our Christ did all this through His own power. There was no one who believed so much in Socrates as to die for his teaching, but not only philosophers and scholars believed in Christ, of whom even Socrates had a vague knowledge (for He was and is the Logos who is in every person, and who predicted things to come first through the prophets and then in person when He assumed our human nature and feelings, and taught us these doctrines), but also workmen and men wholly uneducated, who all scorned glory, and fear, and death. Indeed, this is brought about by the power of the ineffable Father, and not through the instrumentality of human reason. . . .

Dialogue With Trypho[9]

"We have now heard your opinion on these matters," interrupted Trypho. "Resume your discourse where you left off, and bring it to an end, for it seems to be entirely absurd and utterly impossible of proof. Your statement that this Christ existed as God before all ages, and then that He consented to be born and become man, yet that He is not of human origin, appears to be not only paradoxical, but preposterous."

"I am aware," I replied, "that my assertion must seem paradoxical, es-

pecially to you Jews, who were never in the least interested in knowing or doing the things of God, but only the things of your teachers, as God Himself testifies. However, Trypho, the fact that this Man is the Christ of God is not to be denied, even if I were unable to prove that He, being God, pre-existed as the Son of the Creator of the universe and became Man through a virgin. Since it has been proved beyond all doubt that He is the Christ of God, whatever that Christ eventually is to be, even if I fail to show that He pre-existed, and

[9] *Ibid.,* p. 220 ff.

consented to become man with a body and feelings like our own, according to the will of the Father; only in this last regard could you rightly claim that I have been wrong. But you cannot deny that He is the Christ, even though He apparently is of human origin, and evidently became the Christ by the Father's choice. For, my friends, there are some of our race, who acknowledge that Jesus is the Christ, but claim that He has a merely human origin. I naturally disagree with such persons, nor would I agree with them even if the majority of those who share my opinions were to say so. For we have been told by Christ Himself not to follow the teachings of men, but only those which have been announced by the holy Prophets and taught by Himself. . . ."

"So, my friends," I said, "I shall now show from the Scriptures that God has begotten of Himself a certain rational Power as a Beginning before all other creatures. The Holy Spirit indicates this Power by various titles, sometimes the Glory of the Lord, at other times Son, or Wisdom, or Angel, or God, or Lord, or Word. He even called Himself Commander-in-chief when He appeared in human guise to Joshua the son of Nun. Indeed, He can justly lay claim to all these titles from the fact both that He performs the Father's will and that He was begotten by an act of the Father's will. But does not something similar happen also with us humans? When we utter a word, it can be said that we beget the word, but not by cutting it off, in the sense that our power of uttering words would thereby be diminished. We can observe a similar example in nature when one fire kindles another, without losing anything, but remaining the same; yet the enkindled fire

seems to exist of itself and to shine without lessening the brilliancy of the first fire. My statements will now be confirmed by none other than the Word of Wisdom, who is this God begotten from the Universal Father, and who is the Word and Wisdom and Power and Glory of Him who begot Him. . . .

"So also was the prophecy beginning with the words, 'Behold a virgin shall conceive and bear a Son,' (Is 7:14) spoken of Him. For, if the one of whom Isaiah spoke was not to be born of a virgin, to whom did the Holy Spirit allude when He said: 'Behold, the Lord Himself shall give you a sign: Behold, a virgin shall conceive and bear a Son'? If He was to be born of human intercourse like any other firstborn son, why did God solemnly announce that He would give a sign, which is not common to all firstborn? What is truly a sign, and what was to be an irrefutable proof to all men, namely, that by means of a virgin's womb the Firstborn of all creatures took flesh and truly became man, was foreknown by the Prophetic Spirit before it took place and foretold by him in different ways, as I have explained to you. Indeed, He foretold this in order that, when it did take place, everyone would understand that it all happened by the power and purpose of the Creator of the world; just as Eve was made from one of Adam's ribs, and as all living beings were created by the Word of God in the beginning. But here, too, you dare to distort the translation of this passage made by your elders at the court of Ptolemy, the Egyptian king, asserting that the real meaning of the Scriptures is not as they translated it, but should read, 'Behold a young woman shall conceive,' as though something of extraordinary importance was signified by a woman conceiving after sexual intercourse, as all young women, except the barren, can do. And even the barren can become fertile by the power of God. Samuel's mother, who had been sterile, gave birth to her child by the will of God. The same thing can be said of the wife of the holy Patriarch Abraham, and of Elizabeth, who bore John the Baptist, and of many other women. You must realize, therefore, that nothing is impossible for God to do, if He wills it. And, especially when it was prophesied that this would happen, you should not venture to mutilate or misinterpret the prophecies, for in doing so you do no harm to God, but only to yourselves."

III. ST. IRENAEUS*

Proof of the Apostolic Preaching[10]

---

* St. Irenaeus (c130–c200), born in Smyrna in Asia Minor and later a student at Rome, became Bishop of Lyons (c177) where he fought heresy and the persecution of the Church at the risk of martyrdom. He ranks as the first great post-Apostolic theologian. In his development of the doctrine of recapitulation he sought to present the humanity of Christ as being in itself the summary of human evolution.

In his *Proof of the Apostolic Preaching* he traces the guidance of mankind by God from Adam to Christ, explaining the essential Christian teaching of the Trinity, the Incarnation and the Redemption. His *Against Heresies*, whose full title is *Detection and Overthrow of the Pretended but False Gnosis*, refutes the Gnostic teachings of the Valentinians and the Marcionites.

Whence, then, comes the substance of the first man? From God's Will and Wisdom, and from virgin earth. "For God had not rained," says the scripture, "before man was made, and there was no man to till the earth" (Gen 2:5). From this earth, then, while it was still virgin, God took dust and fashioned the man, the beginning of humanity. So the Lord, summing up afresh this man, reproduced the scheme of his incarnation, being born of a virgin by the Will and Wisdom of God, that He too might copy the incarnation of Adam, and man might be made, as was written in the beginning, "according to the image and likeness" of God (Gen 1:26).

And just as it was through a virgin who disobeyed that man was stricken and fell and died, so too it was through the Virgin, who obeyed the word of God, that man resuscitated by life received life. For the Lord came to seek back the lost sheep, and it was man who was lost; and therefore He did not become some other formation, but He likewise, of her that was descended from Adam, preserved the likeness of formation; for Adam had necessarily to be restored in Christ, that mortality be absorbed in immortality, and Eve in Mary, that a virgin, become the advocate of a virgin, should undo and destroy virginal disobedience by virginal obedience.

And the sin that was wrought through the tree was undone by the obedience of the tree, obedience to God whereby the Son of man was

---

[10] Joseph P. Smith, *Proof of the Apostolic Preaching* (Westminster, Md.: The Newman Press, 1952), pp. 68–73.

nailed to the tree, destroying the knowledge of evil, and bringing in and conferring the knowledge of good; and evil is disobedience to God, as obedience to God is good. And therefore the Word says through Isaiah the prophet, foretelling what was to come to pass in the future — for it was because they told the future that they were "prophets" — the Word says through him as follows: "I refuse not, and do not gainsay, my back have I delivered to blows and my cheeks to buffets, and I have not turned away my face from the contumely of them that spat" (Is 50:6). So by the obedience, whereby He obeyed unto death, hanging on a tree, He undid the old disobedience wrought in the tree. And because He is Himself the Word of God Almighty, who in His invisible form pervades us universally in the whole world, and encompasses both its length and breadth and height and depth — for by God's Word everything is disposed and administered — the Son of God was also crucified in these, imprinted in the form of a cross on the universe; for He had necessarily, in becoming visible, to bring to light the universality of His cross, in order to show openly through His visible form that activity of His: that it is He who makes bright the height, that is, what is in heaven, and holds the deep, which is in the bowels of the earth, and stretches forth and extends the length from East to West, navigating also the Northern parts and the breadth of the South, and calling in all the dispersed from all sides to the knowledge of the Father. . . .

In such wise, then, was His triumph of our redemption, and His fulfillment of the promise to the patriarchs, and His doing away with the primal disobedience: the Son of God became a son of David and a son of Abraham; for in the accomplishment of these things, and in their summing up in Himself, in order to give us His own life, the Word of God was made flesh through the instrumentality of the Virgin, to undo death and work life in man; for we were in the bonds of sin, and were to be born through sinfulness and to live with death.

Great, then, was the mercy of God the Father: He sent the creative Word, who, when He came to save us, put Himself in our position, and in the same situation in which we lost life; and He loosed the prison-bonds, and His light appeared and dispelled the darkness in the prison, and He sanctified our birth and abolished death, loosing those same bonds by which we were held. And He showed forth the resurrection, becoming Himself, "the firstborn from the dead" (Col 1:18), and raised in Himself prostrate man, being lifted up to the heights of heaven, at the right hand of the glory of the Father, as God had promised through the prophet, saying: "I will raise up the tabernacle of David, that is fallen" (Am 9:11), that is, the body sprung from David; and this was in truth accomplished by our Lord Jesus Christ, in the triumph of our redemption, that He raise us in truth, setting us free to the Father. And if anyone accept not His virgin birth, how shall he accept His resurrection from the dead? For it is nothing marvellous, nothing astonishing, nothing unheard-of, if one who was not born rose from the dead — but we can not even speak of the "resurrection" of one who came into being without birth, for he who is not born is not immortal; and he who was not subject to birth will not be subject to death either; for how can one who did not take on man's beginning receive his end?

So, if He was not born, neither did He die; and if He did not die, neither was He raised from the dead; and if He was not raised from the dead, He has not conquered death, nor is its reign abolished; and if death is not conquered, how are we to mount on high into life, being subject from the beginning to death?

So those who exclude redemption from man, and do not believe God will raise them from the dead, despise also our Lord's birth, which the Word of God underwent for our sake, to be made flesh, that He might manifest the resurrection of the flesh, and take the lead of all in heaven: as the firstborn, first-begotten of the thought of the Father, the Word, Himself in the world making all things perfect by His guidance and legislation; as the firstborn of the Virgin, a just and holy man, a servant of God, good, pleasing to God, perfect in all things, freeing those who follow Him from Hell; as the firstborn of the dead, head and source also of the life unto God.

Thus, then, does the Word of God "in all things hold the primacy" (Col 1:18), for He is true man and "Wonderful Counsellor and God the Mighty" (Is 9:6), calling man back again into communion with God, that by communion with Him we may have part in incorruptibility.

Against Heresies[11]

The Spirit, then, descended according to the prearranged plan, and the Son of God, who was also the Word of the Father, came in the fullness of time and became incarnate in man, and fulfilled the whole human economy, even our Lord Jesus, ever one and the same, as the Lord himself bears witness, the Apostles confess and the prophets proclaim. Their doctrine is false who have devised ogdoads, tetrads and unreal appearances, who destroy the Spirit and divide Jesus Christ. Wherefore it behooves thee and all who attend to this Scripture, and are anxious for their salvation, not to yield without a struggle when they hear their discourses. For they say the same things as believers, but with a different meaning. Indeed, their meaning is contrary to ours and blasphemous, and destructive to those who, be-

guiled by the similarity of terms, are inoculated by the poison of their different opinion, just as if one, giving another gypsum mixed with water instead of milk, should mislead him by the color. So said one superior to us about all who in any way corrupt the things of God and adulterate the truth: "Gypsum is wrongly mixed with the Divine milk."[12]

Since we have clearly shown that the Word who was in the beginning with God, through whom all things were made and who was always present with the human race, even he in the last times according to the time appointed of the Father, was united with His creation, and became man subject to suffering, the argument of those who say, "If he was born *then,* he was not Christ *before,*" is over-

---

[11] *Irenaeus: Against Heresies* (London: S.P.C.K., 1916), pp. 128–131, 140–141.

[12] Gypsum in liquid preparation was used by the Roman nobles as a poison. See Pliny, N. H. 36. 24.

come. For we have shown that the Son of God, who was always existent with the Father, did not begin to be then; for when he became incarnate and man, he summed up in himself the long roll of humanity, supplying us in a concise manner with salvation. So that what we lost in Adam, namely the being in the image and likeness of God, we might recover in Christ Jesus.

Because it was impossible for that man who had been once beaten and knocked out through disobedience to refashion himself and obtain the reward of victory, and also it was impossible that the man who had fallen under the power of sin should receive salvation, the Son accomplished both things, being the Word of God, descending from the Father, and becoming incarnate, and descending to death, and consummating the plan of our salvation. And he (Paul) explains the reason why the Word of God did this saying, "For this cause Christ both lived and died and rose again, that he might be the Lord, both of the living and the dead" (Rom 14:9).

[He quotes 1 Cor 15:3 f., 12; Rom 14:15; Gal 3:13; 1 Cor 8:11, to show that Paul on every occasion when speaking of his suffering, humanity, death and atonement used the name Christ.]

For it was Jesus Christ who suffered for us, who died and rose, who descended and ascended, the Son of God who became the Son of man, as the very name signifies. For in the name of Christ is implied the Anointer, the Anointed, and the Unction wherewith the Anointment has been made. It is the Father who anoints, the Son who is anointed, and the Spirit who is the Unction, as the Word declares by Isaiah: "The Spirit of the Lord is upon me because He hath anointed me," thus indicating the anointing Father, the anointed Son, and the Unction which is the Spirit.[13]

[He proceeds to quote sayings of our Lord with regard to his own suffering and crucifixion, Mt 16:13 f., 21–25; 10:17 f., 28 and 38, and concludes:]

For he himself promised that he would confess them before his Father who confessed his name before men; but would deny those who denied him, and would bring to shame those who were ashamed to confess him. But in spite of this certain [ones] have waxed audacious that they even spurn the martyrs and abuse those who are slain for their confession of their Lord, and suffer all things foretold by our Lord, and in this respect attempt to follow in his steps, becoming the witnesses in death of him who died, whom we reckon among the martyrs.[14]

[He is now concerned to prove the reality of our Lord's suffering, which the Gnostics denied.]

For if he did not suffer, there is no thanks to him, since there was no Passion. And we have been deceived by him who exhorts us to endure what he did not endure himself. We, too, shall be superior to the Master through suffering and bearing what he never suffered nor bore. But as our Lord alone is truly Master, the Son of God is truly good and enduring, even the Word of God the Father, who was made the Son of man. For he agonized and conquered. As a man he con-

---

[13] Cf. *Apostolic Preaching*, c. 47. See also III. 6. I, where an explanation of Ps. 45:7, "therefore God hath anointed thee," is given. The reference is to Is 41:1.

[14] Passibilis *martyres* facti. "Martyr" is used here in both senses of *witness* and *suffer*.

tended on behalf of the fathers, and through his obedience he discharged the debt of disobedience; for he bound the strong man, set free the weak, and gave salvation to his own creation by destroying sin. For he is a most holy and merciful Lord, and one who loveth the race of men.

Therefore, as we have said, he caused human nature to cling to God and to be one with God. For had not man banished the enemy of man, that enemy had not been justly vanquished. And had not God granted salvation, we had never possessed it securely. And had not man been joined to God, he could never have shared in incorruptibility. For it behooved him, who was the mediator of God and man, by his relationship with both to lead both into friendship and harmony, presenting man to God and revealing God to man. In what manner could we be partakers of His adoption unless we had received from Him (God) through the Son that communion which is with Himself? Unless His Word incarnate had imparted it to us. Wherefore he came through every age, restoring to each its communion with God. Therefore they who do not believe in a real incarnation are still under the old condemnation, and are *patrons of sin,* not believing in the conquest of death. . . .

If, therefore, the first Adam had a human father, it would be natural to expect that the second Adam was born of Joseph. But if the first were taken from the soil and formed by God, it behooved the man, who recapitulated in himself the man formed by God, to have a similar kind of birth. Why, then, did not God again take

earth, instead of causing the formation to be from Mary? In order to prevent another creation taking place, lest that creation might be the one to be saved, and in order that the very same creation might be recapitulated, the likeness being retained throughout. They are far astray, then, who say that he took nothing of the Virgin in order that they may get rid of his inheritance of the flesh and his likeness to us. For if he did not take the substance of the flesh from man, he neither became man nor the Son of man, and if he was not made that which we were, there was nothing wonderful in his sufferings. Everyone will allow that we consist of body taken from the ground, and soul receiving spirit from God. Such the Word of God became, recapitulating his own creation in himself. [He quotes Gal 1:4; Rom 4:3, 4.1.]

Otherwise his coming down (κάθοδος) to Mary was superfluous. For why did he come down to her if he was to take nought from her? And if he took nought from Mary, he could not have received earthly food by which the earthly body is sustained; he had not felt hunger after fasting forty days; John had never said, "Jesus sat, being wearied of his journey" (Jn 4:6); he had never wept over Lazarus nor sweated drops of blood; nor had he said, "my soul is exceeding sorrowful" (Mt 24:38); and blood and water had not issued from his pierced side (Jn 19:34). For all these things are indications of the flesh which is taken from the earth and which he recapitulated in himself, saving his own handiwork.

IV. TERTULLIAN*

The Apology[15]

* Tertullian (c160–220), born in Carthage, received the classical Roman education of his day and later became a lawyer in Rome. Upon his conversion he returned to Carthage where he became a catechist and finally a priest. His attraction to asceticism led him to the extreme of joining the montanists, a heretical sect which prohibited second marriages, forbade flight from persecution, and condemned the Church's "lax" discipline. Tertullian called Catholics "psychics," or "animal men," and his fellow rigorists "Pneumatics," or "Spirit-inspired."

However, in general his theology is orthodox and his exposition of the mysteries of the Trinity and Incarnation rank him with St. Augustine. He was the first Christian theologian to write in Latin. His logical and legal mind forged a language which became the tool of Western theology. His *Apology*, addressed to the governors of the Roman Provinces, defends Christ as God. His *On the Flesh of Christ* is directed against the Gnostics and Docetists. Praxeas was a Patripassian, who identified Father and Son in the Trinity.

We have already said that God fashioned this whole world by His word, His reason, His power. Even your own philosophers agree that *logos*, that Word and Reason, seems to be the maker of the universe.

This *logos* Zeno defines as the maker who formed everything according to a certain arrangement; the same *logos* (he says) is called Destiny, God, the Mind of Jupiter, and the inevitable Fate of all things. Cleanthes combines all these predicates into Spirit, which, according to him, permeates the universe. Moreover, we, too, ascribe Spirit as its proper substance to that Word, Reason, and Power by which, as we have said, God made everything. For, in Spirit giving utterance, there would be the Word; with Spirit arranging all things, Reason would cooperate; and in Spirit perfecting all things, Power would be present. This, as we have been taught, has been uttered by God and begotten by this utterance, and is, therefore, called the Son of God and God on account of the unity

of nature; for God, too, is Spirit. When a ray is shot forth from the sun, a part is taken from the whole; but there will be sun in the ray because it is a sun ray; its nature is not separated, but extended. Thus, spirit proceeds from spirit and God from God just as light is kindled from light. The source of the substance remains whole and unimpaired, although you may borrow from it many offshoots of its quality. Thus, too, what proceeds from God is God and the Son of God, and both are one; similarly, Spirit proceeds from Spirit and God from God, making two by the measure of existence, plurality by graduation, but not by condition; He has not separated from, but proceeded from the producing cause.

This ray of God, then, as was ever foretold in the past, descended into a certain virgin and, becoming flesh in her womb, was born as one who is man and God united. The flesh, provided with a soul, is nourished, matures, speaks, teaches, acts, and *is* Christ.

Therefore, since they considered Him merely a man, on the basis of

[15] R Arbesmann *et al.*, *Tertullian: Apologetical Works* (New York: Fathers of the Church, Inc., 1950), pp. 63–65.

His lowliness, it followed that they came to esteem Him as a wonder-worker because of His power. For, with a word, He drove evil spirits from men, gave sight again to the blind, cleansed lepers, healed paralytics, and finally, by a word, restored the dead to life; He reduced to obedience the very elements of nature, calming storms, walking upon the water, manifesting that He was the Word of God. In other words, He is that original, firstborn *Logos,* endowed with power and reason and sustained by spirit, the same who, by a mere word, still creates and did create all things.

On the Flesh of Christ[16]

The professors of this world's wisdom find it easier to believe that Jupiter became a bull or a swan than Marcion finds it to believe that Christ veritably became man.

There are, I submit, other things too that are foolish enough, those concerned with the reproaches and sufferings of God. If not, let them call it prudence that God was crucified. Excise this also, Marcion — or rather, this for preference. For which is more beneath God's dignity, more a matter of shame, to be born or to die, to carry about a body or a cross, to be circumcised or to be crucified, to be fed at the breast or to be buried, to be laid in a manger or to be entombed in a sepulcher? You will be the wiser if you refuse to believe these either. Yet wise you cannot be, except by becoming a fool in the world through believing the foolish things of God. Or was your reason for not tearing out of your scriptures the sufferings of Christ that as a phantasm he was free from the perception of them? I have already suggested that he could equally well have undergone the unsubstantial ridicule of an imaginary nativity and infancy. But your answer is now required, murderer of the truth: was not God truly crucified? did he not, as truly crucified, truly die? was he not truly raised again, seeing of course he truly died? Was it by fraud that Paul determined to know nothing among us save Jesus crucified (cf. 11 or 2:2), was it by fraud that he represented him as buried (cf. 1 Cor 15:4), by fraud that he insisted that he was raised up again? (Cf. 1 Cor 15:17-19.) Fraudulent in that case is also our faith, and the whole of what we hope for from Christ will be a phantasm, you utter scoundrel, who pronounce innocent the assassins of God. For of them Christ suffered nothing, if he in reality suffered nothing. Spare the one and only hope of the whole world: why tear down the indispensable dishonor of the faith? Whatever is beneath God's dignity is for my advantage. I am saved if I am not ashamed of my Lord. "Whosoever is ashamed of me," he says, "of him will I also be ashamed" (Mt 10:33; Mk 8:38; Lk 9:26). I find no other grounds for shame, such as may prove that in contempt of dishonor I am nobly shameless and advantageously a fool. The Son of God was crucified: I am not ashamed — because it is shameful. The Son of God died: it is immediately credible — because it is silly. He was buried, and rose again: it is certain

[16] E. Evans (tr.), *Tertullian's Treatise on the Incarnation* (London: S.P.C.K., 1956), pp. 17-21, 37-39, 61-63.

— because it is impossible. But how can these acts be true in him, if he himself was not true, if he had not truly in himself that which could be crucified, which could die, which could be buried and raised up again — this flesh, in fact, suffused with blood, scaffolded of bones, threaded through with sinews, intertwined with veins, competent to be born and to die, human unquestionably, as born of a human mother? And in Christ this flesh will be mortal precisely because Christ is man, and Son of Man. Else why is Christ called Man, and Son of Man, if he has nothing that is man's, and nothing derived from man? — unless perchance either man is something other than flesh, or man's flesh is derived from somewhere else than from man, or Mary is something other than human, or Marcion's god is a man. Unless one of these suppositions were true, Christ could not be described in the Scripture as man except with reference to his flesh, nor as Son of Man except with reference to some human parent: as neither could be described as God without the Spirit of God, nor as the Son of God without God for his Father. Thus the official record of both substances represents him as both man and God: on the one hand born, on the other not born: on the one hand fleshly, on the other spiritual: on the one hand weak, on the other exceeding strong: on the one hand dying, on the other living. That these two sets of attributes the divine and the human, are each kept distinct from the other, is of course accounted for by the equal verity of each nature, both flesh and spirit being in full degree what they claim to be: the powers of the Spirit of God proved him God, the sufferings proved there was the flesh of

man. If the powers postulate the Spirit, no less do the sufferings postulate the flesh. If the flesh along with the sufferings was fictitious, it follows that the Spirit also along with the powers was a fraud. Why make out that Christ was half a lie? He was wholly the truth. He thought it better, I am sure, to be born than to be partially a liar, a liar too against himself, by wearing flesh without bones yet hard, without muscles yet firm, without blood yet gory, without a cloak yet clothed, flesh that hungered without appetite, ate without teeth, and spoke without a tongue, so that his discourse should be a phantasm conveyed to the ears by the ghost of a voice. In such a case he was a phantasm even after the resurrection when he offered his hands and feet for his disciples to examine, saying, "Behold that I am I, because a spirit hath not bones as ye see me having" (Lk 24:18) — undoubtedly meaning hands and feet and bones which a spirit has not but flesh has. How do you interpret this saying, Marcion, when you deduce Jesus from a god who is supremely good and candid and free from all evil? See how he beguiles and deceives and circumvents the eyes of all, their perceptions, their approaches, their contacts. In that case you ought not to have brought Christ down from heaven, but from some band of strolling mountebanks, not as God without manhood but as a man and a magician, not as the high priest of salvation, but as the producer of a pantomime, not as the raiser of the dead but as a seducer of the living: except that even if he was a magician he was born. . . .

My next contention is that nothing that is derived from something else, though it be other than that from which it is derived, is to such an extent other as not to suggest that from which it is derived. No material loses all evidence of its origin, though it be changed into a new identity. Certainly this body of ours, the fact of whose formation from clay the truth has passed on even to the mythologies of the Gentiles, confesses both elements of its origin, earth by its flesh, water by its blood. For though its quality manifests itself under another aspect, this is because it comes into existence as one thing derived from another. Yet what is blood but reddened water, and what is flesh but earth transformed into shapes still its own? Consider its attributes one by one, the muscles as turf, the bones as rocks, even a sort of pebbles round the nipples. Look upon the clinging bands of the sinews as the fibres of roots, the branching meanderings of the veins as the twisting of rivers, the down as moss, the hair as grass, even the very treasures of the marrow in its secret place as the goldmines of the flesh. All these tokens of a terrestrial origin were also in Christ, and these it is which hid the fact that he was the Son of God, since for no other reason was he supposed to be merely man than because he consisted of a human bodily substance. If not, point to something in him that was celestial, begged and borrowed from the Great Bear of the Pleiades or the Hyades: for the things I have enumerated are no less evidence that his flesh was terrestrial than it was ours. I find no trace of anything novel or anything outlandish. In fact it was only for his words and works, solely for his doctrine and power, that they were astonished at Christ as man: whereas a new kind of flesh in him would even have been remarked upon and taken for a marvel. But it was precisely the non-marvelous character of his terrestrial flesh which made the rest of his activities things to marvel at, when they asked, "Whence hath this man this doctrine and these signs?" (Mt 17:54.) These were the words of men who even despised his outward appearance, so far was his body from being of human comeliness, not to speak of celestial glory. Also, though among you the prophets are silent regarding his ignoble presence, the very sufferings, the very revilings tell the tale: the sufferings proved his flesh human, the revilings proved it uncomely. Would any one have dared even to scratch a novel kind of body with the end of his fingernail, or to defile his face with spittings unless it seemed to deserve it? Why do you allege that flesh is celestial which you have no data for thinking celestial, why deny that that is terrestrial which you have no data for recognizing as terrestrial? It hungers when with the devil, is athirst with the Samaritan woman, weeps over Lazarus, trembles at the prospect of death — "The flesh," he says, "is weak" — and at last sheds its blood. You take these, I suppose, for celestial signs. But, say I, how could he, as he said would happen, be despised and suffer, if in that flesh there had shone any radiance from his celestial nobility? By this means, then, we prove our case that in that flesh there was nothing brought down from the skies, and that that was so for the express purpose that it should be capable of being despised and of suffering.

I turn to others, equally wise in their own eyes, who insist that Christ's flesh was composed of soul, in that soul was made into flesh. In that case his soul was flesh, and as his flesh was composed of soul, so also his soul was turned into flesh. Here, as before, I ask for reasons. If it was for the salvation of soul in himself that Christ assumed soul — because it could not have been saved except through him, by being in him — I do not see why he made it into flesh by clothing himself with flesh composed of soul, as though he were unable to save soul except it were turned into flesh. . . .

Now let us put our case less figuratively. It was not feasible for the Son of God to be born of human seed, lest, if he were wholly the son of man, he should not also be the Son of God, and should be in no sense greater than Solomon or than Jonah, as in Ebion's view we should have to regard him. Therefore, being already the Son of God, of the seed of God the Father (that is, spirit), that he might also be the Son of Man all he needed was to take to him flesh out of human flesh without the action of a man's seed: for a man's seed was uncalled-for in one who had the seed of God. And so, as while not yet born of the Virgin it was possible for him to have God for his father, without a human mother, equally, when being born of the Virgin, it was possible for him to have a human mother without a human father. Thus, in short, is there man with God, when there is man's flesh with God's spirit — from man flesh without seed, from God spirit with seed. Therefore if there was an ordinance of reason regarding the need for the Son of God to be brought forth from a virgin, what room is there for doubt that he received from the Virgin that body which he did bring forth from the Virgin, seeing that which he received from God is something else? "It is," say they, "because 'the Word was made flesh' " (Jn 1:14). This saying testifies and declares what it was that was made flesh, while yet there is

no risk that, in spite of this, something else, and not the Word, was made flesh, if it was out of flesh that the Word was made flesh. Or else, if out of himself he was made flesh, let Scripture say so. Since the Scripture says no more than what the Word was made, and not also from what he was so made, it follows that its suggestion is that he was so made out of something else, and not out of himself. If not out of himself but out of something else, beginning with that admission discuss of what it is more fitting to believe the Word was made flesh, if not of that flesh within which he was made flesh — if for no other reason because the Lord himself has judicially and categorically stated, "That which is born of the flesh is flesh, because it has been born of flesh" (Jn 3:6). If he said this of man only, and not also of himself, openly deny that Christ is man, and thus maintain that it did not apply to him. "Nay," but he adds, " 'And that which is born of the Spirit is Spirit' (Jn 3:6), because 'God is spirit' (Jn 4:24), and 'He was born of God' (Jn 1:13); this certainly has him in view, the more so if it has also those who believe in him." Then if this too applies to him, why not also that other? For you cannot divide them, this to him, the other to the rest of men: for you do not deny the two substances of Christ, that of flesh and that of spirit. But if he possessed flesh no less than spirit, when he makes a statement concerning the condition of the two substances which he bore within himself, he cannot be thought to have made a pronouncement concerning spirit as being his but flesh as not his. Thus, since he was himself by the Spirit of God . . . born of God, he was also of human flesh and as man conceived and born in the flesh.

Against Praxeas[17]

But why shall I delay over things so evident, when I ought to be attacking those [arguments] by which they seek to cast darkness over [these] evident things? For, convicted on all sides by the distinctness of the Father and the Son, which we say is ordained without disturbing the permanence of the union as of the sun and the beam and of the spring and the river, they attempt to interpret this [distinctness] in another way, not less in accordance with their opinion, so as no less [than before] to distinguish Father and Son both in one person, while they say that the Son is the flesh, that is, the Man, Jesus, while the Father is the Spirit, that is, God, Christ. These who contend that the Father and the Son are one and the same, now begin to divide them rather than to call them one. For if Jesus is one and Christ is another, the Son will be one and the Father another, because Jesus is the Son and Christ is the Father. This sort of monarchy they perhaps learned of from Valentinus, to make two of Jesus and Christ. But this assumption of theirs has already had its point blunted by our previous discussion, because he whom they make the Father is described as the Word of God, or the Spirit of God and the power of the Most High: for these are not he to whom they are described as belonging, but are from him and belong to him. Yet they will be refuted also in another way in that text. "Behold," they say, "it was announced by the angel, 'Therefore that which shall be born of thee shall be called

holy, the Son of God' (Lk 1:35): and so it was flesh that was born, and so the flesh will be the Son of God." And yet the statement was made concerning the Spirit of God. For certainly it was of the Holy Spirit that the virgin conceived, and what she conceived that she brought to birth. Therefore that must have been born which was conceived and was to be brought to birth, that is, the Spirit, whose name also shall be called "Emmanuel, which is interpreted, God with us" (Mt 1:23). But flesh is not God, that of it should be said, "It shall be called holy, the Son of God"; but he who as God was born in it, of whom also the psalm [speaks], "Because God as man was born in her and hath builded her by the will of the Father" (Ps 87:5). Who, being God, was born in her? The Word, and the Spirit who with the Word was born by the Father's will. Therefore the Word is in flesh; while we must also enquire about this, how the Word was made flesh, whether as transformed into flesh or as having clothed himself with flesh. Certainly as having clothed himself. God however must necessarily be believed to be immutable and untransformable, as being eternal. But change of form is a destruction of what was there first: for everything that is transformed into something else ceases to be what it was and begins to be what it was not. But God neither ceases to be, nor can be anything else. And the Word is God, and "the Word of God abideth forever" (Is 40:8), evidently by continuing in his own form. And if it is not feasible for him to be conformed [to something else], it follows that he

---

[17] E. Evans (tr.), *Tertullian's Treatise Against Praxeas* (London: T. and A. Constable, Ltd., 1948), pp. 173–175.

must be understood to have been made flesh in the sense that he comes to be in flesh, and is manifested and seen and handled by means of the flesh (cf. 1 Jn 1:1, 2), because the other considerations also demand this acceptation. For if the Word was made flesh as the result of a transformation or mutation of substance, Jesus will then be one substance [composed] of two, flesh and spirit, a kind of mixture, as electrum is [composed] of gold and silver: and he begins to be neither gold (that is, spirit) nor silver (that is, flesh), seeing that the one thing is changed by the other and a third thing is brought into being. In that case Jesus will not be God, for he has ceased to be the Word, since it has become flesh: neither will his manhood be flesh, for it is not properly flesh, seeing it has been the Word. Thus out of both things there is neither: there is some third thing far other than both. Yet we find that he is, not in genitive dependence, set forth as both God and Man, the psalm itself making this suggestion, "Because God as man was born in her, he hath builded her by the will of the Father" (Ps 87:5), certainly [we find him set forth] as in every respect Son of God and Son of man, since [we find him] as both God and Man, without doubt according to each substance as it is distinct in what itself is, because neither is the Word anything else but God nor the flesh anything else but man. Thus also the apostle teaches of both his substances: "Who was made," he says, "of the seed of David" — here he will be man, and Son of Man: "Who was defined as Son of God according to the Spirit" (Rom 1:3–4) — here he will be God, and the Word, the Son of God: we observe a double quality, not confused but combined, Jesus in one Person God and Man. I postpone [the consideration] of "Christ." And to such a degree did there remain unimpaired the proper being of each substance, that in him, the Spirit carried out its own acts, that is powers and works and signs, while the flesh accomplished its own passions, hungering in company of the devil, thirsting in company of the Samaritan woman, weeping for Lazarus, sore troubled unto death — and at length it also died. But if there had been some third thing, a confusion of both, like electrum, there would not be in evidence such distinct proofs of both substances; but the Spirit would have performed the functions of the flesh and the flesh the functions of the Spirit, by interchange, or else neither those of the flesh nor those of the Spirit, but those of some third form, by confusion: yes, either the Word would have died or the flesh would not have died, if the Word had been converted into flesh, for either the flesh would have been immortal or the Word mortal. But because both substances acted distinctively each in its own quality, therefore to them accrued both their own activities and their own destinies. Learn therefore with Nicodemus that "what is born in the flesh is flesh and what is born of the Spirit is spirit" (Jn 3:6). Flesh does not become spirit nor spirit flesh: evidently they can [both] be in one [person]. Of these Jesus is composed, of flesh as Man and of spirit as God: and on that occasion the angel, in respect of that part in which he was spirit, pronounced him the Son of God, reserving for the flesh the designation Son of Man. Thus also the apostle, in calling him even the mediator of God and of man, (cf. 1 Tim 2:5) confirms [the fact that he is] of both substances. Lastly, you who interpret "Son of God" as the flesh, show me who the Son of Man may be. Or is he to be the Spirit? But you wish the Spirit to be taken to be the Father himself, since God is spirit: as though, just as the Word is God, God's Spirit might not also be God's Word.

And so you make Christ into the Father, you great fool, because you do not even examine the very force of this name, if indeed "Christ" is a name and not rather a title: for it signifies "anointed." Yet "anointed" is no more a name than "clothed" or "shod," but is something attributive to a name. If as a result of some quibbling Jesus were also called "clothed," as he is called Christ from the sacrament of anointing, would you, as you do here, call Jesus the Son of God but believe "clothed" to be the Father? Now concerning "Christ." If the Father is Christ, the Father is anointed, and by someone else at that: or if by himself, prove it. But that is not the teaching of the Acts of the Apostles in that cry of the church to God, "For in this city have all assembled together, Herod and Pilate with the gentiles, against the holy Son whom thou hast anointed" (Acts 4:27). Thus they testified both that Jesus is the Son of God and that the Son was anointed by the Father: consequently Jesus will be the same as Christ who was anointed by the Father, not [the same as] the Father who anointed the Son. So also Peter: "Therefore let all the house of Israel know assuredly that God hath made both Lord and Christ" — that is, anointed — "this Jesus whom ye crucified" (Acts 2:36). But John even brands as a liar him who has denied that Jesus is Christ, (cf. 1 Jn 2:22), and in contrast [says] that everyone who believes that Jesus is Christ is born of God (cf. 1 Jn 5:1): for which

reason he also exhorts us to believe in the name of his Son Jesus Christ, so that, he says, we may have fellowship with the Father and with his Son Jesus Christ" (1 Jn 1:3). Thus also Paul in every place puts "God the Father and our Lord Jesus Christ": when he writes to the Romans he gives thanks to God through our Lord Jesus Christ (Rom 1:8); when to the Galatians, he represents himself as an apostle, not from men nor through man, but through Jesus Christ and God the Father (Gal 1:1). And you have, throughout all his collected works, [texts] which make statements in this manner and set forth as two God the Father and our Lord Jesus Christ the Son of the Father, and [say] that Jesus himself is Christ, and, under another name also, the Son of God. For continually, by that right by which both names belong to one, that is, the Son of God, one even without the other belongs to the same one: and if "Jesus" alone is written "Christ" also is understood because Jesus was anointed; while if only "Christ" is written, the same is also Jesus because the anointed is Jesus. And of these names one is a proper name which was conferred by the angel, while the other as an attributive accrues from the anointing, yet only so long as Christ is the Son and not the Father. Finally, how blind is the man who does not understand that if he ascribes the name of Christ to the Father the presage of another god is implied in the name of Christ. For if Christ the Father is God who says, "I ascend to my Father and your Father and my God and your God," evidently he reveals another father and god above himself. Also if the Father is Christ, there is another "who establisheth the thunder and createth the spirit and announceth unto men his Christ." And if "the kings of the earth are stood up and the rulers are gathered together into one against the Lord and against his Christ," there will be another lord against whose Christ the kings and rulers are gathered together. And if "Thus saith the Lord to my Lord Christ," there will be another lord who is speaking to Christ the Father. And when the apostle writes, "That the God of our Lord Jesus Christ may give you the Spirit of wisdom and knowledge," there will be another god of Jesus Christ, the bestower of spiritual gifts. Certainly, so as not to wander over the whole ground, he who raised up Christ and is also to raise up our mortal bodies, will be as it were another raiser up than the Father who died and the Father who was raised up, if it is the case that Christ who died is the Father.

CHAPTER 2. ALEXANDRIAN AND ANTIOCHENE THEOLOGY: ARIANISM, NESTORIANISM

INTRODUCTION

The Christology of the Schools of Antioch and Alexandria[1]

by Karl Adam

The Christological controversies of the early Church were settled by two schools of theology, the school of Alexandria and the school of Antioch. The former favored a metaphysical and contemplative view of God and the world; the second tended to stress empirical data, i.e., what is historically given. Where the school of Antioch aspired to God from the world of experience, the Alexandrians labored to understand the world of historical data from the divine. Where the school of

Antioch worked from the depths to the heights, Alexandrian speculation moved from the heights to the depths.

This characteristic distinction between the two schools became the more apparent as the question became more important of *how* divinity and humanity were united in Christ. The school of Antioch started from the historical appearance of Jesus: Christ came into the world wholly man, with a consciousness of human identity. The disputes with Apollinaris had clearly established that Christ possessed a consciousness not only of divine but also of human identity. This

[1] *The Christ of Faith: The Christology of the Church* (New York: Pantheon, 1957; London: Burns & Oates, 1957), p. 34.

27

led them to the conclusion that Christ also had a human self. Hence their question: If Christ's human self is historically given, indeed has priority, how can the divine self be united with this human self? From the start this question involved the danger of deducing the existence of an autonomous human self from the peculiarity of the human consciousness of self, and thus of destroying the unity of Christ's person. The school of Antioch was strongly tempted to regard the union of divinity and humanity in Christ not as an inner union of essence, but as merely external, accidental. It would regard the human self as coexistent with the divine self.

Their unity would be not physical, but moral; not of being, but of will; a mere reciprocal relationship (ἕνωσις σχετεκή) which arises out of the loving inclination of divine and human selves toward each other, and thus must be renewed. Thus a continual exchange of love, a constant movement of love, would take place in Christ between the divine self of the Logos and the human self. The continual obligation of love (συνάφεια) elevates even the human self to the Son of God. So there are two sons of God in Christ, the natural and the adopted. Mary bore only this adopted son. Hence she cannot strictly be called the mother of God, but only the mother of Christ.

I. ORIGEN*

Dialogue With Heraclides[2]

* Origen (c185–254), born in Egypt, received a thorough Christian education. During persecution his father was murdered. His enflamed desire also to die for the faith was forestalled by his mother who kept him home by hiding all his clothes. He later became head of the Christian school at Alexandria where he led a deeply ascetical life and studied the pagan philosophers, the more surely to gain influence on his pupils. After a Palestinian bishop had ordained Origen, his own bishop Demetrius, in punishment for the irregularity of his ordination, deposed and exiled him. He was later imprisoned under the persecution of Decius, was tortured and soon died. In his *Dialogue with Heraclides,* a complete recording of an actual discussion, Origen develops his teaching concerning the relations between the Father and the Son in the Trinity. In Book II of his *Concerning First Principles,* the first systematic presentation of Christian theology, he treats of the redemption of man by the incarnate Logos.

Heraclides: I also believe what the sacred Scriptures say: "In the beginning was the Word, and the Word was with God, and the Word was God. He was in the beginning with God. All things were made by him, and without him nothing was made" (Jn 1:1–3).

[2] Oulton and Chadwick, *Alexandrian Christianity* (Philadelphia: Westminster Press, 1950), pp. 437–439.

Accordingly, we hold the same faith that is taught in these words, and we believe that Christ took flesh, that he was born, that he went up to heaven in the flesh in which he rose again, that he is sitting at the right hand of the Father, and that thence he shall come and judge the living and the dead, being God and man.

Origen: Since once an inquiry has begun it is proper to say something upon the subject of the inquiry, I will speak. The whole church is present and listening. It is not right that there should be any difference in knowledge between one church and another, for you are not the false church.

I charge you, father Heraclides: God is the almighty, the uncreated, the supreme God who made all things. Do you hold this doctrine?

Heracl.: I do. That is what I also believe.

Orig.: Christ Jesus who was in the form of God (cf. Phil 2:6), being other than the God in whose form he existed, was he God before he came into the body or not?

Heracl.: He was God before.

Orig.: Was he God before he came into the body or not?

Heracl.: Yes, he was.

Orig.: Was he God distinct from this God in whose form he existed?

Heracl.: Obviously he was distinct from another being and, since he was in the form of him who created all things, he was distinct from him.

Orig.: Is it true then that there was a God, the Son of God, the only begotten of God, the firstborn of all creation, and that we need have no fear of saying that in one sense there are two Gods, while in another there is one God?

Heracl.: What you say is evident. But we affirm that God is the almighty, God without beginning, without end, containing all things and not contained by anything; and that his Word is the Son of the living God, God and man, through whom all things were made, God according to the spirit, man inasmuch as he was born of Mary.

Orig.: You do not appear to have answered my question. Explain what you mean. For perhaps I failed to follow you. Is the Father God?

Heracl.: Assuredly.

Orig.: Is the Son distinct from the Father?

Heracl.: Of course. How can he be Son if he is also Father?

Orig.: While being distinct from the Father is the Son himself also God?

Heracl.: He himself is also God.

Orig.: And do two Gods become a unity?

Heracl.: Yes.

Orig.: Do we confess two Gods?

Heracl.: Yes. The power is one.

Orig.: But as our brethren take offence at the statement that there are two Gods, we must formulate the doctrine carefully, and show in what sense they are two and in what sense the two are one God. Also the holy Scriptures have taught that several things which are two are one. And not only things which are two, for they have also taught that in some instances more than two, or even a very much larger number of things, are one. Our present task is not to broach a problematic subject only to pass it by and deal cursorily with the matter, but for the sake of the simple folk to chew up, so to speak, the meat, and little by little to instill the doctrine in the ears of our hearers. . . . Accordingly, there are many things which are two that are said in the Scriptures to be one. What passages of Scripture? Adam is one person, his wife another. Adam is distinct from his wife, and his wife is distinct from her husband. Yet it is said in the story of the creation of the world that they two are one: "For the two shall be one flesh" (Gen 2:24; Mt 19:5). Therefore, sometimes two beings can become one flesh. Notice, however, that in the case of Adam and Eve it is not said that the two shall become one spirit, nor that the two shall become one soul, but that they shall become one flesh. Again, the righteous man is distinct from Christ; but he is said by the apostle to be one with Christ: "For he that is joined to the Lord is one spirit" (1 Cor 6:17). Is it not true that the one is of a subordinate nature or of a low and inferior nature, while Christ's nature is divine and glorious and blessed? Are they therefore no longer two? Yes, for the man and the woman are "no longer two but one flesh," and the righteous man and Christ are "one spirit." So in relation to the Father and God of the universe, our Savior and Lord is not one flesh, nor one spirit, but something higher than flesh and spirit, namely, one God. The appropriate word when human beings are joined to one another is flesh. The appropriate word when a righteous man is joined to Christ is spirit. But the word when Christ is united to the Father is not flesh, nor spirit, but more honorable than these — God. That is why we understand in this sense "I and the Father are one" (Jn 10:30). When we pray, because of the one party let us preserve the duality, because of the other party let us hold to the unity. In this way we avoid falling into the opinion of those who have been separated from the Church and turned to the illusory notion of monarchy, who abolish the Son as distinct from the Father and virtually abolish the Father also. Nor do we fall into the other blasphemous doctrine which denies the deity of Christ. What then do the divine Scriptures mean when they say: "Beside me there is no other God, and there shall be none after me," and "I am and there is no God but me"? (Is 43:10; Dt 32:39.) In these utterances we are not to think that the unity applies to the God of the universe . . . in separation from Christ, and certainly not to Christ in separation from God. Let us rather say that the sense is the same as that of Jesus' saying, "I and my Father are one."

II. ARIUS*

Letter of Arius to Eusebius of Nicomedia[3]

* Arius (c250–c336), heresiarch, met with great success as a preacher in Alexandria after his ordination. He propagated subordinationist doctrine concerning the person of Christ and was excommunicated for defense of his condemned position. Largely through the efforts of St. Athanasius, the Council of Nicea met in 325 and publicly condemned him and his teachings. Until death he defended his position: "The Son has a beginning."

To my very dear lord, the faithful and orthodox man of God Eusebius, Arius, unjustly persecuted by Pope Alexander for the sake of the all-conquering truth of which you are also a defender, sends greetings in the Lord.

Since my father Ammonius was coming to Nicomedia, it seemed to me fitting and proper to send you greetings by him, and also to bring to your attention, in the natural love and

[3] *The Christology of the Later Fathers* (London: S.C.M. Press, 1950), p. 329.

affection which you have for the brethren, for the sake of God and his Christ, that the bishop greatly injures and persecutes us and does all he can against us, trying to drive us out of the city as godless men, since we do not agree with him when he says publicly, "Always Father, always Son," "Father and Son together," "The Son exists unbegottenly with God," "The eternal begotten," "Unbegotten-only-one," "Neither in thought nor by a single instant is God before the Son," "Always God, always Son," "The Son is of God himself."

And since your brother Eusebius in Caesarea and Theodotus and Paulinus and Athanasius and Gregorius and all the bishops of the East say that God exists without beginning before the Son, they are anathematized, except Philogonius, Hellanicus, and Macarius, [and such] heretical and uninstructed men, some of whom speak of the Son as an emission, others as a projection, others as co-unbegotten. But we cannot bear even to listen to such im-pieties, though the heretics should threaten us with a thousand deaths. What is it that we say, and think, and have taught, and teach? That the Son is not unbegotten, nor a part of the unbegotten in any way, nor [formed out] of any substratum, but that he was constituted by [God's] will and counsel, before times and before ages, full (of grace and truth), divine, unique, unchangeable. And before he was begotten or created or ordained or founded, he was not. For he was not unbegotten. We are per-secuted because we say, "The Son has a beginning, but God is without be-ginning." For this we are persecuted, and because we say, "He is [made] out of things that were not." But this is what we say, since he is neither a part of God nor [formed] out of any substratum. For this we are persecuted, and you know the rest. So I pray that you may prosper in the Lord, remem-bering our afflictions, fellow Lucianist, truly Eusebius.

The Creed of Ariminum[4]

INTRODUCTION

During the sole reign of Constan-tius, 350–361, a confusing series of Arian and Semi-Arian creeds were issued, many of them prepared at what has been called "the imperial creed factory" at Sirmium in the western Balkans. The "Dated Creed" of 359 is a good statement of the Semi-Arian position, declaring the Son to be "like the Father in all respects," *kata panta*. This was propounded to the double Council for which the Western bishops were summoned to

[4] *Ibid.*, pp. 341–342.

Ariminum in Italy and the Eastern to Seleucia in Isauria. But the Western bishops insisted on the Creed of Nicaea and the Easterners preferred the fairly high Christology of the Second Creed of the Council of Anti-och of 341. Nevertheless delegates from Ariminum were induced to ac-cept, at Nice in Thrace, a revision of the Dated Creed in a more definitely Arian direction, replacing "like in all respects" by simply "like." The bish-ops at Ariminum were forced to follow them, and on the last day of 359 delegates from Seleucia were badgered into the same action by the emperor himself at Constantinople. As formally accepted at a council at Constantinople in January, 360, this was the Creed which Ulfilas took to the Goths. It represents central or moderate Arianism, asserting the likeness of the Son to the Father, but refusing to specify the degree or quality of that likeness — the faith of the Homoeans as distinguished from the Semi-Arian Homoousians and the radical Anomoeans. It is the last of the Arian creeds, and the longest-lived, since it survived among the Germanic Arian Churches until their extinction in the seventh century. The text is to be found in Athanasius, *On the Synods,* 30.

The Text

We believe in one God, Father almighty, from whom are all things,

And in the unique Son of God, who was begotten of God before all ages and before all beginning, through whom all things came into being, both visible and invisible, begotten uniquely, only from the Father only, God of God, like to the Father who begot him, according to the Scriptures, whose generation no one knows except only the Father who begot him. We know that this unique Son of God came from heaven, the Father sending him, as it is written, for the destruction of sin and death, and was born of [the] Holy Spirit, of Mary the virgin according to the flesh, as it is written, and companied with the disciples, and when all the dispensation was fulfilled according to the Father's will, was crucified and died and was buried and descended into the lower regions, before whom hell [hades] itself trembled, who also rose again from the dead on the third day and sojourned with the disciples, and when forty days were fulfilled was taken up into heaven, and sits on the right hand of the Father, [and] is to come on the last day, of the resurrection, in the Father's glory, to render to each according to his works,

And in the Holy Spirit, whom the unique Son of God himself, Christ our Lord and God, promised to send to the race of men as a Paraclete, as it is written, "the Spirit of truth," whom he sent to them when he had ascended into heaven. But as to the word "essence" (*ousia*), which was used by the Fathers in simplicity, but, being unknown to the people caused scandal, because the Scriptures do not contain it, it seems best that it should be taken away and no mention made of it in the future, since the divine Scriptures nowhere made mention of the essence of Father and Son; nor, similarly, should the word *hypostasis* be used of Father and Son and Holy Spirit. But we say that the Son is like the Father, as the divine Scriptures say and teach; and let all heresies which have been condemned before and such recent ones as may have arisen and are contrary to this statement be anathema.

III. ST. ATHANASIUS*

The Incarnation of the Word of God[5]

---

* St. Athanasius (c296–373), Bishop of Alexandria, incurred the enmity of the influential Arians during the reigns of Constantine and Constantius. He was exiled and fled to Rome. He later returned, but was exiled twice again by Constantius and Julian. He returned finally in 366, continued to fight against the powerful Arian sect and tried to reconcile it to the *homoousios*, "of one substance," formula. In *The Incarnation of the Word of God*, Athanasius defends Christian faith in the incarnation against both Jew and pagan. In it he expounds how God the Word, the Logos, by his union with manhood, restored to fallen man the image of God in which he had been first created, and how, by his death and resurrection, he had met and defeated death, the consequence of sin. As Anselm will later do in his *Cur Deus Homo?* Athanasius here presents the incarnation as the necessary remedy for fallen man and his restoration.

. . . Because death and corruption were gaining ever firmer hold on them, the human race was in process of destruction. Man, who was created in God's image and in his possession of reason reflected the very Word Himself, was disappearing, and the work of God was being undone. The law of death, which followed from the Transgression, prevailed upon us, and from it there was no escape. The thing that was happening was in truth both monstrous and unfitting. It would, of course, have been unthinkable that God should go back upon His word and that man, having transgressed, should not die; but it was equally monstrous that beings which once had shared the nature of the Word should perish and turn back again into non-existence through corruption. It was unworthy of the goodness of God that creatures made by Him should be brought to nothing through the deceit wrought upon man by the devil; and it was supremely unfitting that the work of God in mankind should dis-

appear, either through their own negligence or through the deceit of evil spirits. As, then, the creatures whom He had created reasonable, like the Word, were in fact perishing, and such noble works were on the road to ruin, what then was God, being Good, to do? Was He to let corruption and death have their way with them? In that case, what was the use of having made them in the beginning? Surely it would have been better never to have been created at all than, having been created, to be neglected and perish; and, besides that, such indifference to the ruin of His own work before His very eyes would argue not goodness in God but limitation, and that far more than if He had never created men at all. It was impossible, therefore, that God should leave man to be carried off by corruption, because it would be unfitting and unworthy of Himself.

Yet, true though this is, it is not the whole matter. As we have already noted, it was unthinkable that God, the Father of Truth, should go back upon His word regarding death in order to ensure our continued exis-

[5] *The Incarnation of the Word of God*, (New York: Macmillan Co., 1946), pp. 32–35.

tence. He could not falsify Himself; what, then, was God to do? Was He to demand repentance from men for their transgression? You might say that that was worthy of God, and argue further that, as through the Transgression they became subject to corruption, so through repentance they might return to incorruption again. But repentance would not guard the Divine consistency, for, if death did not hold dominion over men, God would still remain untrue. Nor does repentance recall men from what is according to their nature; all that it does is to make them cease from sinning. Had it been a case of a trespass only, and not of a subsequent corruption, repentance would have been well enough; but when once transgression had begun men came under the power of the corruption proper to their nature and were bereft of the grace which belonged to them as creatures in the Image of God. No, repentance could not meet the case. What — or rather *Who* was it that was needed for such grace and such recall as we required? Who, save the Word of God Himself, Who also in the beginning had made all things out of nothing? His part it was, and His alone, both to bring again the corruptible to incorruption and to maintain for the Father His consistency of character with all. For He alone, being Word of the Father and above all, was in consequence both able to recreate all, and worthy to suffer on behalf of all and to be an ambassador for all with the Father.

For this purpose, then, the incorporeal and incorruptible and immaterial Word of God entered our world. In one sense, indeed, He was not far from it before, for no part of creation had ever been without Him Who, while ever abiding in union with the Father, yet fills all things that are. But now He entered the world in a new way, stooping to our level in His love and self-revealing to us. He saw the reasonable race, the race of men that, like Himself, expressed the Father's Mind, wasting out of existence, and death reigning over all in corruption. He saw that corruption held us all the closer, because it was the penalty for the Transgression; He saw, too, how unthinkable it would be for the law to be repealed before it was fulfilled. He saw how unseemly it was that the very things of which He Himself was the Artificer should be disappearing. He saw how the surpassing wickedness of men was mounting up against them; He saw also their universal liability to death. All this He saw and, pitying our race, moved with compassion for our limitation, unable to endure that death should have the mastery, rather than that His creatures should perish and the work of His Father for us men come to nought, He took to Himself a body, a human body even as our own. Nor did He will merely to become embodied or merely to appear; had that been so, He could have revealed His divine majesty in some other and better way. No, He took *our* body, and not only so, but He took it directly from a spotless, stainless virgin, without the agency of human father — a pure body, untainted by intercourse with man. He, the Mighty One, the Artificer of all, Himself prepared this body in the virgin as a temple for Himself, and took it for His very own, as the instrument through which He was known and in which He dwelt. Thus, taking a body like our own, because all our bodies were liable to the corruption of death, He surrendered His body to death instead of all, and offered it to the Father. This He did out of sheer love for us, so that in His death all might die, and the law of death thereby be abolished because, having fulfilled in His body that for which it was appointed, it was thereafter voided of its power for men. This He did that He might turn again to incorruption men who had turned back to corruption, and make them alive through death by the appropriation of His body and by the grace of His resurrection. Thus He would make death to disappear from them as utterly as straw from fire.

The Word perceived that corruption could not be got rid of otherwise than through death; yet He Himself, as the Word, being immortal and the Father's Son, was such as could not die. For this reason, therefore, He assumed a body capable of death, in order that it, through belonging to the Word Who is above all, might become in dying a sufficient exchange for all, and, itself remaining incorruptible through His indwelling, might thereafter put an end to corruption for all others as well, by the grace of the resurrection. It was by surrendering to death the body which He had taken, as an offering and sacrifice free from every stain, that He forthwith abolished death for His human brethren by the offering of the equivalent. For naturally, since the Word of God was above all, when He offered His own temple and bodily instrument as a substitute for the life of all, He fulfilled in death all that was required. Naturally also, through this union of the immortal Son of God with our human nature, all men were clothed with incorruption in the promise of the resurrection. For the solidarity of mankind is such that, by virtue of the Word's indwelling in a single human body, the corruption which goes with death has lost its power over all. You know how it is when some great king enters a large city and dwells in one of its houses; because of his dwelling in that single house, the whole city is honored, and enemies and robbers cease to molest it. Even so is it with the King of all; He has come into our country and dwelt in one body amidst the many, and in consequence the designs of the enemy against mankind have been foiled, and the corruption of death, which formerly held them in its power, has simply ceased to be. For the human race would have perished utterly had not the Lord and Savior of all, the Son of God, come among us to put an end to death.

IV. ST. CYRIL OF JERUSALEM*

Catechetical Lecture XI[6]

---

* St. Cyril (c315–386). Arian bishops had Cyril banished several times. He was also suspected by Rome of being unorthodox because he disliked the term *homoousios* the ground of Nicene faith. St. Gregory of Nyssa was sent to investigate the Jerusalem Church and cleared Cyril of suspicions. In the eleventh of his twenty-four *Catecheses*, catechumenal instructions delivered at Lent and Easter, Cyril states clearly the divinity of Jesus, countering Arian contentions that there was a time when he was not and that he was the Son of God only by adoption.

6 *Cyril of Jerusalem and Nemesius of Emesa* (London: S.C.M. Press, 1955), pp. 141–143.

Believe, then, in Jesus Christ, Son of the living God. He is only-begotten as the Gospel says, "For God so loved the world that he gave his only-begotten Son, that whosoever believeth in him should not perish, but have everlasting life" (Jn 3:16), and "He that believeth on him is not condemned" (Jn 3:18), "but is passed from death unto life" (Jn 5:24). "But he that believeth not the Son, shall not see life, but the wrath of God abideth on him" (Jn 3:36); "because he hath not believed on the only-begotten Son of God" (Jn 3:18). Of him John bore witness saying, "And we beheld his glory, the glory as of the only-begotten of the Father, full of grace and truth" (Jn 1:14), and him the demons trembling hailed, "Let us alone; what have we to do with thee, Jesus thou Son of the most high God?" (Mk 5:7.)

So, being begotten of the Father, he is Son of God by nature, not by adoption. And "he that loveth him that begat, loveth him also that is begotten of him" (1 Jn 5:1), while he who sets at nought him who is the begotten insults by implication him who begat. Now when you hear of God begetting, do not fall athinking in corporeal terms, or risk blaspheming by imagining corruptible generation. "God is a Spirit" (Jn 4:24). Divine generation is spiritual. Bodies are begotten from bodies, and there has to be an interval of time for it to be completed. But time does not come into the begetting of the Son from the Father. Bodies are begotten in an imperfect state, but the Son of God was begotten perfect. For what he is now, that has he been timelessly begotten from the beginning. We are begotten so as to develop from childishness to rationality. Being man, your first state

is imperfect and your advance is by stages. But do not imagine anything of that sort in divine generation, or charge the Begetter with lack of power. For you might charge the Begetter with lack of power, if the Begotten was first imperfect and then reached perfection in time; that is if the Begetter did not fully grant from the beginning what was by supposition granted after the lapse of time.[7]

Do not think, therefore, in terms of human generation, as when Abraham begat Isaac. For Abraham truly begat Isaac, but what he begat was not the product of his will, but what another rendered to him. But when God the Father begat, it was not as unknowing what should be, or only after some deliberation.[8] It would be the extreme of blasphemy to say that God did not know whom he was begetting; nor would it be any less blasphemous to say that the Father became Father only after deliberating. For God was not at first childless, and then after lapse of time became Father, but he had his Son from all eternity, not begetting him as men beget men,

----

[7] This is a new argument against the "adoption" doctrine of Paul of Samosata, against whom bishop Hymenaeus of Jerusalem had taken the field. Paul had argued that the Father is honored by having unique Godhead, and by being believed to have divinized the Son of Mary by *prokopē,* or advance in grace. Cyril replies that if God is supposed to need time to produce a Son thus, the thought is dishonoring to God.

[8] The Arians posed the dilemma: either God begat because he could not help himself and without knowing the outcome, or he thought first and begat deliberately. In the latter case, "there was when the Son was not." Cyril parries this argument by indicating a number of ways in which the analogy of begetting cannot be pressed, in theology, and that the Arian dilemma is based on such an illegitimate pressing of analogy.

but as he alone knows who begat him true God before all ages.

The Father, being himself true God begat a Son like to himself, true God.[9] Do not compare it with teachers "begetting" disciples, or as Paul says to some of his, "For in Christ Jesus I begat you through the gospel" (1 Cor 4:15). For in such cases, someone who was not by nature a "son," becomes such by discipleship. But the Son of God is Son by nature, true Son. You *photizomenoi* are now becoming sons of God, but do not liken Christ's Sonship to that. For your sonship is one of adoption by grace, as it is written, "But as many as received him, to them gave he the right to become children of God, even to them that believe on his name; which were begotten not of blood, nor of the will of the flesh, nor of the will of man, but of God" (Jn 1:12–13). We indeed were begotten "of water and of the Spirit" (Jn 3:5), but it was not thus that the Son was begotten of the Father, who at the time of his baptism addressed him, saying "This is my Son" (Mt 3:17), He did not say, This man is now become my Son, but "This is my Son," to show that he was Son prior to anything baptism might bring about.

Neither did the Father beget the Son in the way in which the human mind begets speech.[10] For mind is something permanently present in us, but speech, spoken and dispersed in the air, perishes. For we know Christ to have been begotten, not as an uttered word, but as indwelling[11] reason, and living, not spoken with lips and dispersed, but eternally and ineffably begotten of the Father, and come into being as a Person,[12] that is to say "In the beginning was the Word, and the Word was with God, and the Word was God" (Jn 1:1). The Word is seated at the Father's right hand, understanding his will, and creating the world at his behest, a Word descending and ascending.[13] For uttered speech neither descends nor ascends. He is Word that speaks and says, "The things which I have seen with my Father, these I speak" (Jn 8:38). He is authoritative Word, reigning over all, for "the Father hath committed all things unto the Son" (Jn 5:22).

So the way in which the Father begat the Son is not attainable by human analogy, but is one that he alone knows. For we do not profess to say how he begat him, but we affirm that it was not in this or that manner. And our ignorance of the way in which the Father begat the Son is shared by every created being.

---

[9] It is impossible to find a nuance of difference between the substance of this confession and the Nicene faith.

[10] This analogy for the divine generation had a great vogue with the second-century apologists, and is given in its crudest form in Theophilus of Antioch, *To Autolycus.* It was a very effective means of commending to the Greeks the Christian claim that one known in recent history is nevertheless the eternal revelation of God. But by the time of Cyril it had become clear what error could follow from pressing this analogy too far.

[11] *Enhypostatos,* having real being within another existent.

[12] *Hypostasis,* already, among the Syrians and Palestinians, beginning to be used of the Persons of the Trinity, in distinction from *Ousia,* the shared reality of Godhead wherein the Three are one God.

[13] Cyril may have before his mind Is 55:8–11, with its notion of God's Word coming down into the world to cause his will to be done, and then "reporting back" the completion of its mission. In the later part of the section, Cyril is reserving, under safeguards, the analogy which he has begun by seeming to reject.

V. ST. BASIL*

Letter to the Sozopolitans[14]

---

* St. Basil the Great (c330–379), after a thorough education in the best that both pagan and Christian schools could offer, settled as a hermit and devoted his time to meditation and preaching. His bishop, Eusebius of Caesarea, called upon him to defend the faith against Valens, the Arian emperor. When the Council of Constanti-nople met, shortly after his death, it practi-cally terminated the Arian controversies. In his *Letter to the Sozopolitans,* (377) he fol-lows his basic concern which is rather to distinguish the divine and human charac-teristics in Christ than to stress the unity of person.

I read the letter, most honorable brethren, which you wrote concerning your troubles. And we rejoiced in the Lord that you associated us with you in your solicitude for the care of things needful for you and de-manding attention. But we felt much sorrow on hearing that, in addition to the disorder brought upon the churches by the Arians, and the con-fusion which they have produced con-cerning the doctrines of faith, still another novelty has appeared among you, throwing the brotherhood into great grief, as you have written to us, namely, that men are introducing in-novations and dogmas unfamiliar to the ears of the faithful as if they were, as they pretend, from the teaching of the Scriptures. You have written, in fact, that there are some among you who are doing away with the Incarna-tion of our Lord Jesus Christ, as much as they are able, and rejecting the grace of the great mystery kept secret from eternity but manifested in His own time (cf. 1 Tim 3:16), when the Lord, after having gone through all things pertaining to the care of the human race, in addition to all else bestowed upon us His own sojourn

among us (cf. Gal 4:4). For He aided His own creature, first through the patriarchs, whose lives have been set forth as examples and rules for those desiring to follow in the footsteps of the saints and through a zeal like theirs to arrive at the perfection of good deeds. Then, He gave a law for his assistance, delivering it by angels through Moses (cf. Gal 13:19); then, Prophets, who proclaimed be-forehand the salvation that was to be (cf. Acts 3:18), judges, kings, and just men, who performed their mighty works with hidden hand. After all these, in the last days, He Himself was manifested in the flesh, "born of a woman, born under the Law, that he might redeem those who were under the Law, that we might receive the adoption of sons" (Gal 4:4–5).

If, therefore, the sojourn of the Lord in the flesh did not take place, the Redeemer did not pay to death the price for us, and He did not by His own power destroy the dominion of death. For, if that which is subject to death were one thing, and that which was assumed by the Lord were another, then death would not have ceased performing its own works, nor would the sufferings of the God-bear-ing flesh have become ours gain; He would not have destroyed sin in the

---

[14] *St. Basil: Letters,* Vol. II (New York: Fathers of the Church, Inc., 1955), pp. 232–235.

flesh (cf. Rom 3:3–4); we who had died in Adam would not have been made to live in Christ (cf. 1 Cor 15:22); that which had fallen asunder would not have been restored; that which was shattered would not have been repaired; that which had been estranged through the deceit of the serpent would not have been again made God's own. For, all these things are done away with by those who say that the Lord made His sojourn with a heavenly body.[15] And what was the need of the blessed Virgin, if the God-bearing flesh was not to be assumed from the substance of Adam? But who is so bold as now to revive once more through sophistic words and the testimony, as they pretend, of the Scriptures the teaching of Valentinus[16] which was silenced long ago? This impiety of the unappearance,[17] in fact, is not something new, but it was begun long ago by the weak-minded Valentinus, who, taking a few detached phrases of the Apostle, constructed the impious fiction for himself, saying that He had taken on "the nature of a slave" (cf. Phl 2:5–8), and not the slave himself, and that the Lord had been made "in the form," but that humanity itself had not been assumed by Him. These men,

---

[15] The doctrine of the Apollinarians.

[16] Valentinus, an Alexandrian, taught in Rome from the year 130 until he was excommunicated in the year 140. He died in Cyprus in 161. He pretended to be a follower of a certain Theudas, the disciple of St. Paul. His system was most elaborate and ingenious, and his sect was the most widely spread of the Gnostic heresies.

[17] Docetism, the common doctrine of many Gnostic sects, signified that Christ had no real human body, but had merely assumed an ethereal or phantom body. However, Valentinus and his followers taught that Christ had assumed a body. Each school had a different teaching on this point, but all denied the real Incarnation.

whom we ought to deplore bitterly since they are bringing new disturbances upon you, seem to be uttering words akin to those.

Now, as to their saying that human feelings pass over to the Godhead Itself, that is characteristic of those who never preserve any consistency in thoughts and are unaware that some feelings are of the flesh and others of flesh endowed with a soul, and still others of a soul using a body. Now, it is a property of flesh to be cut and lessened and destroyed, and, again, of flesh endowed with a soul to suffer weariness and pain and hunger and thirst and to be overcome by sleep; and the properties of a soul using a body are griefs and anxieties and cares and all such things. Some of these are natural and necessary to the living creatures, but some are due to a depraved will, brought on by a life that is dissolute and not trained to virtue. Therefore, it is evident that the Lord took on the natural feelings for a confirmation of the true Incarnation and not of one according to appearance, but rejected as unworthy of the undefiled Godhead the feelings arising from vice which soil the purity of our souls. For this reason it is said that He was "made in the likeness of sinful flesh" (Rom 8:3), not, indeed, in the likeness of flesh, as these men think, but in the likeness of sinful flesh. Accordingly, He took our flesh with its natural feelings, but He "did not sin" (1 Pet 2:22). Yet, even as death in the flesh, which was handed down to us through Adam, was swallowed up by the Godhead, so also sin was utterly destroyed by the justice which is in Jesus Christ, so that in the resurrection we resume our flesh, which is neither liable to death nor subject to sin (cf. Rom 5:12, 17).

These are, brothers, the mysteries of the Church; these are the traditions of the Fathers. We earnestly beg every man who fears the Lord and is awaiting the judgment of God not to be led astray by various teachings. If anyone teaches otherwise than right and does not have recourse to the sound words of faith, but, rejecting the sayings of the Spirit, makes his own teaching of greater authority than the evidence from the Gospels, guard against such a one.

May the Lord grant that at some time we may meet together, so that whatever has now escaped our explanation we may supply by a personal interview. Out of many things we have written few to you, since we do not wish to go beyond the limits of a letter, and since at the same time we are convinced that for those who fear the Lord even a brief reminder is sufficient.

VI. ST. JOHN CHRYSOSTOM*

Christmas Morning[18]

---

*St. John Chrysostom (c347–407), Doctor of the Church, had been educated for law but became interested in theological studies and finally embraced the monastic life. His bishop at Antioch assigned him to preaching, at which he excelled and earned the title "goldenmouthed." He incurred the displeasure of Empress Eudoxia, who successfully had him falsely condemned for heretical views. Banished, he died from the severities of continued exile and travel. He emphasized throughout his homilies and sermons the complete and perfect divinity of Christ against the Arians and the complete and perfect humanity against the Apollinarists.

I behold a new and wondrous mystery. My ears resound to the Shepherd's song, piping no soft melody, but chanting full forth a heavenly hymn. The Angels sing. The Archangels blend their voice in harmony. The Cherubim hymn their joyful praise. The Seraphim exalt His glory. All join to praise this holy feast, beholding the Godhead here on earth, and man in heaven. He Who is above, now for our redemption dwells here below; and he that was lowly is by divine mercy raised.

Bethlehem this day resembles heaven; hearing from the stars the singing of angelic voices; and in place of the sun, enfolds within itself on every side, the Sun of Justice. And ask not how: for where God wills, the order of nature yields. For He willed, He had the power, He descended, He redeemed; all things move in obedience to God. This day He Who is, is Born; and He Who is, becomes what He was not. For when He was God, He became man; yet not departing from the Godhead that is His. Nor yet by any loss of divinity became He man, nor through increase became He God from man; but being the Word He became flesh, His nature, because of impassibility, remaining unchanged. . . .

Yet He has not forsaken His angels, nor left them deprived of His care, nor because of His Incarnation has He

[18] *The Sunday Sermons of the Great Fathers*, Vol. I (Chicago: Henry Regnery Co., 1955), pp. 110–113.

departed from the Godhead. And behold kings have come, that they might adore the heavenly King of glory; soldiers that they might serve the Leader of the Hosts of Heaven; women, that they might adore Him Who was born of a woman so that He might change the pains of childbirth into joy; virgins, to the Son of the Virgin, beholding with joy, that He Who is the Giver of milk, Who has decreed that the fountains of the breast pour forth in ready streams, receives from a Virgin Mother the food of infancy; infants, that they may adore Him Who became a little child, so that *out of the mouth of infants and of sucklings,* He might perfect praise; children, to the Child Who raised up martyrs through the rage of Herod; men, to Him Who became man, that He might heal the miseries of His servants; shepherds, to the Good Shepherd Who has laid down His life for His sheep; priests, to Him Who has become a High Priest according to the order of Melchisedech; servants, to Him Who "took upon Himself the form of a servant" that He might bless our servitude with the reward of freedom (Phil 2:7); fishermen, to Him Who from amongst fishermen chose catchers of men; publicans, to Him Who from amongst them named a chosen Evangelist; sinful women, to Him Who exposed His Feet to the tears of the repentant; and that I may embrace them all together, all sinners have come, that they may look upon the Lamb of God who taketh away the sins of the world. . . .

This day He Who was ineffably begotten of the Father, was for me born of the Virgin, in a way no tongue can tell. Begotten according to His nature before all ages from the Father: in what manner He knows Who has begotten Him; born again this day

from the Virgin, above the order of nature, in what manner knoweth the power of the Holy Spirit. And His heavenly generation is true, and His generation here on earth is true. As God He is truly begotten of God; so also as man is He truly born from the Virgin. In heaven He alone is the Only-Begotten of the One God; on earth He alone is the Only-Begotten of the unique Virgin.

And as in the heavenly generation, to imply a mother is heretical, so in this earthly generation, to speak of a father is blasphemy. The Father begot in the spirit (*Pater absque defluxu genuit*), and the Virgin brought forth without defilement. The Father begot without the limitations of flesh, since He begot as became the Godhead; so neither did the Virgin endure corruption in her childbearing, since she brought forth miraculously. Hence, since this heavenly birth cannot be described, neither does His coming amongst us in these days permit of too curious scrutiny. Though I know that a Virgin this day gave birth, and I believe that God was begotten before all time, yet the manner of this generation I have learned to venerate in silence, and I accept that this is not to be probed too curiously with wordy speech. For with God we look not for the order of nature, but rest our faith in the power of Him who works.

It is indeed the way of nature that a woman in wedlock brings forth; when an unwed virgin, after she has borne a child, is still a virgin, then nature is here surpassed. Of that which happens in accord with nature we may enquire; what passes above it we honor in silence; not as something to be avoided, passed over, but as that which we venerate in silence, as something sublime, beyond all telling. . . .

And in what manner was the Almighty with her? Who in a little while came forth from her? He was as the craftsman, who coming on some suitable material, fashions to himself a beautiful vessel; so Christ, finding the holy body and soul of the Virgin, builds for Himself a living temple, and as He had willed, formed there a man from the Virgin; and, putting Him on, this day came forth; unashamed of the lowliness of our nature. For it was to Him no lowering to put on what He Himself had made. Let that handiwork be forever glorified, which became the cloak of its own Creator. For as in the first creation of flesh, man could not be made before the clay had come into His hand, so neither could this corruptible body be glorified, until it had first become the garment of its Maker.

What shall I say! And how shall I describe this Birth to you? For this wonder fills me with astonishment. The Ancient of days has become an infant. He Who sits upon the sublime and heavenly Throne, now lies in a manger. And He Who cannot be touched, Who is simple, without complexity, and incorporeal, now lies subject to the hands of men. He Who has broken the bonds of sinners, is now bound by an infant's bands. But He has decreed that ignominy shall become honor, infamy be clothed with glory, and total humiliation the measure of His Goodness. For this He assumed my body, that I may become capable of His Word; taking my flesh, He gives me His Spirit; and so He bestowing and I receiving, He prepares for me the treasure of Life. He takes my flesh, to sanctify me; He gives me His Spirit, that He may save me. . . .

Yet in becoming man He was born, not as man is born, but as God. If He had been born from an ordinary union, as I was, He would have been reckoned a fraud. And for this cause He is now born of a Virgin, but in being born He preserves undefiled this womb, and protects that spotless virginity; so that this unheard of manner of bringing forth is for me a pledge of its sublime truthfulness.

For this day the ancient slavery is ended, the devil confounded, the demons take to flight, the power of death is broken, paradise is unlocked, the curse is taken away, sin is removed from us, error driven out, truth has been brought back, the speech of kindliness diffused, and spreads on every side. . . .

Why is this? Because God is now on earth, and man in heaven; on every side all things commingle. He has come on earth, while being Whole in heaven; and while complete in heaven, He is without diminution on earth. Though He was God, He became Man; not denying Himself to be God. Though being the impassable Word, He became flesh; that He might dwell amongst us, He became Flesh. He did not become God. He was God. Wherefore He became flesh, so that He Whom heaven did not contain, a manger would this day receive. He was placed in a manger, so that He, by whom all things are nourished, may receive an infant's food from His Virgin Mother. So, the Father of all ages, as an infant at the breast, nestles in the virginal arms, that the Magi may more easily see Him. Since this day the Magi too have come, and made a beginning of withstanding tyranny; and the heavens give glory, as the Lord is revealed by a star.

VII. ST. AUGUSTINE*

Letter to Volusian[19]

* St. Augustine (354–430), Bishop of Hippo, North Africa, a Doctor of the Church, was born of a pagan father and a Christian mother, St. Monica. After studying law at Carthage, he devoted his time to literary pursuits. He abandoned the Christian life, took a mistress, and his deep interest in philosophy led him to join the Manichaeans. Disillusioned by the inability of their leader Faustus to solve many basic philosophical problems, Augustine went to Rome and opened a school of rhetoric. Unsatisfied, he later went to Milan where St. Ambrose exerted great influence over him. After his baptism in 387, he returned to Africa and established a religious community. Augustine's mark on Christian theology has been immense and deep. He practically molded the theology of the West which later under St. Thomas Aquinas received a new mold and new directions. Later the Reformers used Augustine against the medieval schoolmen, and still later Jansenists used him as an authority in their own behalf. In his Letter to Volusian Augustine tries to remove this pagan's objections to the incarnation on the ground of the radical impossibility of the union of God and man by having recourse to the analogy of the union of body and soul in man.

You must understand the Word of God, by whom all things were made, without thinking that anything of Him passes away or changes from future to past. He remains as He is and He is everywhere totally present. But He comes when He reveals Himself and goes away when He is hidden. However, He is present whether He is revealed or hidden, as light is present to the eyes of one who sees as well as of one who is blind, but it is present to him who sees as something actual, while to the blind it is something missing. So, also, the sound of the voice is present to ears that hear; it is also present to deaf ears: to the former it is actual, from the latter it is hidden. What more strange than what happens when our voices utter words in obviously rapid sequence? For, when we speak, there is no chance for even a second syllable until the first has stopped sounding, yet, if one hearer is present, he hears all that we say; and if two are present, both hear the same whole sound which each one hears; and if a silent crowd hears it, they do not divide the sounds among them by particles as if it were food, but the whole sound is heard wholly by all and by each. So, then, is it harder to believe that the eternal Word of God should have the same effect on material things as the word of a man has on human ears, and that the Word should be wholly present everywhere, as the sound is heard entirely by each one?

Therefore, we need have no fear about that tiny body of infancy, that so great a God should seem to be confined in it. God's greatness is not in mass but in power; He has given a greater sense of foresight to tiny ants and bees than to asses and camels; He creates the immense spread of the fig tree from the smallest seed, while many much smaller things grow from much larger seeds; He has endowed the minute pupil of the eye with the

[19] St. Augustine: Letters, Vol. III (New York: Fathers of the Church, Inc., 1953), pp. 23–28.

power of sight by which in an instant it sweeps across almost half the sky; He has centered all the senses in one spot of the brain, and from there sends out their fivefold activity; He radiates the life-giving impulse through all the parts of the body from the heart, an organ of insignificant size: in these and other like instances, He who is not small in small things produces great things from the least. For, that very greatness of His power, which feels no narrowness in narrow quarters, enriched the Virgin's womb, not by an externally caused but by an intrinsic childbirth; that power took to itself a rational soul and thereby also a human body, and chose to better all mankind without suffering any diminution itself, deigning to take the name of humanity from man, while granting him a share in the divinity. That same power brought forth the body of the infant from the inviolate virginal womb of the mother, as afterward the Body of the Man penetrated closed doors (Jn 20:19, 26). It will not be wondered at if an explanation is asked of this; it will not be remarkable if an example is demanded. Let us grant that God can do something which we confess we cannot fathom. In such matters the whole explanation of the deed is in the power of the doer.

Turning, now, to the fact of his relaxing in sleep and being nourished by food, and experiencing all human feelings: it proves to men that He took on human nature, He did not destroy it. Behold, that is how it happened, yet certain heretics, by excessive admiration and praise of ˙ His power, refuse to acknowledge the human nature which is undoubtedly His. Herein is all the worth of grace, by which He saves those who believe,

containing in itself deep treasures of wisdom and knowledge (Col 2:3), and steeping in faith the minds which it draws to the eternal contemplation of unchangeable truth. Suppose the omnipotent had created His manhood by forming it otherwise than in a mother's womb, and had presented Himself suddenly to our sight; suppose He had not passed through the stages from childhood to youth, had taken no food, no sleep: would He not have given ground for the erroneous opinion which believed that He had not really become man? And by doing everything miraculously, would He not have obscured the effect of His mercy? But now He has appeared as Mediator between God and men, in such wise as to join both natures in the unity of one Person, and has both raised the commonplace to the heights of the uncommon and brought down the uncommon to the commonplace.

What wonders does God not perform in the activities of created life, and how commonplace they have become through daily usage! Again, how many customary things are trampled under foot which would fill us with awe, if we considered them carefully! Take the force which is found in seeds: who can grasp in his thought or describe in language their numbers, their urge to live and grow, their hidden strength, their power to unfold their littleness into something great? He, then, who in the world of nature does not need seeds to make seeds, did not need seed to make himself a human body; He who, without any change in Himself, has woven the course of centuries by means of change submitted His Body to the sequence of time and the limitations of age. What began outside of time took growth in the course of time, but in the beginning the Word by whom all time was made chose the time when He was to take flesh; He did not wait for the time that He might become flesh, for, in truth, it was man who drew near to God, not God who went far off from Himself.

But there are some who request an explanation of how God is joined to man so as to become the single person of Christ, as if they themselves could explain something that happens every day, namely, how the soul is joined to the body so as to form the single person of a man. For, as the soul makes use of the body in a single person to form a man, so God makes use of man in a single Person to form Christ. In the former Person there is a mingling of soul and body; in the latter Person there is a mingling of God and man; but the hearer must abstract from the property of material substance by which two liquids are usually so mingled that neither retains its separate character, although among such substances, light mingled with air remains unchanged. Therefore, the person of man is a mingling of soul and body, but the Person of Christ is a mingling of God and man, for when the Word of God is joined to a soul which has a body, it takes on both the soul and the body at once. The one process happens daily in order to beget men; the other happened once to set men free. However, it ought to be easier to believe in the intermingling of two incorporeal things than of one incorporeal and the other corporeal. For, if the soul is not deceived about its own nature, it grasps the fact that it is incorporeal, but the Word of God is much more incorporeal, and for this reason it ought to be easier to believe in the intermingling of the Word of God and a soul

than of a soul and a body. The one truth we experience in ourselves; the other we are bidden to believe in Christ. But, if we were ordered to believe both these truths, and they were both equally outside our experience, which of them would we be more ready to believe? Granted that the term mingling or intermingling is not unworthily taken from the usage of corporeal things of far different nature and origin, would we not admit that it would be easier for two incorporeal things to be mingled than for one corporeal and the other incorporeal?

Therefore, the Word of God and the same Son of God, co-eternal with the Father, and the same power and wisdom of God (Col 1:24), reaching mightily from the lofty end of rational creation to the lowly end of material creation, and ordering all things sweetly (Wis 8:1), present and hidden, nowhere confined, nowhere divided, nowhere extended, but everywhere wholly present without physical bulk, in a far other mode than that in which He is present to the rest of creation; this Word took on human nature, and thereby became the one Jesus Christ, Mediator between God and men (1 Tim 2:5), equal to the Father in His divinity, less than the Father according to the flesh, that is, as man; unchangeably immortal according to His divinity which is equal to the Father, but likewise subject to change and death according to the weakness derived from us. In this same Christ, at the time which He had recognized as most fitting, and had ordained before time was, there came to men a Master and helper that we might gain eternal salvation. He was a Master, indeed, whose authority, manifested here in the flesh, was to confirm those vital truths, previously spoken not only by the holy Prophets, whose utterances were wholly true, but even by the philosophers and the very poets and authors of various kinds of works — and who doubts that they mingled many of their truths with falsehood? — and even before He became man He was present to all who could be sharers of His truth, for the sake of those who were not able to penetrate into the depths of truth and to distinguish what truth was. But, most of all, since men generally in their intense longing for the divinity thought that God was to be approached through the powers of heaven, which they imagined to be gods, and through the various rites of forbidden and sacrilegious worship, carried out with more pride than piety — and thus the demons, through their kinship with pride, substitute them-selves for the holy angels — by the example of His Incarnation He led man to know that whereas they had been trying to approach Him through subordinate beings, as though He were afar off, He was so close to their affectionate desire that He condescended to become man and to be united to him. He did this in such manner that the whole of man was thus joined to Him, as the soul is to the body, but without the change-ableness of matter, into which God is not changed, but which we see present in the body and the soul. But, He is our help, because, without the grace of faith which comes from Him, no one can overcome his sinful lusts, or be cleansed by the remission and par-don of the remains of sin which he has not overcome.

The City of God[20]

You speak expressly of the Father and of His Son whom you call the intellect or understanding of the Father. You speak, also, of one who is between these two and by whom, we suppose, you mean the Holy Spirit. According to your way of speaking, you call these three Gods. On this point, in spite of inaccurate termi-nology, you catch at least a glimpse, through the mist of your imaginings, of the end toward which we must strive. Yet you refuse to acknowledge the Incarnation of the immutable Son of God by which we are saved and enabled to reach those realities in which we believe and which, in part, we understand. Thus, you see, how-ever dimly and at a great distance, the country where you should dwell, but you will not take the road that leads there.

You confess, in the same way, the reality of grace when you say that it is granted to a few to reach God by virtue of their intelligence. You do not say: "It has pleased a few" or "Few have wished." You say: "It has been granted." Surely, you are admitting the grace of God and the insufficiency of man. You even use this very word in a passage where, following Plato, you say you are sure that, in this life, no man can arrive at the perfection of wisdom, but that those who live ac-cording to their conscience can make up, by the providence and grace of God, in the life to come, for all that was lacking on earth. Now, if only

[20] St. Augustine: *The City of God* (New York: Fathers of the Church, Inc., 1953), pp. 170–174.

you could have known "the grace of God through Jesus Christ, our Lord" (Rom 7:25), and the Incarnation by which He assumed a human soul and body, you would have seen that there is no greater example of grace than this.

But, why this apostrophe? I know that, so far as you are concerned, now that you are dead, it is a waste of words. But, as for those who esteem you and love you either out of love for wisdom or out of curiosity about those arts which you should never have learned, it is these I am addressing, in your name and, perhaps, not in vain. The grace of God could not, cious as when, in the Incarnation, the only Son of God, remaining unchangeable in Himself, clothed Himself with our humanity and gave the promise of His love to men, by the mediation in any other way, have been so gra- of a man — gave men hope that they might come to Him who, before, had been as distant as the immortal is from the mortal, the unchangeable from the changeable, the holy from the unholy, the happy from the unhappy. And, because He had endowed our nature with the desire both of happiness and of immortality, He joined His happiness with our mortality and, by suffering, He taught us to despise what we fear so that He might give us what we desire.

But, to acquiesce in this truth you needed humility, and that is a virtue to which your stiff neck does not easily bend. For, what is so incredible in this teaching, especially for you whose philosophy should predispose you to this belief? What is incredible in the doctrine that God assumed a human soul and body? After all, you have a high enough idea of the intellectual soul and, therefore, of the human soul to believe it capable of consubstantiality with the intelligence of the Father which, you admit, is the Son of God.

What, then, is so incredible in the fact that one intellectual soul has been assumed in an ineffable and unique manner for the salvation of many? Now, that a body must be united to the soul, if a man is to be whole and complete, we know from the experience of our own nature. Yet, if this were not the most common experience in the world, it would be very hard indeed to believe, for it is much easier to believe in a union of spirit with spirit, or, to use your terminology, of the incorporeal with the incorporeal, even though the union were between a human and a divine or a mutable and an immutable spirit, than to believe in a union between body and soul.

But do you, perhaps, find a difficulty in the extraordinary birth of this body from a virgin? Surely, it ought not to be a difficulty but rather an inducement to embrace our religion that a miraculous being should be born in a miraculous manner. Or, perhaps, you cannot believe that this body, which was laid aside in death and transformed in its resurrection, ascended incorruptible and immortal into heaven merely because Porphyry, in his "The Return of the Soul," which I have cited so often, has insisted that the soul must escape from every kind of a body if it is to be forever happy with God?

But, surely, you ought to have corrected him and his doctrines, since you share his incredible opinions about the soul of this visible world which is an immense material body. For, as Platonists, you say that the universe is not merely alive but very happy, and you even hope that it will live forever. How, then, can the soul of the world be never detached from its body nor ever cease to be happy, if it is true that, for the soul to be happy, it must flee from every kind of a body? You also admit in your writings that the sun and all the other stars are bodies — as everyone else can see and unhesitatingly admits. But, with what you think is even more profound insight, you add that these living beings are utterly happy and, in union with their bodies, are eternal.

Yet, the moment the Christian faith is in question, you forget or pretend to be ignorant of the doctrines that you are accustomed to discuss or teach. Why is this so, and why do you repudiate Christianity for the very opinions which you yourself repudiate? The answer is: Because Christ came in humility and you are proud.

VIII. NESTORIUS*

Letter of Nestorius to Celestine[21]

---

* Nestorianism, attributed to Nestorius the Syrian (died c451), proposed that there are two separate Persons in Christ, one human and the other divine. It is characterized by the rejection of the term *theotokos,* which designates Mary actually to be the Mother of God. Cyril of Alexandria persuaded Pope Celestine to summon a synod at Rome in 430 to condemn Nestorius. This done, he had the condemnation repeated in his own synod at Alexandria and sent notice of both decrees to Nestorius with a letter of explanation and twelve anathemas. This letter, which epitomized Cyril's faith, was formally approved by the Council of Ephesus (431) and later at the Council of Chalcedon (451). As the most brilliant representative of the Alexandrian theological tradition, he put into systematic form, on the basis of the teaching of St. Athanasius and the Cappadocian Fathers, the classical Greek doctrines of the Trinity and of the Person of Christ.

We have also found no slight corruption of orthodoxy among some of those here, which we have treated with both sternness and gentleness, [as demanded]. It is no small error, but similar to the corruption of Apollinaris and Arius, blending together the Lord's appearance as man into a kind of confused combination — so much so that certain of our clergy, some from inexperience, others from heretical error long kept concealed, as often happened even in the times of the apostles, err like heretics, and openly blaspheme

[21] *The Christology of the Later Fathers* (London: S.C.M. Press, 1950), pp. 347–348.

God the Word consubstantial with the Father, as if he took up his beginning from the Christ-bearing Virgin, and grew up with his temple and was buried with [it] in the flesh; they even say that his flesh after the resurrection did not remain flesh, but was changed into the nature of Godhead. To speak briefly, they refer the Godhead of the Only-begotten to the same origin as the flesh joined [with it], and kill it with the flesh, and blasphemously say that the flesh joined with the Godhead was turned into deity by the deifying Word, which is nothing more nor less than to corrupt both. They even dare to treat of the Christ-bearing

Virgin in a way as along with God, for they do not scruple to call her *theotokos,* when the holy and beyond-all-praise Fathers at Nicea said no more of the holy Virgin than that our Lord Jesus Christ was incarnate of the Holy Spirit and the Virgin Mary — not to mention the Scriptures, which everywhere, both by angels and apostles, speak of the Virgin as mother of Christ, not of God the Word. I presume that rumor has already informed Your Blessedness what conflicts we have endured for these things, and you have also learned that we have not struggled in vain, but many of those who had gone astray have by the grace of the Lord repented, learning from us that what is born is properly consubstantial with the parent, and that it was to the creature of the Lord's humanity, joined with God, [being] of the Virgin by the Spirit, that what was seen among men was committed. If anyone wishes to use this word *theotokos* with reference to the humanity which was born, joined to God the Word, and not with reference to the parent, we say that this word is not

appropriate for her who gave birth, since a true mother should be of the same essence as what is born of her. But the term could be accepted in consideration of this, that the word is used of the Virgin only because of the inseparable temple of God the Word which was of her, not because she is the mother of God the Word — for none gives birth to one older than herself.

I suppose that rumor has already told you of these things, but we expound what has been happening to us, in order to show in fact that it is in a brotherly spirit that we wish to know about the affairs of those whom we mentioned before, not out of mere importunate curiosity — since we tell you of our affairs as among brothers, sharing with each other the facts of [these] divisions, so that the beginning of this letter of mine may be indeed correct — for I said as I began this letter that we ought to enjoy brotherly converse with each other.

I and those who are with me greet all the brotherhood in Christ which is with you.

The Third Letter of Cyril to Nestorius[22]

. . . Following in every respect the confessions of the holy Fathers, which they drew up as the Holy Spirit spoke in them, and pursuing the track of their thoughts, and taking as it were the royal road, we say that the unique Word of God himself, who was begotten of the very substance of the Father, who is true God of true God, the Light of Light, through whom all things came into being, both things in heaven and things in earth, coming down for the sake of our salvation,

and humbling himself even to emptying, was made flesh and became man. That is, taking flesh of the holy Virgin, and making it his own from the womb, he underwent a birth like ours, and came forth a man of woman, not throwing off what he was, but even though he became [man] by the assumption of flesh and blood, yet still remaining what he was, that is, God indeed in nature and truth. We do not say that the flesh was changed into the nature of Godhead, nor that the ineffable nature of the Word of

---

[22] *Ibid.,* pp. 350–354.

God was transformed into the nature of flesh, for he is unchangeable and unalterable, always remaining the same according to the Scriptures. But when seen as a babe and wrapped in swaddling clothes, even when still in the bosom of the Virgin who bore him, he filled all creation as God, and was enthroned with him who begot him. For the Divine cannot be numbered or measured, and does not admit of circumscription.

So confessing the Word united hypostatically to flesh, we worship one Son and Lord Jesus Christ, neither putting apart and dividing man and God, as joined with each other by a union of dignity and authority — for this would be an empty phrase and no more — nor speaking of the Word of God separately as Christ, and then separately of him who was of a woman as another Christ, but knowing only one Christ, the Word of God the Father with his own flesh. For then he was anointed in human wise like us, though he himself gives the Spirit to those who are worthy to receive it, and not by measure, as says the blessed Evangelist John. Neither do we say that the Word of God tabernacled in him who was begotten of the holy Virgin as an ordinary man — lest Christ should be thought of as a God-bearing man. For though the Word did tabernacle among us, and it is said that in Christ dwelt all the fullness of the Godhead bodily, yet we so conceive [of this] that when he was made flesh, we do not define the indwelling in him in precisely the same manner as that in which one speaks of an indwelling in the saints; but being united by nature and not changed into flesh, he effected such an indwelling as the soul of man might be said to have in its own body.

[There is] therefore one Christ and Son and Lord, not as if man were conjoined with God by a union of dignity or authority. For equality of honor does not unite the natures, and Peter and John, for instance, are of equal honor with each other, as both apostles and holy disciples, but the two are not [made] into one. Nor do we think of the mode of conjunction as by association, for this is not enough for a natural union; nor as by an acquired relation, as we, being joined to the Lord, as it is written, are one spirit with him. Indeed we reject the term "conjunction," as not sufficiently indicating the union . . . [nor is the Word the God or Lord of Christ, since God the Word and his flesh are united in one *hypostasis* though as man he was under God and under the law].

We refuse to say of Christ, "I adore him who was born for the sake of him who bore him, I worship him who was seen for the sake of the invisible," and it is horrible to say in addition to this, "He who was assumed is styled as God with him who assumed." He who says this divides him again into two Christs, and puts a man apart separately and God similarly. For he confessedly denies the union, according to which he is not worshipped as one [person] along with another, nor does he [merely] share the style of God. But one Christ Jesus is thought of, the unique Son, honored by one worship with his own flesh. And we confess that he who was begotten from God the Father as Son and God only-begotten, though being by his own nature impassible, suffered in the flesh for us, according to the Scriptures, and he was in the crucified flesh impassibly making his own the sufferings of his own flesh. So by the grace of God he tasted death for everyone, giving up his own body to it, although by nature he was life, and was himself the resurrection. . . .

We must necessarily add this: proclaiming the death in the flesh of the unique Son of God, that is, Jesus Christ, and confessing his return to life from the dead, and his reception into heaven, we celebrate the unbloody service in the churches. So we approach to the mystical gifts and are sanctified, becoming partakers of the holy flesh and the honorable blood of Christ the Savior of us all, not receiving it as ordinary flesh — God forbid — nor as that of a man sanctified and conjoined with the Word by a unity of honor, or as one who had received a divine indwelling, but as truly lifegiving and the Word's own flesh. For being by nature, as God, life, when he had become one with his own flesh, he made it life-giving. . . .

We do not divide the terms used in the Gospels of the Savior as God or man between two *hypostases,* or Persons, for the one and only Christ is not twofold, though he is thought of as out of two, and as uniting different entities into the indivisible unity — as man is thought of as of body and soul, and yet not as twofold, but one out of both. . . . For it is necessary to believe that, being God by nature, he became flesh, that is, man ensouled with a rational soul, for what reason should some be embarrassed by some of his sayings that may be such as befit humanity? . . . All the terms used in the Gospels are to be referred to one Person, the one incarnate *hypostasis* of the Word. There is one Lord Jesus Christ, according to the Scriptures. . . .

Since the holy Virgin gave birth after the flesh to God who was united by *hypostasis* with flesh, therefore we say that she is *theotokos,* not as though the nature of the Word had the beginning of its existence from flesh . . . [nor that the Word needed human birth, but that by accepting it he blessed the beginning of our existence, and removed the curse from it]. . . . For this cause we say that he also in his [earthly] dispensation blessed marriage itself, and went when he had been invited to Cana of Galilee with the holy apostles.

We have learned to hold these things from the holy apostles and Evangelists and all the God-inspired Scripture, and by the true confession of the blessed Fathers. All these it is necessary for Your Reverence to accept and support without deceit; and what Your Reverence must anathematize is subjoined to this our letter:

1. If anyone does not confess that Emmanuel is God in truth, and therefore the holy Virgin is *theotokos* — for she bore in the flesh the Word of God become flesh — let him be anathema.

2. If anyone does not confess that the Word of God the Father was united by *hypostasis* to flesh and is one Christ with his own flesh, that is, the same both God and man together, let him be anathema.

3. If anyone divides the *hypostases* in the one Christ after the union, joining them only by a conjunction in dignity, or authority or power, and not rather by a coming together in a union by nature, let him be anathema.

4. If anyone distributes between two persons or *hypostases* the terms used in the evangelical and apostolic writings, whether spoken of Christ by the saints or by him about himself, and attaches some to a man thought of separately from the Word of God, and others as befitting God to the

Word of God the Father alone, let him be anathema.

5. If anyone dares to say that Christ was a God-bearing man, and not rather God in truth, being by nature one Son, inasmuch as the Word became flesh, and is made partaker of blood and flesh precisely like us, let him be anathema.

6. If anyone says that the Word of God the Father was the God or Master of Christ, and does not rather confess the same both God and man, the Word having become flesh according to the Scriptures, let him be anathema.

7. If anyone says that Jesus was energized as a man by the Word from God, and clothed with the glory of the Only-begotten, as being another besides him, let him be anathema.

8. If anyone dares to say that the man who was assumed ought to be worshiped with God the Word and glorified with him, and with him styled God, as being one [being] in a different one — for the constantly added "with" forces one to think this — and does not rather honor Emmanuel with one veneration, and send up to him one doxology, inasmuch as the Word has become flesh, let him be anathema.

9. If anyone says that the one Lord Jesus Christ was glorified by the Spirit, as making use of an alien power that worked through him, and received from him the power to prevail over unclean spirits and to ac-complish divine wonders among men, and does not rather say that it was his own Spirit, through whom he also worked the divine wonders, let him be anathema.

10. The divine Scripture speaks of Christ as the High Priest and Apostle of our confession, and [says that] he offered himself for us for an odor of sweet savor to his God and Father. If anyone says that the Word of God himself did not become our High Priest and Apostle, when he became flesh and man for us, but as it were another [who was] separately from him man of woman — or if anyone says that he offered the offering for himself, and not rather for us alone, for he who knew no sin had no need of offering, let him be anathema.

11. If anyone does not confess that the flesh of the Lord is life-giving, and the own [flesh] of the Word of God the Father, but as of another besides him, associated with him in dignity, or having received merely a divine indwelling — and not rather life-giving, as we said, because it became the own [flesh] of the Word who is able to give life to all things, let him be anathema.

12. If anyone does not confess that the Word of God suffered in the flesh and was crucified in the flesh and tasted death in the flesh, and became the first-born of the dead, although he is as God Life and life-giving, let him be anathema.

IX. BOETHIUS*

Treatise Against Eutyches and Nestorius[23]

* Boethius (c480–c524), Roman consul, philosopher and statesman, was friend and adviser of the Emperor Theodoric. His defense of an ex-consul on the charge of treason brought about his own accusation, conviction and final execution. He wrote works on logic; his *On the Consolation of* *Philosophy*, written in prison, attempts to direct the soul through philosophy to divine contemplation. Besides a work on the Trinity, his *Treatise Against Eutyches and Nestorius* was written to defend the teachings of the Council of Chalcedon.

It remains for us to show how in accordance with the affirmation of Catholic belief Christ consists at once in and of both natures.

The statement that a thing consists of two natures bears two meanings; one, when we say that anything is a union of two natures, as e.g., honey and water, where the union is such that in the combination, however the elements be confounded, whether by one nature changing into the other, or by both mingling with each other, the two entirely disappear. This is the way in which according to Eutyches Christ consists of two natures.

The other way in which a thing can consist of two natures is when it is so combined of two that the elements of which it is said to be combined continue without changing into each other, as when we say that a crown is composed of gold and gems. Here neither is the gold converted into gems nor is the gem turned into gold, but both continue without surrendering their proper form.

Things then like this, composed of various elements, we say consist also in the elements of which they are composed. For in this case we can say that a crown is composed of gems and gold,

[23] Boethius, *The Theological Tractates* (Cambridge: Harvard University Press, 1918), pp. 120–127 *passim*.

for gems and gold are that in which the crown consists. For in the former mode of composition honey and water is not that in which the resulting union of both consists.

Since then the Catholic Faith confesses that both natures continue in Christ and that they both remain perfect, neither being transformed into the other, it says with right that Christ consists both in and of the two natures; *in* the two because both continue, *of* the two because the One Person of Christ is formed by the union of the two continuing natures.

But the Catholic Faith does not hold the union of Christ out of two natures according to that sense which Eutyches puts upon it. For the interpretation of the conjunction out of two natures which he adopts forbids him to confess consistence in two or the continuance of the two either; but the Catholic adopts an interpretation of the consistence out of two which comes near to that of Eutyches, yet keeps the interpretation which confesses consistence in two.

"To consist of two natures" is therefore an equivocal or rather a doubtful term of double meaning denoting different things; according to one of its interpretations the substances out of which the union is said to have been composed do not continue, according to another the union effected of the two is such that both natures continue.

When once this knot of doubt or ambiguity has been untied, nothing further can be advanced to shake the true and solid content of the Catholic Faith, which is that the same Christ is perfect man and God, and that He who is perfect man and God is One God and Son of Man, that, however, quaternity is not added to the Trinity by the addition of human nature to perfect Godhead, but that one and the same Person completes the number of the Trinity, so that, although it was the manhood which suffered, yet God can be said to have suffered, not by manhood becoming Godhead but by manhood being assumed by Godhead. Further, He who is man is called Son of God not in virtue of divine but of human substance, which latter none the less was conjoined to Godhead in a unity of natures. And although thought is able to distinguish and combine the manhood and the Godhead, yet one and the same is perfect man and God, God because He was begotten of the substance of the Father, but man because He was engendered of the Virgin Mary. And further He who is man is God in that manhood was assumed by God, and He who is God is man in that God was clothed with manhood. And although in the same Person the Godhead which took manhood is different from the manhood which It took, yet the same is God and man. For if you think of man, the same is man and God, being man by nature, God by assumption. But if you think of God, the same is God and man, being God by nature, man by assumption. And in Him nature becomes double and substance double because He is God-man, and

One Person since the same is man and God. This is the middle way between two heresies, just as virtues also hold a middle place. For every virtue has a place of honor midway between extremes. For if it stands beyond or below where it should it ceases to be virtue. And so virtue holds a middle place.

Wherefore if the following four assertions can be said to be neither beyond or below reason, viz., that in Christ are either two Natures and two Persons as Nestorius says, or one Person and one Nature as Eutyches says, or two Natures but one Person as the Catholic Faith believes, or one Nature and two Persons, and inasmuch as we have refuted the doctrine of two Natures and two Persons in our argument against Nestorius and incidentally have shown that the one Person and one Nature suggested by Eutyches is impossible — since there has never been anyone so mad as to believe that His Nature was single but His Person double — it remains that the article of belief must be true which the Catholic Faith affirms, viz., that the Nature is double, but the Person one. But as I have just now remarked that Eutyches confesses two Natures in Christ before the union, but only one after the union, and since I proved that under this error lurked two opposite opinions, one, that the union was brought about by conception although the human body was certainly not taken from Mary; the other, that the body taken from Mary formed part of the union by means of the Resurrection, I have, it seems to me, argued the twofold aspect of the case as completely as it deserves. What we have now to inquire is how it came to pass that the two Natures were combined into one Substance.

Nevertheless, there remains yet another question which can be advanced by those who do not believe that the human body was taken from Mary, but that the body was in some other way set apart and prepared, which in the moment of union appeared to be conceived and born of Mary's womb. For they say: if the body was taken from man while every man was, from the time of the first disobedience, not only enslaved by sin and death but also involved in sinful desires, and if his punishment for sin was that, although he was held in chains of death, yet at the same time he should be guilty because of the will to sin, why was there in Christ neither sin nor any will to sin? And certainly such a question is attended by a difficulty which deserves attention. For if the body of Christ was assumed from human flesh, it is open to doubt of what kind we must consider that flesh to be which was assumed.

In truth, the manhood which He assumed He likewise saved; but if He assumed such manhood as Adam had before sin, He appears to have assumed a human nature complete indeed, but one which was in no need of healing. But how can it be that He assumed such manhood as Adam had when there could be in Adam both the will and the desire to sin, whence it came to pass that even after the divine commands had been broken, he was still held captive to sins of disobedience? But we believe that in Christ there was never any will to sin, because especially if He assumed such a human body as Adam had before his sin, He could not be mortal, since Adam, had he not sinned, would in no wise have suffered death. Since, then, Christ never sinned, it must be asked why He suffered death if

He assumed the body of Adam before sin. But if He accepted human conditions such as Adam's were after sin, it seems that Christ could not avoid being subject to sin, perplexed by passions, and, since the canons of judgment were obscured, prevented from distinguishing with unclouded reason between good and evil, since Adam by his disobedience incurred all these penalties of crime.

To whom we must reply that there are three states of man to envisage: one, that of Adam before his sin, in which, though free from death and still unstained by any sin, he could yet have within him the will to sin; the second, that in which he might have suffered change had he chosen to abide steadfastly in the commands of God, for then it could have been further granted him not only not to sin or wish to sin, but to be incapable of sinning or of the will to transgress. The third state is the state after sin, into which man needs must be pursued by death and sin and the sinful will. Now the points of extreme divergence between these states are the following: one state would have been for Adam a reward if he had chosen to abide in God's laws; the other was his punishment because he would not abide in them; for in the former state there would have been no death nor sin nor sinful will, in the latter there was both death and sin and every desire to transgress, and a general tendency to ruin and a condition helpless to render possible a rise after the Fall. But that middle state from which actual death or sin was absent, but the power for both remained, is situated between the other two.

Each one, then, of these three states somehow supplied to Christ a cause for his corporeal nature; thus His assumption of a mortal body in order to drive death far from the human race belongs properly to that state which was laid on man by way of punishment after Adam's sin, whereas the fact that there was in Christ no sinful will is borrowed from that state which might have been if Adam had not surrendered his will to the frauds of the tempter. There remains, then, the third or middle state, to wit, that which was before death had come and while the will to sin might yet be present. In this state, therefore, Adam was able to eat and drink, digest the food he took, fall asleep, and perform all the other functions which always belonged to him as man, though they were allowed and brought with them no pain of death.

There is no doubt that Christ was in all points thus conditioned; for He ate and drank and discharged the bodily function of the human body. For we must not think that Adam was at the first subject to such need that unless he ate he could not have lived, but rather that, if he had taken food from every tree, he could have lived for ever, and by that food have escaped death; and so by the fruits of the Garden he satisfied a need. And all know that in Christ the same need dwelt, but lying in His own power and not laid upon Him. And this need was in Him before the Resurrection, but after the Resurrection He became such that His human body was changed as Adam's might have been but for the bands of disobedience. Which state, moreover, our Lord Jesus Christ Himself taught us to desire in our prayers, asking that His Will be done as in heaven so on earth, and that His Kingdom come, and that He may deliver us from evil. For all these things are sought in prayer by those members of the human family who rightly believe and who are destined to undergo that most blessed change of all.

So much have I written to you concerning what I believe should be believed. In which matter if I have said aught amiss, I am not so well pleased with myself as to try to press my effusions in the face of wiser judgment. For if there is no good thing in us there is nothing we should fancy in our opinions. But if all things are good as coming from Him who alone is good, that rather must be thought good which the Unchangeable Good and Cause of all Good indites.

X. LEONTIUS OF JERUSALEM

Three Books Against the Nestorians and Eutychians[24]

Of those things which exist substantially and are united in substance, some even in union preserve the proper character of their existence, while others are mixed together and injured so as to destroy the precise identity of the things united. The relation of things of the first kind, when observed with each other and in each other, produces one thing out of the two,

[24] This work, formerly attributed to Leontius of Byzantium (6th century), an anti-Monophysite theologian, is now known to be the product of a hitherto unrecognized Leontius of Jerusalem. From *The Christology of the Later Fathers* (London: S.C.M. Press, 1950), pp. 376–377.

and, as one might say, shows it to be one in number, still preserving the difference of being [existence] in the identity of the union. An example of this among living beings is our humanity, and among simple or natural objects the kind of relation to each other of things which have their own *hypostasis* and can exist by themselves. Such can be seen in the case of a torch; for the stock is one thing and the flamy nature of fire is another, but when they exist with each other and in each other, they make both into one torch. And as one might say, forcing it a little, fire is made wooden and wood fiery, the one sharing in the brightness of the fire, the other the earthy heaviness found in the firebrand, and each exchanges qualities with the other, while remaining in its own and unmixed identity. . . .

Having distinguished these points, we must note that things which are exchanged with each other and transformed, being constituted out of different forms and substances, retain nothing unmixed after the composition of the things involved in the composition. But mixing and confusing the peculiar properties of all, all of them together, it has produced another mixed-up form, and there has been a jumbling and confusion in the mixture of many *hypostases* and natures, preserving neither the individuality of the *hypostasis* nor the common quality of the nature, but producing something else which has come into being out of these, yet is not the same as any of its constituent parts. So then if Godhead and manhood, when united in substance, do not retain even in the union the natural property of each, they are mixed together, and there remains neither Godhead nor manhood, but another kind of substance has been produced, formed out of them and yet not the same. What could be more impious or abominable than even to conceive of this, not to speak of affirming it and teaching it as a dogma? It remains, then, that from this examination of the character of substantial union, we should grasp the unmixed [respective] identity of deity and humanity, according to the previous examples, gathering a faint image from all these things of the truth which is above all things, which shows that one entity is produced out of these, of which I do not care whether you call it Person or *hypostasis* or indivisible being or substratum, or anything else you may prefer. For the argument has now beaten and put to flight those who separate [them] in their relationship [speaking] of dignity or authority or some other relation of divided things, showing that they divide the natures into separate *hypostases,* and [such natures] can have no real fellowship or share in an exchange [of qualities]. . . .

[A later passage comments significantly on the relation of nature to supernature, as of man to indwelling deity:]

And let us not pass it over unnoticed, that three causes may be observed from which every [kind of] energy is produced. One is from natural force, another from a corrupt state contrary to nature, and the other is observed to be a kind of advance or progress toward the better. These are and are called natural, unnatural, and supernatural respectively. The unnatural, as the name indicates, being a certain falling away of natural states and powers, injures the substance itself and its natural energies. The natural is produced from the unimpeded [natural] cause operating precisely according to nature. But the supernatural raises and elevates, and gives power for more perfect things, and such as could not be done while remaining in the natural [alone]. The supernatural does not destroy the natural [forces], but leads them on and impels them, so that they are both able to perform their own [functions], and also receive power for what is beyond them.

PART TWO: THE CHURCH SPEAKS

Chapter 3. Basic Christological Formulations

INTRODUCTION

The Christological Problems[1]

by J. M. Carmody and T. E. Clark

The mystery of Christ, Karl Adam has written, is not that he is God, but that he is the God-man (*The Son of God*). The Christological problem in the strict sense is concerned with the relationship of the humanity and divinity co-present in the savior. So it arises only when the co-presence of genuine humanity and divinity has been established. This is obvious logically; but it is also by and large true of what happened historically. The strict Christological problem arose in acute form only in the late fourth century, when the true and integral humanity and the perfect divinity of

[1] *Word and Redeemer* (Glen Rock, N. J.: Paulist Press, 1966), pp. 4–7.

Christ had finally been clearly affirmed. Let us trace the development in a brief and somewhat abstract outline.

1. HUMANITY

a) *The body*: The first truth about Christ to be challenged and defended was his humanity and particularly his bodily reality. From the beginning gnostic dualism, wishing to keep God as pure spirit from direct contact with the impurities of matter, denied the reality of the human body, birth, suffering and death of the savior. This was the heresy of *docetism* (Gk: *dokein*, to seem, appear). And from Ignatius of Antioch on, the Church

vigorously asserted that Christ had a
true body of flesh, truly born from
Mary, and that he truly suffered and
died.

b) *The soul:* The attack on the
human mind of Christ came in the
fourth century, from . . . Arianism
and especially Apollinarianism. Both
thought that the Word (for Arians a
creature, for Apollinarians true God)
took the place of a human mind in
the savior. Both of these views followed the Word-flesh schema . . .
The first Council of Constantinople in
381 met this error in its condemnation
of Apollinarianism.

2. DIVINITY

The divinity of Christ had also been
questioned or compromised from early
days. The Ebionites, a Judaeo-Chris-
tian sect, considered Jesus to be a
mere man with special relationship to
God. Various forms of adoptionism
(seeing Jesus as God's "adopted son")
sprang up in the first few centuries.
But the main challenge to the divinity
of Christ came from Arius, who considered the Son to be the most perfect of creatures, subordinate to the
Father-Creator. The Council of Nicaea
(325) defined in its creed the equal
divinity of the Son with the Father.
Several decades of the fourth century
after Nicaea were required to confirm
and clarify the Nicene dogma.

By 381, the orthodox patristic portrait of Christ was as follows: He is
truly man, with a body subject to
death (against docetism), and a human mind or spiritual soul (against
Arianism and Apollinarianism). He
is truly and perfectly God, equal to
and distinct from the Father (against
Arianism). Now, finally, the time is
ripe for the Christological question in
the strict sense, the question of the

relationship of humanity and divinity,
to take the center of the stage.

Logically, two sets of answers are
possible. Historically, these two possibilities took the form of two Christologies: the Word-flesh (roughly,
Alexandrian) Christology, and the
Word-man (Antiochene) Christology.

a) *The Word-flesh Christology of
Alexandria:* This view stressed the
unity of Christ, the fact that it is one
and the same who is both God and
man, it ran the risk, however, of lessening the reality and completeness of
his humanity. Its characteristic formula was the Joannine "The Word
was made flesh" (Jn 1:14). It insisted
that the Word took to himself and
made his own the flesh drawn from
Mary. Largely through stoic influence,
it tended to make the divine Word
(*logos* or reason) preempt in Christ
the place of his human *logos* or mind.
In its moderate form (Athanasius,
Cyril of Alexandria), it did not deny
the presence of a human mind in the
savior, but Athanasius, and, to a lesser
extent Cyril, failed to give the human
mind and will of Christ an active role
in our salvation. In its extreme form,
the Word-flesh Christology led Arianism and Apollinarianism to deny the
need and possibility of a human mind
in Christ; the divine Word assumed
this function. For them, too, as for
Dioscorus, Eutyches and the monophysites (who said Christ has only
one nature), divinity and humanity
formed not only a single person but
a single nature. The Word-flesh
Christology, as defended by Cyril,
triumphed at Ephesus (431) in the
condemnation of Nestorius. Twenty
years later, however, monophysitism
was condemned by Chalcedon (451).

b) *The Word-man Christology of
Antioch:* This approach stressed the

reality and integrality of both natures in Christ. It did so out of concern for the divine transcendence of the Word, who must not, it was felt, become enmeshed in the weaknesses of the flesh; and there was also concern for the synoptic gospels' portrayal of Jesus as fully a man. Antioch's characteristic formula spoke of the "Man assumed" (*Homo assumptus*) by the Word. The son of Mary is spoken of as distinct from the Word, and assumed by or united to him in a perfect union. In its extreme form (Nestorianism), this view refused to attribute the actions and sufferings of Jesus to the Word of God, and denied that Mary was genuinely the *theotokos* (mother of God), insisting she was only the mother of Christ. There is a good deal of discussion today as to whether the leading representatives of this view, Theodore of Mopsuestia and Nestorius, were really heretical in their thought. John of Antioch is a good example of the moderate Antiochene view. Nestorianism met defeat at Ephesus, as we have said. But in 433 Cyril and John of Antioch agreed on a *Formula of Union*. Antioch also made a prominent contribution to the definition of Chalcedon (451), which rejected both extremes by defining that Christ is one hypostasis, one person, in two abidingly distinct natures. We may note also that the Christology of the West, mainly a Word-man

Christology, also contributed to the definition of 451, particularly through Pope Leo's *Tome to Flavian*. With these two ecumenical councils, we are at the peak of the great Christological debate and its resolution.

Cyril's more radical followers would not accept Chalcedon, and there resulted an unfortunate schism of the monophysite churches of Egypt and Syria. Many scholars today feel that their monophysitism was more verbal than real. The next few centuries witnessed two major but unsuccessful efforts to reconcile them. The first of these attempts, under Emperor Justinian, culminated in the Second Council of Constantinople (551), which condemned the writings of Theodore and of two other Antiochenes of the previous century. The other effort took the form of a willingness on the part of some, encouraged by Pope Honorius, to deny that there are two wills and two kinds of activity in the God-man. The Third Council of Constantinople (681) ended this threat of monothelitism (the heresy that Christ has only one will). The import of this council was that it applied the Chalcedonian solution (one person and two natures), to the sphere of volition and action (one person but two wills and two levels of action). But Chalcedon remains the decisive early council even to our own day.

The Soteriological Argument in the Christological Disputes

The second theme . . . is the soteriological concern of the fathers. It is important to stress this today, when there is a tendency to set the Christological (ontological), and the soteriological (functional), i.e., what Christ was and

what he did, in sharp opposition to each other. Scholastic theology of recent centuries has, unfortunately, too much separated the two. Harnack's charge that the gospel was hellenized by the fathers, while now commonly rejected, still finds more subtle echoes. And the ontological preoccupations of Nicaea and Chalcedon are often looked upon as regrettable, even if necessary, displacements of Christian focus. While the conciliar definitions and the immediate issues at stake were Christological, the underlying concern was soteriological. Against docetism, Arianism, Apollinarianism, Nestorianism, monophysitism, monothelitism, the same soteriological principle constantly recurs: *What was not assumed* (i.e., whatever in humanity was not united in Christ with the divine person of the Word) *was not healed*. Each of these heresies was seen not merely as falsifying the constitution of Christ but as threatening our salvation by Christ. The fathers, especially the Greek fathers, began from the so-called *physico-mystical* conception of the redemption: in the incarnation there occurred a *physical union* between the Word and a single human nature, which somehow *mystically contained* all men. Thus the presence and the action of the Word in this humanity, which is *our* humanity, is of itself a presence and action which saves humanity. This view drew on the scriptural doctrine of our solidarity with Christ (e.g., Heb 2:11); it also drew on Platonic ideas about the unity of mankind. It was and remains a rich and attractive link between Christology and soteriology.

I. THE COUNCIL OF NICEA, A.D. 325*

Letter of Eusebius of Caesarea Describing the Council of Nicea[2]

---

* The Council of Nicea (Iznik, Turkey), convoked in 325 by Constantine and approved by Pope Sylvester I, condemned Arianism. After each bishop expressed his position on the nature of the Incarnation, Arius was allowed to expound his own teachings, which were clearly seen to be contrary to the belief of the Church. The Council declared that Christ as Son of God is divine, of the same substance as the Father. The term *homoousios*, "consubstantial," was chosen to express this relationship.

As I received my tradition from the bishops before me, both in my first instruction and when I was baptized, and as I have learned from the divine Scriptures and as I believed and taught both in the office of the presbyterate and in the episcopate itself — so still believing I present to you my Creed, which is this:

"We believe in one God, Father,

[2] *The Christology of the Later Fathers* (London: S.C.M. Press, 1950), pp. 337–339.

Almighty, the maker of all things visible and invisible,

"And in one Lord Jesus Christ, the Word of God, God of God, Light of Light, Life of Life, unique Son, first-born of all creation, begotten of the Father before all the ages, through whom also all things came to be, who for our salvation was incarnate and dwelt among men and suffered and rose on the third day and ascended to the Father and will come again with glory to judge living and dead.

"We also believe in one Holy Spirit.

"Believing that each of these is and exists, the Father truly [as] Father, the Son truly Son, and the Holy Spirit truly Holy Spirit, as also our Lord said when sending forth his disciples for the preaching, 'Go and make disciples of all nations, baptizing them in the name of the Father and of the Son and of the Holy Spirit' — of which I firmly assert that this is what I hold, and so I am convinced, and so I have held, and will stand for this faith till death, anathematizing every godless heresy.

"That I have always been convinced of these things, heart and soul, since I was first conscious of myself, and so I am now convinced and profess — [this] I witness in truth before God Almighty and our Lord Jesus Christ, and am prepared to demonstrate and prove to you that so I believed and preached in times gone by."

When I had presented this statement of faith there was no room for opposition — indeed our most pious emperor himself, first of all, testified that its contents were very sound. He further confessed that he himself was so convinced, and urged all to agree to it and to subscribe and assent to these very teachings, with the addition of the one word "consubstantial," which he himself interpreted as follows: "The Son is not to be called 'consubstantial' according to what happens to bodies, nor is he constituted by a division or some kind of cutting up of the Father, nor can the immaterial and intellectual and bodiless nature undergo what happens to bodies, but these things must be conceived of in divine and ineffable terms." Such were the theological observations of our most learned and pious emperor. But [the bishops], on the ground of adding

the *homoousios*, produced the following statement:

[The Creed drawn up at the Council]

"We believe in one God, Father, Almighty, maker of all things, visible and invisible,

"And in one Lord Jesus Christ, begotten of the Father uniquely, that is, of the substance of the Father, God of God, Light of Light, true God of true God, begotten, not made, consubstantial with the Father, through whom all things were made, both things in heaven and those in earth, who for us men and for our salvation came down and was incarnate, [and] became man; he suffered and rose on the third day, ascended into heaven, and is coming to judge living and dead,

"And in the Holy Spirit.

"But those who say, there was once when he was not, and before he was begotten he was not and he came into being out of things that are not, or allege that the Son of God is of a different subsistence or essence, or created or alterable or changeable, the catholic and apostolic Church anathematizes."

When they formulated this statement, I did not let it pass without examination in what sense they said "of the substance of the Father" and "consubstantial with the Father." So questions were raised and answered and the meaning of the phrases was tested by reason. Thus it was declared that they used the phrase "of the substance" to indicate his being of the Father, but not as if he were a part of the Father. So I agreed to subscribe to this in the sense of the pious teaching which declares that the Son is of the Father, but not as being a part of his essence. So I agreed to this idea, not rejecting the word *homoousios*, having before me the aim of peace, and that of not falling away from the sound doctrine.

In the same way I also accepted the phrase "begotten and not made," since they alleged that "made" is a term shared with the other creatures of God which came into being through the Son, which the Son is in no way like, since he is not a work of God comparable to those things that came into being through him, but is of a nature superior to everything made, which the divine oracles teach was begotten of the Father, the manner of his generation being ineffable and indescribable for every nature that came into being.

So also the phrase "the Son is consubstantial with the Father" stands up if properly examined — not in the manner of bodies or similarly to mortal animals, nor by division or cutting up of the essence — nor by any suffering or alteration or change of the essence and power of the Father; for the unbegotten nature of the Father is free from all these things. But the phrase "consubstantial with the Father" indicates that the Son of God bears no similarity with the creatures of God that came into being, but is in every way made like only to the Father who begot him, and is not of any other *hypostasis* or essence, but of the Father. It seemed proper to assent to the term itself, expounded in this manner, since I knew of some learned and distinguished bishops and writers among the ancients who made use of the term *homoousios* in the doctrinal discussion about the Father and the Son.

This will be sufficient with reference to the Creed that was set forth, to which we all assented — not without examination, but according to the senses indicated, which were inquired into in the presence of our most devout emperor himself, and supported by the arguments given above. And I did not find the anathematism set forth by them after the Creed distressing, since it forbids the use of non-scriptural terms, from which has come almost all the disorder and confusion of the Church. For as none of the inspired Scriptures uses the phrases "Out of things that are not" and "There was once when he was not," and the others that follow, it did not seem proper to use or teach them. I agreed to this too as a sound decision, since I had not been accustomed to use these terms previously.

Nor did I think it improper to anathematize the term, "Before he was begotten he was not," since all confess that the Son of God was before [his] generation according to the flesh. Our most pious emperor similarly supported the principle that he existed before all ages according to his divine generation, since before he was actually begotten he existed potentially in the Father, unbegottenly. For the Father is always Father as he is always King and Savior, being all potentially, and always standing in the same relations and [being in himself] the same.

I have thought it necessary to report to you these things, beloved, showing you the process of our examination and assent. I properly resisted up to the last moment, as long as what was written in unaccustomed language was offensive, but then I accepted without disputing what was unobjectionable, when it became clear to me, on examining fairly the meaning of the terms, that they harmonized with what I myself had professed in the Creed that I previously issued.

II. THE COUNCIL OF EPHESUS 431 A.D.*

The Epistle of Cyril to Nestorius[3]

---

* The Council of Ephesus was convened by the Eastern Roman Emperor Theodosius II in 430 to condemn Nestorianism, which held that there are two separate Persons in Christ and that Mary is not the Mother of God but merely mother of Christ's human nature. The Council defined the hypostatic union of two natures, divine and human, in the one divine Person of Jesus Christ.

To the most religious and beloved of God, fellow minister Nestorius, Cyril sends greeting in the Lord. . . . I urge you, as a brother in the Lord, to propose the word of teaching and the doctrine of the faith with all accuracy to the people, and to consider that the giving of scandal to one even of the least of those who believe in Christ, exposes a body to the unbearable indignation of God. . . . But this we shall accomplish most excellently if we shall turn over the words of the holy Fathers, and are zealous to obey their commands, proving ourselves, whether we be in the faith according to that which is written, and conform our thoughts to their upright and irreprehensible teaching.

The holy and great Synod [Ephesus] therefore says, that the only begotten Son, born according to nature of God the Father, very God of very God, Light of Light, by whom the Father made all things, came down, and was incarnate, and was made man, suffered, and rose again the third day, and ascended into heaven. These words and these decrees we ought to follow considering what is meant by the Word of God being incarnate and made man. For we do not say that the nature of the Word was changed and became flesh, or that it was converted into a whole man consisting of soul and body; but rather that the Word having personally united to himself flesh animated by a rational soul, did in an ineffable and inconceivable manner become man, and was called the Son of Man, not merely as willing or being pleased to be so called, neither on account of taking to himself a person, but because the two natures being brought together in a true union, there is of both one Christ and one Son; for the difference of the natures is not taken away by the union, but rather the divinity and the humanity make perfect for us the one Lord Jesus Christ by their ineffable and inexpressible union. So then he who had an existence before all ages and was born of the Father, is said to have been born according to the flesh of a woman, not as though his divine nature received its beginning of existence in the holy Virgin, for it needed not any second generation after that of the Father (for it would be absurd and foolish to say that he who existed before all ages, coeternal with the Father, needed any second beginning of existence), but since, for us and for our salvation, he personally united to himself to a human body, and came forth of a woman, he is in this way said to be born after the flesh;

---

[3] *Nicene and Post-Nicene Fathers of the Christian Church* (Grand Rapids, Mich.: Wm. B. Eerdmans Pub. Co., 1956), pp. 197–198.

for he was not first born a common man of the holy Virgin, and then the Word came down and entered into him, but the union being made in the womb itself, he is said to endure a birth after the flesh, ascribing to himself the birth of his own flesh. On this account we say that he suffered and rose again; not as if God the Word suffered in his own nature stripes, or the piercing of the nails, or any other wounds, for the Divine nature is incapable of suffering, inasmuch as it is incorporeal, but since that which had become his own body suffered in this way, he is also said to suffer for us; for he who is in himself incapable of suffering was in a suffering body. In the same manner also we conceive respecting his dying; for the Word of God is by nature immortal and incorruptible, and life and life-giving; since, however, his own body did, as Paul says, by the grace of God taste death for every man, he himself is said to have suffered death for us, not as if he had any experience of death in his own nature (for it would be madness to say or think this), but because, as I have just said, his flesh tasted death. In like manner his flesh being raised again, it is spoken of as his resurrection, not as if he had fallen into corruption (God forbid), but because his own body was raised again. We, therefore, confess one Christ and Lord, not as worshipping a man *with* the Word (lest this expression "with the Word" should suggest to the mind the idea of division), but worshipping him as one and the same, forasmuch as the body of the Word, with which he sits with the Father, is not separated from the Word himself, not as if two sons were sitting with him, but one by the union with the flesh. If,

however, we reject the personal union as impossible or unbecoming, we fall into the error of speaking of two sons, for it will be necessary to distinguish, and to say, that he who was properly man was honored with the appellation of Son, and that he who is properly the Word of God, has by nature both the name and the reality of Sonship. We must not, therefore, divide the one Lord Jesus Christ into two Sons. Neither will it at all avail to a sound faith to hold, as some do, an union of persons; for the Scripture has not said that the Word united to himself the person of man, but that he was made flesh. This expression, however, "the Word was made flesh," can mean nothing else but that he partook of flesh and blood like to us; he made our body his own, and came forth man from a woman, not casting off his existence as God, or his generation of God the Father, but even in taking to himself flesh remaining what he was. This the declaration of the correct faith proclaims everywhere. This was the sentiment of the holy Fathers; therefore they ventured to call the holy Virgin, the Mother of God, not as if the nature of the Word or his divinity had its beginning from the holy Virgin, but because of her was born that holy body with a rational soul, to which the Word being personally united is said to be born according to the flesh. These things, therefore, I now write unto you for the love of Christ, beseeching you as a brother, and testifying to you before Christ and the elect angels, that you would both think and teach these things with us, that the peace of the Churches may be preserved and the bond of concord and love continue unbroken amongst the Priests of God.

III. THE COUNCIL OF CHALCEDON 451 A.D.*

The Chalcedonian Decree⁴

---

* The Council of Chalcedon (451) re-affirmed the definitions of Nicea and of the First Council of Constantinople (381). It declared their positions on the Person of Christ to be orthodox Catholic belief. It asserted Mary to be *Theotokos,* Mother of God.

The Symbol of the One Hundred and Fifty at Constantinople:

We believe in one God, Father Almighty, maker of heaven and earth, and of all things visible and invisible.

And in one Lord Jesus Christ, the unique Son of God, begotten of the Father before all the ages, Light of Light, true God of true God, begotten, not made, through whom all things came into being; who for us men and for our salvation came down from heaven, and was incarnate of [the] Holy Spirit and Mary the Virgin, and became man; he was crucified also for us under Pontius Pilate, and suffered, and was buried, and rose again on the third day according to the Scriptures; ascended into heaven, and sits on the right hand of the Father, and is coming again with glory to judge living and dead; of whose Kingdom there will be no end.

And in the Holy Spirit, the Lord, and the Life-giver, who proceeds from the Father, who with the Father and the Son is worshiped and glorified, who spoke through the prophets — [and] in one Holy Catholic and Apostolic Church; we confess one Baptism for the remission of sins. We look for the resurrection of the dead, and the life of the age to come. Amen.⁵

---

⁴ *The Christology of the Later Fathers* (London: S.C.M. Press, 1950), pp. 372–373.

⁵ The additions to the Creed in West-

[The Nicene Creed should have been enough, the decree continues, but the Fathers of Constantinople found it necessary to clarify the teaching on the Holy Spirit. Now that others either confuse or divide the Person of Christ, the Council has received as standards of orthodoxy the Synodical Letters of Cyril to Nestorius and the Easterns and the Letter of Leo to Flavian, that is, the Tome. Finally it proceeds to its own definition.]

For [the Council] opposes those who try to divide the mystery of the dispensation⁶ into a dyad of Sons; and those who dare to say that the Godhead of the only-begotten is passible it expels away from the company of the priests; and it resists those who think of a mixture or confusion of the two natures of Christ; and it drives away those who fancy that the form of a servant (cf. Phil 2:7), which he took of us was of a heavenly or some

---

ern use may be noted here; both Latin and English versions retain the Nicene phrase "God of God" before "Light of Light"; the addition of the *filioque* ("and from the Son") after "proceeds from the Father" was made almost casually in Spain at the reconciliation of the Spanish Arians in 589, later spread, and since the ninth century has been considered in the East to mark an error in doctrine as well as an unauthorized addition.

⁶ A phrase suggested by Eph 1:9, 10; the "dispensation" (*oikonomia*) is so often used with reference to the incarnation as practically to become a term for it.

other substance; and those who imagine two natures of the Lord before
the union but invent one after the
union it anathematizes.

Following therefore the holy Fathers, we confess one and the same
our Lord Jesus Christ, and we all
teach harmoniously [that he is] the
same perfect in Godhead, the same
perfect in manhood, truly God and
truly man, the same of a reasonable
soul and body; consubstantial with
the Father in Godhead, and the
same consubstantial with us in manhood, like us in all things except
sin; begotten before ages of the Father in Godhead, the same in the
last days for us; and for our salvation
[born] of Mary the virgin *theotokos*
in manhood, one and the same Christ,
Son, Lord, unique; acknowledged in
two natures without confusion, without change, without division, without
separation — the difference of the natures being by no means taken away
because of the union, but rather the
distinctive character of each nature
being preserved, and [each] combining in one Person and *hypostasis* —

not divided or separated into two Persons, but one and the same Son and
only-begotten God, Word, Lord Jesus
Christ; as the prophets of old and
the Lord Jesus Christ himself taught
us about him, and the symbol of the
Fathers has handed down to us.

Since we have determined these
things with all possible accuracy and
care, the holy and ecumenical Council
has decreed that no one shall be allowed to bring forward another Creed,
nor to compose or produce or think
out or teach [such] to others. But
those who dare either to compose
another Creed, or propound, or teach,
or deliver another Symbol to those
who wish to turn to the knowledge of
the truth from paganism or Judaism,
or from any kind of heresy[7] if they
are bishops or clerics, the bishops
shall be expelled from the episcopate,
the clerics from the clergy; if they
are monks or laymen, they shall be
anathematized.

[7] In the ancient catechumenate the *tra-
ditio Symboli,* or delivery of the Creed to
converts, both as a sacred formula and as a
scheme of instruction, was an important
part of preparation for Baptism.

IV. LEO THE GREAT*

The Tome of Leo[8]

---

* Leo the Great (died 461), Pope and
Doctor of the Church, greatly established
and advanced the authority of the Roman
See, though his jurisdiction was not recognized in the East. His legates presided at
the Council of Chalcedon which accepted
his *Tome* as a standard of Christological
orthodoxy.

Leo to his beloved brother Flavian:
Having read Your Affection's letter,
the late arrival of which is a matter of

[8] *The Christology of the Later Fathers*
(London: S.C.M. Press, 1950), pp. 361–
367.

surprise to us, and having gone
through the record of the proceedings
of the bishops, we have now, at last,
gained a clear view of the scandal
which has risen up among you, against
the integrity of the faith; and what at

first seemed obscure has now been elucidated and explained.

By this means Eutyches, who seemed to be deserving of honor under the title of presbyter, is now known to be exceedingly thoughtless and sadly inexperienced, so that to him may apply what the prophet said, "He refused to understand that he might act well; he meditated unrighteousness on his bed." What, indeed, is more unrighteous than to entertain ungodly thoughts, and not to yield to persons wiser and more learned? But into this folly do they fall who, when hindered by some obscurity from knowing the truth, have recourse, not to the words of the prophets, not to the letters of the apostles, nor to the authority of the Gospels, but to themselves; and become teachers of error, just because they have not been disciples of the truth. For what learning has he received from the sacred pages of the New and Old Testaments, who does not so much as understand the very beginning of the Creed? And that which, all the world over, is uttered by the voices of all applicants for regeneration is still not apprehended by the mind of this aged man.

If, then, he knew not what he ought to think about the incarnation of the Word of God, and was not willing, for the sake of obtaining the light of intelligence, to make laborious search through the whole extent of the Holy Scriptures, he should at least have received with heedful attention that general confession common to all, whereby the whole body of the faithful profess that they "believe in God the Father Almighty, and in Jesus Christ his only Son our Lord, Who was born of the Holy Spirit and the Virgin Mary." By which three clauses the engines of almost all heretics are shattered. For when God is believed to be both "Almighty" and "Father," it is found that the Son is everlasting together with himself, differing in nothing from the Father, because he was born as "God from God," Almighty from Almighty, Coeternal from Eternal; not later in time, not unlike him in glory, not divided from him in essence; and the same only-begotten and everlasting Son of an eternal Parent was "born of the Holy Ghost and the Virgin Mary." This birth in time in no way detracted from, in no way added to, that divine and everlasting birth; but expended itself wholly in the work of restoring man, who had been deceived, so that it might both overcome death, and by its power "destroy the devil who had the power of death." For we could not have overcome the author of sin and of death, unless he who could neither be contaminated by sin nor detained by death had taken upon himself our nature and made it his own. For, in fact, he was "conceived of the Holy Ghost" within the womb of a virgin mother, who bore him, as she had conceived him, without loss of virginity. . . .

Possibly his reason for thinking that our Lord Jesus Christ was not of our nature was this: that the angel who was sent to the blessed and ever-virgin Mary said, "The Holy Ghost shall come upon thee and the power of the Highest shall overshadow thee, and therefore also that holy thing which shall be born of thee shall be called Son of God" (Lk 1:35), as if, because the Virgin's conception was caused by a divine act, therefore the flesh of him whom she conceived was not of the nature of her who conceived him. But we are not to understand that "generation," peerlessly wonderful, and wonderfully peerless, in such a sense as that the newness of the mode of production did away with the proper character of the kind. For it was the Holy Ghost who gave fecundity to the Virgin, but it was from a body that a real body was derived; and "when Wisdom was building herself a house," "the Word was made flesh, and dwelt among us" (Pr 9:1; Jn 1:14), that is, in that flesh which he assumed from a human being, and which he animated with the spirit of rational life.

Accordingly, while the distinctness of both natures and substances is preserved, and both meet in one Person, lowliness is assumed by majesty, weakness by power, mortality by eternity; and in order to pay the debt of our condition, the inviolable nature has been united to the passible, so that as the appropriate remedy for our ills, one and the same "Mediator between God and men, the man Christ Jesus," (1 Tim 2:5), might from one element be capable of dying, and from the other be incapable. Therefore in the entire and perfect nature of very Man was born very God, whole in what was his, whole in what was ours. (By "ours" we mean what the Creator formed in us at the beginning, and what he assumed in order to restore;) for of that which the deceiver brought in, and man, thus deceived, admitted, there was not a trace in the Savior; and the fact that he took on himself a share in our infirmities did not make him a partaker in our transgressions. He took on him "the form of a servant" without the defilement of sins, augmenting what was human, not diminishing what was divine; because that "emptying of himself" (Phil 2:7), whereby the Invisible made himself visible, and the Creator and Lord of all things willed to be one among mortals, was a stooping down of compassion, not a failure of power. Accordingly, the same who, remaining in the form of God, made man, was made Man in the form of a servant. For each of the natures retains its proper character without defect; and as the form of God does not take away the form of a servant, so the form of a servant does not impair the form of God. For since the devil was glorying in the fact that man, deceived by his craft, was bereft of divine gifts, and, being stripped of this endowment of immortality, had come under the grievous sentence of death, and that he himself, amid his miseries, had found a sort of consolation in having a transgressor as his companion, and that God, according to the requirements of the principle of justice, had changed his own resolution in regard to man, whom he had created in so high a position of honor, there was need of a dispensation of secret counsel, in order that the unchangeable God, whose will could not be deprived of its own benignity, should fulfill by a more secret mystery his original plan of loving kindness towards us, and that man, who had been led into fault by the wicked subtlety of the devil, should not perish contrary to God's purpose.

Accordingly, the Son of God, descending from his seat in heaven, yet not departing from the glory of the Father, enters this lower world, born after a new order, by a new mode of birth. After a new order, because he who in his own sphere is invisible became visible in ours; he who could not be enclosed in space willed to be enclosed; continuing to be before times, he began to exist in time; the Lord of the universe allowed his infinite majesty to be overshadowed, and took upon him the form of a servant: the impassible God did not disdain to become passible, and the immortal one to be subject to the laws of death. And born by a new mode of birth, because inviolate virginity, while ignorant of concupiscence, supplied the matter of his flesh. What was assumed from the Lord's mother was nature, not fault; and the fact that the nativity of our Lord Jesus Christ is wonderful, in that he was born of a virgin's womb, does not imply that his nature is unlike ours. For the selfsame who is very God is also very Man: and there is no illusion in this union, while the lowliness of man and the loftiness of Godhead meet together. For as "God" is not changed by the compassion [exhibited], so "Man" is not consumed by the dignity [bestowed]. For each "form" does the acts which belong to it, in communion with the other; the Word, that is, performing what belongs to the Word, and the flesh carrying out what belongs to the flesh. The one of these shines out in miracles; the other succumbs to injuries.

And as the Word does not withdraw from equality with the Father in glory, so the flesh does not abandon the nature of our kind. For, as we must often be saying, he is one and the same, truly Son of God, and truly Son of Man: God, inasmuch as "in the beginning was the Word, and the Word was with God, and the Word was God" (Jn 1:1); Man, inasmuch as "the Word was made flesh, and dwelt among us" (Jn 1:3). God, inasmuch as "all things were made by him, and without him nothing was made" (Jn 1:14); Man, inasmuch as he was "made of a woman, made under the law" (Gal 4:4). The nativity of the flesh is a manifestation of human nature: the Virgin's child-bearing is an indication of divine power. The infancy of the babe is exhibited by the humiliation of swaddling clothes; the greatness of the highest is declared by the voices of angels. He whom Herod impiously designs to slay is like humanity in its beginnings; but he whom the Magi rejoice to adore on their knees is Lord of all. Now when he came to the baptism of John his forerunner, lest the fact that the Godhead was covered with a veil of flesh should be concealed, the voice of the Father spoke in thunder from heaven, "This is my beloved son, in whom I am well pleased" (Mt 3:17). Accordingly, he who, as man, is tempted by the devil's subtlety is the same to whom, as God, angels pay duteous service. (Cf. Mt 4:11; Mk 1:13.) To hunger, to thirst, to be weary, and to sleep is evidently human. But to feed five thousand men with five loaves, and to bestow on the woman of Samaria that living water, to drink of which can secure one from thirsting again; to walk on the surface of the sea with feet that sink not, and by rebuking the storm to bring down the "uplifted waves," is unquestionably divine (cf. Ps 93 (92):3, 4; Mt 8:26; Mk 4:39; Lk 8:24, 25). As then — to pass by many points — it does not belong to the same nature to weep with feelings of pity over a dead friend and, after the mass of stone had been removed from the grave where he had lain four days, by a voice of command to raise him up to life again; or to hang on the wood and to make all the elements tremble after daylight had been turned into night; or to be transfixed with nails and to open the gates of paradise to the faith of the robber, so it does not belong to the same nature to say, "I and the Father are one" (Jn 10:30), and to say, "The Father is greater than I" (Jn 14:28). For although in the Lord Jesus Christ there is one Person of God and man, yet that whereby contumely attaches to both is one thing, and that whereby glory attaches to both is another: for from what belongs to us he has that manhood which is inferior to the Father; while from the Father he has equal Godhead with the Father.

Accordingly, on account of this unity which is to be understood as existing in both the natures, we read, on the one hand, that "the Son of Man came down from heaven" (Jn 3:13), inasmuch as the Son of God took flesh from that Virgin of whom he was born; and, on the other hand, the Son of God is said to have been crucified and buried, inasmuch as he underwent this, not in his actual Godhead, wherein the Only-begotten is coeternal and consubstantial with the Father, but in the weakness of human nature. Wherefore we all, in the very Creed, confess that "the only-begotten Son of God was crucified and buried," according to that saying of the apostle, "For if they had known it, they would not have crucified the Lord of majesty" (1 Cor 2:8). And when our Lord and Savior himself was by his questions instructing the faith of the disciples, he said, "Who do men say that I the Son of Man am?" And when they had mentioned various opinions held by others, he said, "But who say ye that I am?" that is, "I who am Son of Man, and whom you see in the form of a servant, and in reality of flesh, who say ye that I am?" Whereupon the blessed Peter, as inspired by God, and about to benefit all nations by his confession, said, "Thou art the Christ, the Son of the living God"

(Mt 16:13–19). Not undeservedly, therefore, was he pronounced blessed by the Lord, and derived from the original Rock that solidity which belonged both to his virtue and to his name, who through revelation from the Father confessed the selfsame to be both the Son of God and the Christ; because one of these truths, accepted without the other, would not profit unto salvation, and it was equally dangerous to believe the Lord Jesus Christ to be merely God and not man or merely man and not God. But after the resurrection of the Lord — which was in truth the resurrection of a real body, for no other person was raised again than he who had been crucified and had died — what else was accomplished during that interval of forty days than to make our faith entire and clear of all darkness? For a while he conversed with his disciples, and dwelt with them, and ate with them, and allowed himself to be handled with careful and inquisitive touch by those who were under the influence of doubt; and this was his purpose in entering in to them when the doors were shut, and by his breath giving them the Holy Ghost and opening the secrets of Holy Scripture after bestowing on them the light of intelligence, and again in his selfsame person showing to them the wound in the side, the prints of the nails, and all the fresh tokens of the passion, saying, "Behold my hands and feet, that it is I myself; handle me and see, for a spirit hath not flesh and bones, as ye see me have" (Lk 24:39); that the properties of the divine and the human nature might be acknowledged to remain in him without causing a division, and that we might in such sort know that the Word is not what the flesh is as to confess that the one Son of God is both Word and flesh.

On which mystery of the faith this Eutyches must be regarded as unhappily having no hold whatever; for he has not acknowledged our nature to exist in the only-begotten Son of God, by way either of the lowliness of mortality or of the glory of resurrection. Nor has he been overawed by the declaration of the blessed Apostle and Evangelist John, saying, "Every spirit that confesseth that Jesus Christ has come in the flesh is of God, and every spirit which dissolveth Jesus is not of God, and this is Antichrist" (1 Jn 4:2–3). Now what is to dissolve Jesus, but to separate the human nature from him, and to make void by shameless inventions that mystery by which alone we have been saved? Moreover, seeing he is blind as to the nature of Christ's body, he must needs be involved in the like senseless blindness with regard to his Passion also. For if he does not think the Lord's crucifixion to be unreal, and does not doubt that he really accepted suffering, even unto death, for the sake of the world's salvation; as he believes in his death, let him acknowledge his flesh also, and not doubt that he whom he recognizes as having been capable of suffering is also man with a body like ours; since to deny his true flesh is also to deny his bodily sufferings.

V. THE SECOND AND THIRD COUNCILS OF CONSTANTINOPLE*

The Anathemas of the Second Council[9]

* The Second Council of Constantinople (553 A.D.) was convoked by Emperor Justinian I to combat continuing Nestorian trends, particularly Monophysite positions, which held that Christ's divine nature had totally absorbed his human nature. The Third Council, called by Emperor Constantine IV in 680, brought about a reconciliation between the Church of Rome and the Eastern Church. It condemned Monotheletism, which claimed that the two natures of Christ are so unified that in him there is only one will and one activity.

1. If anyone does not confess one nature or substance, one power and authority, of Father and Son and Holy Spirit, Consubstantial Trinity, one Deity worshiped in three *hypostases* or persons, let him be anathema. For [there is] one God and Father, of whom are all things, and one Lord Jesus Christ, through whom are all things, and one Holy Spirit, in whom are all things.

2. If anyone does not confess that there are two generations of God the Word, one before ages of the Father, non-temporal and bodiless, the other at the last days when the same came down from heaven and was incarnate of the holy, glorious *theotokos,* and ever-virgin Mary, and born of her, let him be anathema.

3. If anyone says that the Word of God who did wonders was one and Christ who suffered was another, or says that God the Word was together with Christ who came of woman, or

[9] *The Christology of the Later Fathers* (London: S.C.M. Press, 1950), pp. 378–385 passim.

was in him as one in another, but not [that he was] one and the same our Lord Jesus Christ, the Word of God incarnate and made man, and [that] the wonders and the sufferings, which he voluntarily endured in flesh, were of the same, let him be anathema.

4. If anyone says that the union of God the Word with man took place [merely] by grace or by energy, or by equality of honor, or by authority or ascription or relation or power, or by good pleasure — as of God the Word being pleased with the man, from his being well and truly satisfied with him, as Theodore insanely says [let him be anathema] — or [if he speaks of a union] by use of the same name, according to which the Nestorians, calling God the Word "Jesus" and "Christ," and naming the man separately "Christ" and "Son," and evidently speaking of two persons with one appellation and honor and dignity and worship, pretend to speak of one person and one Christ — but does not confess that the union of God the Word with flesh ensouled with a reasonable and intellectual soul took place by composition, that is, by *hypostasis,* as the holy Fathers taught — and because of this, his *hypostasis* [is] one, namely, the Lord Jesus Christ, one of the holy Trinity — let him be anathema. For, thinking of the union in diverse ways, some, in accordance with the ungodliness of Apollinaris and Eutyches, assuming the disappearance of the components, affirm the union by confusion; while those who accept the ideas of Theodore and Nestorius, rejoicing in division, introduce the union of relation. But the holy Church of God, rejecting the impiety of each heresy, confesses the union of

God the Word with the flesh by composition, that is, by *hypostasis.* For the union by composition in the mystery about Christ not only preserves the components unconfused, but accepts no separation.

[*"5" reaffirms the ideas of "4" and "6" reasserts the propriety of the use of the term theotokos.]*

7. If anyone who says "in two natures" does not confess that our one Lord Jesus Christ is made known in Godhead and manhood, in order that he may indicate the distinction of the natures, from which the ineffable union took place without confusion, neither the Word being changed into the nature of the flesh nor the flesh transferred into the nature of the Word — for each remains what it was by nature, even when the union by *hypostasis* has taken place — but takes the phrase with reference to division into parts in the mystery of Christ [let him be anathema]. Or when [anyone] confessing the number of natures in the same our one Lord Jesus Christ, God the Word incarnate, does not take the distinction of the elements of which he was constituted, which was not taken away by the union, in contemplation only — for [he is] one of both and both [are] through one — but uses the number as if he possessed separated natures with their own *hypostases,* let him be anathema.

8. If anyone who confesses that the union was effected out of two natures, deity and humanity, or speaks of one incarnate nature of God the Word, does not so take these [terms], as the holy Fathers taught, that out of the divine nature and the human, when the union by *hypostasis* took place, one Christ was formed, but out of these phrases tries to introduce one

nature or substance of the Godhead and flesh of Christ, let him be anathema. For when saying that the unique Word was united by *hypostasis,* we do not mean that there was any mixture of the natures with each other, but rather we think of the Word as united with flesh, each remaining what it is. Therefore Christ is one, God and man, the same consubstantial with the father in Godhead, in the same consubstantial with us in manhood. Equally therefore does the Church of God reject and anathematize those who divide into parts or cut up, and those who confuse the mystery of the divine dispensation of Christ.

9. If anyone says that Christ is to be worshiped in two natures, from which two adorations are introduced, one proper to God the Word and one to the man — or if anyone in terms of destruction of the flesh, or of confusion of the Godhead and the manhood, or strangely contriving one nature or substance of the components, so worships Christ — but does not with one adoration worship God the Word incarnate with his own flesh,

as the Church of God has received from the beginning, let him be anathema.

10. If anyone does not confess that our Lord Jesus Christ who was crucified in flesh is true God and Lord of glory and one of the holy Trinity, let him be anathema.

11. If anyone does not anathematize Arius, Eunomius, Macedonius, Apollinaris, Nestorius, Eutyches, and Origen,[10] with their godless writings, and all other heretics who were condemned and anathematized by the holy catholic and apostolic Church and the holy four councils, . . . and those who have held or hold the like to the above-mentioned heretics, and remain till the end in their own impiety, let him be anathema.

[10] This casual and incidental condemnation of Origen is surprising and its authenticity has been doubted; however, Justinian was interested in securing a condemnation of Origen's more eccentric speculations, which reappeared from time to time in the more learned and sophisticated monastic circles, and probably did succeed in this incidental manner. Whether the specific anathemas against Origen ascribed to this Council are genuine is uncertain.

The Statement of Faith of the Third Council of Constantinople

Following the holy and ecumenical five councils, and the holy and approved Fathers, and unanimously defining that our Lord Jesus Christ, our true God, one of the holy and life-bestowing Trinity, is to be confessed perfect in Godhead and the same perfect in manhood . . . [the Chalcedonian definition is then repeated, with the one additional phrase that Mary is called "genuinely and in truth *theotokos"]. . . .*

We also proclaim two natural willings or wills in him and two natural

operations, without separation, without change, without partition, without confusion, according to the teaching of the holy Fathers — and two natural wills not contrary [to each other], God forbid, as the impious heretics have said [they would be], but his human will following, and not resisting or opposing, but rather subject to his divine and all-powerful will. For it was proper for the will of the flesh to be moved [naturally], yet to be subject to the divine will, according to the all-wise Athanasius.

For as his flesh is called and is the flesh of God the Word, so also the natural will of his flesh is called and is God the Word's own will, as he himself says: "I came down from heaven, not to do my own will, but the will of the Father who sent me," calling the will of the flesh his own, as also the flesh had become his own. For in the same manner that his all-holy and spotless ensouled flesh, though divinized, was not destroyed, but remained in its own law and principle, so also his human will, divinized, was not destroyed, but rather preserved, as Gregory the divine says: "His will, as conceived of in his character as the Savior, is not contrary to God, [being] wholly divinized." We also glorify two natural operations in the same our Lord Jesus Christ, our true God, without separation, without change, without partition, without confusion, that is, a divine operation and a human operation, as the divine preacher Leo most clearly says: "For each form does what is proper to it, in communion with the other; the Word, that is, performing what belongs to the Word, and the flesh carrying out what belongs to the flesh." We will not therefore grant [the existence of] one natural operation of God and the creature, lest we should either raise up into the divine nature what is created, or bring down the pre-eminence of the divine nature into the place suitable for things that are made. For we recognize the wonders and the sufferings as of one and the same [person], according to the difference of the natures of which he is and in which he has his being, as the eloquent Cyril said.

Preserving therefore in every way the unconfused and undivided, we set forth the whole [confession] in brief; believing our Lord Jesus Christ, our true God, to be one of the holy Trinity even after the taking of flesh, we declare that his two natures shine forth in his one *hypostasis*, in which he displayed both the wonders and the sufferings through the whole course of his dispensation, not in phantasm but truly, the difference of nature being recognized in the same one *hypostasis* by the fact that each nature wills and works what is proper to it, in communion with the other. On this principle we glorify two natural wills and operations combining with each other for the salvation of the human race.

PART THREE: DEVELOPMENTS IN CHRISTOLOGY

Chapter 4. Medieval Developments

INTRODUCTION

Medieval Scholastic Development[1]

by Karl Adam

"Nature" is the essence of a thing, what makes a being what it is. More precisely, "nature" is the essence of a thing insofar as it is the principle of its functioning, of its peculiar activity and passivity. It answers the question *quid?* – what?

The person asks who? – *quis?* It is defined as the *hypostasis rationalis,* the spiritual self. Literally, the concept [of] hypostasis implies an autonomy, a self-sufficiency, a "standing-in-itself." The hypostasis as an autonomy is thus distinguished from the acci-

dent, which subsists in something other than itself; in Scholastic terms the accident is an *ens in alio,* whereas the hypostasis is an *ens in se.* As a thing-in-itself, however, it cannot be a merely intellectual being, but must also have an individual concrete reality of being. In other words, the hypostasis cannot be a *substantia secunda,* as Aristotle puts it; it cannot be a mere generic concept. It is an individual, concrete substance – in Aristotelian terms, *substantia prima.* This concept of autonomy (*inseitas*) thus does away with the accidental on the one hand, and the merely abstract and intellectual on the other. It is essentially a concrete substance, for example, this

---

[1] *The Christ of Faith: The Christology of the Church* (London: Burns & Oates, 1957; New York: Pantheon, 1957), pp. 193–194.

stone, this Cephas. However, there are also substances, for example, the human body, or the arm or foot of an organism, which are certainly concrete and individual, but are not entire in themselves, and attain their whole being only by being united with another concrete substance. These are called *substantiae incompletae*. So as well as the concept of autonomy, *inseitas*, the concept of hypostasis also requires that of *integritas*, organization as a whole. The hypostasis must be a *substantia prima completa*. But even then the complete concept of hypostasis has not yet been reached. There is a possibility — and in Christ it became a reality — that a complete individual substance, such as Christ's humanity, however closed and independent its being, nevertheless might in fact lose this closed autonomy because it is integrated into a higher substance. In this case, it is no longer an hypostasis, because it receives its definiteness and completion not in its own being but only in a higher being. So for the concept of hypostasis to be complete, it is also necessary that this last possibility of an ordination of being towards a higher hypostasis should be excluded, that the hypostasis should be "totally in itself," or entirely autonomous. In this sense, Scholastic terminology speaks of a *totietas in se*, or a *perseitas*. So the concept of hypostasis includes three things: the *inseitas*, the *integritas*, and finally the *totietas in se*, or *perseitas*. As such a closed and autonomous whole, it excludes any kind of synthesis or composition; it is incommunicable, unique, and unrepeatable (*incommunicabilitas*). In positive terms, it is a closed entirety, with an independent autonomy. The mark of the hypostasis is this very quality of a *closed* being.

That is why it is defined as *substantia prima, integra, tota in se*.

A purely formal evaluation of what gives the complete substance this incommunicability would be to call it *subsistence*. Subsistence is that mode of being, *modus essendi*, which gives to the substantial essence its incommunicability.

Only now have we reached a definition of the concept "hypostasis." But, even a crystal can be this kind of hypostasis. How is this to be distinguished from a "person"? Something new must also be added — *rationalitas*, the faculty of reason. The person is the *hypostasis rationalis*. The person arises only when the incommunicable, autonomous substance is also a spiritual, rational substance, only when it has that independent spiritual possession of its autonomy which is the basis for the development of a consciousness of self-sufficiency. It is true, being a person does not condition one's actual knowledge of one's own autonomy, but it certainly conditions one's capability of reaching this consciousness, this conscious self-possession. This faculty of reason, this *rationalitas*, is what transforms the hypostasis from a purely static, dead, frozen, *totietas in se* into one that is dynamic, spiritual, profound. The autonomy of being becomes an autonomy of self-possession, the faculty of self-consciousness. So person cannot be separated from intellectuality. The person is necessarily *sui juris*, subject to law, and, being subject to law, bears the responsibility of the activities of its nature. It is not as if the *rationalitas*, although a characteristic of the "nature," had no effect upon being a person. Because it is a question of a spiritual rational being, the autonomy is *in ipsa ratione hypostaseos* intensified, to the extent that only then is its independent self-possession and self-belonging fully realized.

Using this terminology, the theologians sought to answer the question of the ultimate basis for unity in the constitution of Christ.

I. ST. ANSELM*

Cur Deus Homo?[2]

---

* St. Anselm (c1033–1109), Archbishop of Canterbury, born in Lombardy, entered a monastic school in Normandy after an undisciplined adolescence. His strong character and penetrating intellect later led to his rise to the archbishopric of Canterbury. He fought against lay investiture, twice exiling himself in protest. As theologian and philosopher he ranks first between St. Augustine and St. Thomas. He differed from earlier theologians in that he prefered to defend and to explain the faith by intellectual reasoning, rather than by exclusive dependence upon Scripture and authority. His *Monologium* and *De Veritate* were efforts in this direction to establish the existence of God. In *Cur Deus Homo?* Anselm makes a foremost contribution to the theology of the atonement.

Chapter VI

How no being, except the God-man can make the atonement by which man is saved.

Anselm. But this cannot be effected, except the price paid to God for the sin of man be something greater than all the universe besides God.

Boso. So it appears.

Anselm. Moreover, it is necessary that he who can give God anything of his own which is more valuable than all things in the possession of God, must be greater than all else but God himself.

Boso. I cannot deny it.

Anselm. Therefore none but God can make this satisfaction.

Boso. So it appears.

Anselm. But none but a man ought to do this, otherwise man does not make the satisfaction.

Boso. Nothing seems more just.

Anselm. If it be necessary, therefore, as it appears, that the heavenly kingdom be made up of men, and this cannot be effected unless the aforesaid satisfaction be made, which none but God can make and none but man ought to make, it is necessary for the God-man to make it.

Boso. Now blessed be God! we have made a great discovery with regard to our question. Go on, therefore, as you have begun. For I hope that God will assist you.

Anselm. Now must we inquire how God can become man.

[2] S. N. Deane (tr.), *St. Anselm: Basic Writings,* revised ed. (Chicago: The Open Court Pub. Co., 1962), pp. 244–251.

Chapter VII

How necessary it is for the same being to be perfect God and perfect man.

Anselm. The Divine and human natures cannot alternate, so that the Divine should become human or the human Divine; nor can they be so commingled as that a third should be produced from the two which is neither wholly Divine nor wholly human. For, granting that it were possible for either to be changed into the other, it would in that case be only God and not man, or man only and not God. Or, if they were so commingled that a third nature sprung from the combination of the two (as from two animals, a male and a female of different species, a third is produced, which does not preserve entire the species of either parent, but has a mixed nature derived from both), it would neither be God nor man. Therefore the God-man, whom we require to be of a nature both human and Divine, cannot be produced by a change from one into the other, nor by an imperfect commingling of both in a third; since these things cannot be, or, if they could be, would avail nothing to our purpose. More-over, if these two complete natures are said to be joined somehow, in such a way that one may be Divine while the other is human, and yet that which is God not be the same with that which is man, it is impossible for both to do the work necessary to be accomplished. For God will not do it, because he has no debt to pay; and man will not do it, because he cannot. Therefore, in order that the God-man may perform this, it is necessary that the same being should be perfect God and perfect man, in order to make this atonement. For he cannot and ought not to do it, unless he be very God and very man. Since, then, it is necessary that the God-man preserve the completeness of each nature, it is no less necessary that these two natures be united entire in one person, just as a body and a reasonable soul exist together in every human being; for otherwise it is impossible that the same being should be very God and very man.

Boso. All that you say is satisfactory to me.

Chapter VIII

How it behooved God to take a man of the race of Adam,
and born of a woman.

Anselm. It now remains to inquire whence and how God shall assume human nature. For he will either take it from Adam, or else he will make a new man, as he made Adam originally. But, if he makes a new man, not of Adam's race, then this man will not belong to the human family, which descended from Adam, and therefore ought not to make atonement for it, because he never belonged to it. For, as it is right for man to make atonement for the sin of man, it is also necessary that he who makes the atonement should be the very being who has sinned, or else one of the same race. Otherwise, neither Adam nor his race would make satisfaction for themselves. Therefore, as through Adam and Eve sin was propagated among all men, so none but themselves, or one born of them, ought to make atonement for the sin of men. And, since they cannot, one born of them must fulfill this work. Moreover, as Adam and his whole race, had he not sinned, would have stood firm without the support of any other being, so, after the fall, the same race must rise and be exalted by means of itself. For, whoever restores the race to its place, it will certainly stand by that being who has made this restoration. Also, when God created human nature in Adam alone, and would only make woman out of man, that by the union of both sexes there might be increase, in this he showed plainly that he wished to produce all that he intended with regard to human nature from man alone. Wherefore, if the race of Adam be reinstated by any being not of the same race, it will not be restored to that dignity which it would have had, had not Adam sinned, and so will not be completely restored; and, besides, God will seem to have failed of his purpose, both which suppositions are incongruous. It is, therefore, necessary that the man by whom Adam's race shall be restored be taken from Adam.

Boso. If we follow reason, as we proposed to do, this is the necessary result.

Anselm. Let us now examine the question, whether the human nature taken by God must be produced from a father and mother, as other men are, or from man alone, or from woman alone. For, in whichever of these three modes it be, it will be produced from Adam and Eve, for from these two is every person of either sex descended.

And of these three modes, no one is easier for God than another, that it should be selected on this account.

Boso. So far it is well.

Anselm. It is no great toil to show that that man will be brought into existence in a nobler and purer manner, if produced from man alone, or woman alone, than if springing from the union of both, as do all other men.

Boso. I agree with you.

Anselm. Therefore must he be taken either from man alone, or woman alone.

Boso. There is no other source.

Anselm. In four ways can God create man, viz., either of man and woman, in the common way; or neither of man nor woman, as he created Adam; or of man without woman, as he made Eve; or of woman without man, which thus far he has never done. Wherefore, in order to show that this last mode is also under his power, and was reserved for this very purpose, what more fitting than that he should take that man whose origin we are seeking from a woman without a man? Now whether it be more worthy that he be born of a virgin, or one not a virgin, we need not discuss, but must affirm, beyond all doubt, that the God-man should be born of a virgin.

Boso. Your speech gratifies my heart.

Anselm. Does what we have said appear sound, or is it unsubstantial as a cloud, as you have said infidels declare?

Boso. Nothing can be more sound.

Anselm. Paint not, therefore, upon baseless emptiness, but upon solid truth, and tell how clearly fitting it is that, as man's sin and the cause of our condemnation sprung from a woman, so the cure of sin and the source of our salvation should also be found in a woman. And that women may not despair of attaining the inheritance of the blessed, because that so dire an evil arose from woman, it is proper that from woman also so great a blessing should arise, that their hopes may be revived. Take also this view. If it was a virgin which brought all evil upon the human race, it is much more appropriate that a virgin should be the occasion of all good. And this also. If woman, whom God made from man alone, was made of a virgin (*de virgine*), it is peculiarly fitting for that man also, who shall spring from a woman, to be born of a woman without man. Of the pictures which can be superadded to this, showing that the God-man ought to be born of a virgin, we will say nothing. These are sufficient.

Boso. They are certainly very beautiful and reasonable.

Chapter IX

How of necessity the Word only can unite in one person with man.

Anselm. Now must we inquire further, in what person God, who exists in three persons, shall take upon himself the nature of man. For a plurality of persons cannot take one and the same man into a unity of person. Wherefore in one person only can this be done. But, as respects this personal unity of God and man, and in which of the Divine persons this ought to be effected, I have expressed myself, as far as I think needful for the present inquiry, in a letter on the Incarnation of the Word, addressed to my lord, the Pope Urban.

Boso. Yet briefly glance at this matter, why the person of the Son should be incarnated rather than that of the Father or the Holy Spirit.

Anselm. If one of the other persons be incarnated, there will be two sons in the Trinity, viz., the Son of God, who is the Son before the incarnation, and he also who, by the incarnation, will be the son of the virgin; and among the persons which ought always to be equal there will be an inequality as respects the dignity of birth. For the one born of God will have a nobler birth than he who is born of the virgin. Likewise, if the Father become incarnate, there will be two grandsons in the Trinity; for the Father, by assuming humanity, will be the grandson of the parents of the virgin, and the Word, though having nothing to do with man, will yet be the grandson of the virgin, since he will be the son of her son. But all these things are incongruous and do not pertain to the incarnation of the Word. And there is yet another reason which renders it more fitting for the Son to become incarnate than the other persons. It is, that for the Son to pray to the Father is more proper than for any other person of the Trinity to supplicate his fellow. Moreover, man, for whom he was to pray, and the devil, whom he was to vanquish, have both put on a false likeness to God by their own will. Wherefore they have sinned, as it were, especially against the person of the Son, who is believed to be the very image of God. Wherefore the punishment or pardon of guilt is with peculiar propriety ascribed to him upon whom chiefly the injury was inflicted. Since, therefore, infallible reason has brought us to this necessary conclusion, that the Divine and human natures must unite in one person, and that this is evidently more fitting in respect to the person of the Word than the other persons, we determine that God the Word must unite with man in one person.

Boso. The way by which you lead me is so guarded by reason that I cannot deviate from it to the right or left.

Anselm. It is not I who lead you, but he of whom we are speaking, without whose guidance we have no power to keep the way of truth.

II. PETER ABELARD*

Christian Theology[3]

---

* Peter Abelard (1079–1142) won philosophical and theological recognition and established his reputation by his refutation of the extreme realism of William of Champeaux. An unfortunate romantic adventure interrupted his career, which was later punctuated by the Church's condemnation of some of his theological standpoints. In his *Christian Theology*, Abelard attempts to explain and defend his teachings on the Trinity, in explanation of which he had applied his dialectical principles.

I turn now to the question as to why the Son only and not the Father or the Holy Spirit became incarnate.

We accept with reason that the same essence is incarnate, that is, the essence of Father, Son, and Holy Spirit. But when it is said that the Son was incarnate, it is meant that the light of divine wisdom shone forth through this incarnation on carnal things. This alone, or this especially, was the benefit God intended to impart to us in the garment of flesh. On this account He was called "Angel of Counsel" or "Counselor."

The Psalmist says: "In Thy light shall we see light" (Ps 36:9). Simeon said: "A light to lighten the Gentiles" (Lk 2:32) and the Platonists assert: "God the Word is the true light."

"The Word was made flesh and dwelt with us" (Jn 1:19). This is as much as to say: "Wisdom was made incarnate so that by its illumination the knowledge of wisdom might dwell with us." In the flesh which He assumed He instructed and taught us perfectly by the converse of His life, by the passion of His death, and by the glory of His resurrection and ascension.

Since then, in all that He did in the flesh, the Lord had the intention of our instruction, it is rightly said that only Wisdom became incarnate.

To the objection that the Incarnation was by divine grace, in pity for us, and not from any merit of ours, and must therefore be assigned to the Holy Spirit rather than the Son, I reply that it is one thing to be conceived by the Spirit: another thing for the Spirit to be conceived, that is, to become incarnate. In the same way, it is one thing to be regenerated

---

[3] J. R. McCallom (tr.), *Abelard's Christian Theology* (Oxford: Basil Blackwell, 1948), pp. 83–88.

by water and the Spirit, and another thing for water and the Spirit to regenerate. To grant the light of true wisdom to His predestined people was the purpose of the Incarnation. There is diversity of work in the three persons, though not of essence, and according to this diversity certain special work is proper to each person.

The Son of God is therefore called "logos," that is, "Word," according to the meaning assigned by the Greeks of a concept of mind or reason, not the actual vocal expression usually implied in "word."

The objection may be raised as to why, if God is operative in all three persons, the Son alone took flesh. My reply is that we cannot say the Father or the Spirit became incarnate or suffered, but we can say that in the Incarnation both the Father and the Spirit were working, for we cannot exclude divine Power or Goodness from the Incarnation. The comparison I should make in this respect is that of a warrior putting on his armor. Various assistants cooperate in the process of his arming himself who themselves do not put on armor.

THE PROBLEMS OF GENERATION AND
PROCESSION

To answer the question about the same thing being born of itself or proceeding from itself, I must now approach the nature of this kind of generation or procession.

Look at a waxen image. Consider that in it is the mixture of wax: that is, the wax itself as substance. From this wax, the image becomes, in philosophical language, materialized out of material. The same essence is both the wax itself and the waxen image. We can predicate of the wax that it is the image, and of the image that it is the wax. None the less, it is also true to say that the waxen image is from the wax. But the wax is not from the waxen image. The wax itself is, however, the material of the image. The waxen image is not the material either of the wax or of itself. Again, we can assert that the image was realized out of the wax of which it is composed. Yet neither the wax itself nor the image itself were composed simply out of the image. Now if we take these names of wax and waxen image absolutely, not relatively to one another, we can assert anything of them that will be true of both because the substance is identical. I mean, for instance, if the wax is yellow and the image an upright figure, then the thing is yellow and upright throughout. If, however, we take the names relatively, in respect, that is, of the generation or composition of the waxen image, thinking of them as the material and the thing materialized from this material, as cause and effect, or the begetter and the begotten, then we cannot link them in respect of their particular functions by a predicating adjective. We cannot say that the material is the same as the thing materialized from it. Apply this comparison to the divine generation and my position is clear. God, the Father, is the divine Power; God, the Son, is divine Wisdom. Now divine Wisdom is a kind of power, since it is the ability to discern and foresee and deliberate aright against anything that may deceive God. Hence divine Wisdom coming from divine Power is a sort of waxen image out of wax. Philosophically, it is a species of a genus. The species is the same as the genus, as a man is the same as an "animal," or a waxen image the same as wax. The wax image is from wax as man is from animal. I mean that, insofar as it is a wax image it must be wax, just as insofar as a man is a man, he must be an animal. But the contrary is not true. Power, therefore, of discernment and doing all kinds of things may be considered like wax which has potentiality either to be a wax image or anything else: or, as the animal species, which may be a man or any other animal. This is my illustration to show that, when I say the Son is begotten of the Father, I mean that divine Wisdom is from divine Power as I have explained.

IS THE SAME THING FROM ITSELF?

I now refute the argument that the same thing generates itself, that is, that because the Son is from the Father, the same thing is therefore from itself. My comparison of a waxen image makes this objection invalid. The wax and the waxen image are essentially the same thing. Since the image is made from the wax it is not, therefore, made from itself. We cannot say: "This wax image is generated from this wax image"; for, in fact, it comes from the wax. The wax and the waxen image are essentially the same, but not the same by property and definition.

So, too, we use the phrase that "God is from God" in respect of the persons. Each of the persons is God: but each one is from the other and not in any way actually the other.

DOES GOD BEGET HIMSELF?

"If God begets God, then He begets either Himself or another God." This comment is another one to be refuted by my image example. It is granted that wax is a material which can go into any sort of materialized form. When it takes on a form it does, it may be said, take on or beget itself. And so it either begets itself or more wax. But the fact is that the wax which is made into some form or other, though essentially the same as the original material wax, is not the same wax by definition. I pointed out above that terms which are relative cannot be applied to the whole of anything, but only to what they define in anything. The wax material is, therefore, the material of some kind of waxen thing, and as Plato points out material is a kind of mother of that which is materialized. So it is not the material or mother of itself, or, in my instance, of some other wax. Hence when God begets God, that is, is the Father of God, He does not therefore beget Himself or another God.

THE QUESTION OF TIME IN GENERATION

On the eternity of generation, the question was whether the Son is always being begotten or was always begotten. I dealt with this matter at the beginning of an earlier treatise.

I said that He is always being begotten and has always been begotten. I mean that full and perfect generation to have been always from the Father. It neither begins nor ceases. Hence I say He always is begotten and always was. For it is the same thing for Him to be begotten and to have been begotten. When we say either that the Son is begotten of the Father or that He was begotten we do not speak according to any distinction of time. That eternal generation has no reference to time. It was before time and is now perfect in time.

III. ST. BONAVENTURE*

*Breviloquium*⁴

---

* St. Bonaventure (1221–1274), the Seraphic Doctor and Franciscan theologian, taught and lectured at Paris until he was made Minister General of his Order in 1257. As a theologian he continued in the tradition of St. Augustine and St. Anselm. A proponent of a mystical theory of knowledge, he had little attraction to the new Aristotelean movement in which St. Thomas figured so prominently. Bonaventure's dogmatic writings are mainly his *Commentary on the Sentences* and his *Breviloquium*. His treatment of the Incarnation does not differ basically from St. Thomas' treatise on the same. He maintains that the Incarnation would not have taken place had Adam not sinned, nor does he exempt the Blessed Virgin from original sin.

THE REASON WHY THE WORD OF GOD OUGHT TO BE INCARNATE

1. After certain statements given above about the Trinity of God, the creation of the world, and the corruption of sin, we turn now to a brief discussion of the incarnation of the Word. Through the Word incarnate, the salvation and redemption of mankind was achieved, not because God could not have saved or freed mankind otherwise, but because no other way was so congruous and fitting for the Redeemer, the redeemed, and the redemptive process.

2. The explanation of this is as follows: Because the effective principle of things could not be and ought not to be anything other than God and because it is surely as important to redeem created things as to create them, just as it is as important to have a good existence as to have a simple existence, it was most fitting that the redeeming principle of things be God the most high so that, just as God created all things through the uncreated Word, so He cures all things through the Word incarnate. Because God made all things effec-

tively, wisely, and best or benevolently, it was fitting that He should so redeem them that He might show His power, wisdom, and benevolence. What shows more power than to join in one person extremes most widely separated? What shows more wisdom and congruity than that for the perfection of the whole universe there should be a union of first and last, namely, of the Word of God, which is the principle of all, and of human nature, which was the last of all creatures? What shows greater benevolence than that God should assume the form of that to be saved because of the salvation of that to be saved? Certainly there is shown here such benignity that nothing more clement, more benign, more amicable can be thought of. It is most fitting, therefore, that this should be the way of God the Redeemer because it demonstrates the divine power, wisdom, and benevolence.

3. Because man when he fell into sin turned away and withdrew himself from the most powerful, wise, and benevolent principle, he was made corrupt in infirmity, ignorance, and perversity, and the result is precedence of the carnal, animal, and sensual over the spiritual. Hence man was un-

---

⁴ E. E. Nemmers (tr.), *Breviloquium* (St. Louis: B. Herder Book Co., 1946), pp. 109–114.

suited for imitating divine virtue, for learning of its light, for choosing its goodness. So that man might be redeemed from that state, it was most fitting that the first principle should descend to him by rendering Himself knowable, lovable, and imitable. Because carnal, animal, and sensual man did not know or love or follow anything except what was proportioned and adapted to his state, "the Word was made flesh" (Jn 1:14) for the rescue of man from this state so that God could be known, loved, and imitated by man who was flesh and in this way, by knowing, loving, and imitating, man might be cured of the sickness of sin.

4. Lastly, because man could not be perfectly redeemed unless he regained innocence of mind, the friendship of God and his own excellence by which he was second only to God, and this could be achieved only through God in the form of that to be saved, it was fitting that the Word should become incarnate. Man could not regain his excellence unless the Redeemer was God for, if the Redeemer were a mere creature, then man would be subject to that mere creature and thus would not regain the state of excellence. Moreover, man could not recover the friendship of God except by a suitable mediator who could place His hand in either or both natures as conforming to and a friend of both. Hence, just as the Redeemer is like God through His divinity, so He is like man through His humanity. Man could not recover his innocence of mind except by the forgiveness of sin, and it was not fitting for divine justice to forgive sin except after a condign satisfaction for that sin. Because man could not make satisfaction for sin unless God did so

for the whole of mankind and it was suitable only if man who had sinned should do so, it was most appropriate that mankind be redeemed by the God-man born of Adam's kind. Because excellence could not be recovered except by a most excellent Redeemer, nor could friendship be regained except by a most amiable mediator, nor could innocence be regained except by a most adequate satisfier, and there is no most excellent Redeemer except God, no most amiable mediator except man, no most adequate satisfier except one equally God and man, the incarnation of the Word was most congruous with our redemption. Just as mankind came into being through the uncreated Word and fell into sin by abandoning the inspired Word, so it should rise from sin through the incarnate Word.

THE INCARNATION: THE UNION OF NATURES

1. We ought to consider three points about the incarnate Word, namely, the union of natures, the plenitude of gifts, and the suffering of the Passion for the redemption of mankind. In regard to the union of natures we should consider these three points in order to understand the mystery of the Incarnation, namely, its operation, mode, and time.

2. According to Christian faith, we should hold these truths in regard to the operation of the Incarnation: that the Incarnation is the operation of the Trinity through whom the assumption of flesh by the Deity and the union of the Deity with the flesh occurred in such a way that the assumption involves not only a sensible flesh but also a rational spirit with its vegetative, sensitive, and intellectual powers, and also in such a way

that there is union not in the unity of nature but of person, not of a human person but of a divine person, not of the assumed but of the assuming, not of any person but of the person of the Word alone. Such is the union that whatever is said of the Son of God, may be said of the Son of man, and conversely, with the exception of those terms in which the union of the divine and human is expressed or absence [of human personality] is implied.

3. The explanation of this is as follows: The operation of the Incarnation proceeds from the first principle not only in so far as it is effective but also in so far as it repairs by redeeming, satisfying, and conciliating. Because the Incarnation, in so far as it bespeaks a certain effect, stems from the first principle, which accomplishes all things by reason of its highest power and substance, power and operation are united and completely undivided in the three persons, hence it must be that the operation of the Incarnation flowed from the whole Trinity.

4. Because the Incarnation is from the first principle insofar as it repairs by redeeming and because all mankind has fallen and sinned in soul and body, the entire nature must be assumed so that all of it may be cured. And because the carnal part is better known to us and more removed from God, the operation should not be called an animation but rather an incarnation so that the selection of this method might be made clearer and a greater humiliation shown and a more profound dignity demonstrated.

5. Again, because the Incarnation is from the first principle insofar as it repairs by satisfying, and there is no satisfaction except when made by

him who ought to make it and can make it, and no one ought to make it but man and no one can make it but God, it was fitting that in the satisfaction there be a concourse of both natures, namely, divine and human. And because it is impossible that divine nature should coincide with another nature as a part of a third nature and it is impossible that the divine nature go over into another nature because of the most perfect simplicity and immutability of the divine nature, divinity and humanity are not united in a unity of nature or of accident but in a unity of person and hypostasis. And because the divine nature cannot exist in any suppositum except in its own hypostasis, this union cannot exist in the hypostasis or person of man but rather of God. Hence by this union the first principle in one of its hypostases makes itself the suppositum of human nature, and thus there is only one personality and personal unity there, namely, on the part of the one assuming.

6. Lastly, because the Incarnation is from the first principle insofar as it repairs by conciliating, and in conciliating it is a mediator, and mediation properly falls to the Son of God, it follows that this is the case with the Incarnation. It is the mediator's part to be the medium between man and God, to lead man back to divine knowledge, conformity, and sonship. No one is more suitable as a medium than the person who produces and is produced, who is the middle one of the three persons. No one is more fitting to lead man back to the divine knowledge than the Word (by whom the Father expresses Himself), which is unitable to flesh, as a word is unitable to the voice. No one is more

fitting to lead man back to divine conformity than He who is the image of the Father. No one is more fitting to lead man back to his adopted sonship than the natural Son. Hence no one is more fitting to become the Son of man than the Son of God.

7. Because the Son of man and of God is in every way the same by reason of the Incarnation and because "whatever things for one and the same reason are the same, are the same among themselves,"[5] it follows that, unless there is a word available

[5] Aristotle, I *Elenchi*, chap. 5.

for the purpose, one necessarily has to communicate by using an idiom, unless there is a word which includes a certain repugnance to one's idea, as is the case with those words used to express the union of one nature with another. Such words are: to unite, to be incarnate, to assume and to be assumed. Such is the case with a denial of something whose opposite belongs to the other [nature], as is the case with the words: to begin to be, to be created, and the like in which an allied meaning exists contrary to the foregoing rule for the foregoing reason.

IV. ST. THOMAS AQUINAS*

Summary Theologiae

Summa Theologiae

* St. Thomas Aquinas (c1225–1274), the Angelic Doctor, Dominican philosopher and theologian, born in Italy, was related both to Italian and to French royalty. After an early Benedictine monastic education, Thomas went to Naples for his higher education and while there he was attracted to the Dominicans and their intellectual apostolate. He joined the Order in 1244 after overcoming his ambitious parents' opposition. He studied in Paris under St. Albert the Great, the most widely learned man of his time, and later lectured at Paris. His philosophical and theological writings form one of the greatest contributions to the thought of the Church and of Western Civilization. His genius lay principally in the ability of his penetrating intellect to seize upon the truth, from whatever source, and to synthesize it masterfully. The *Summa Theologiae* is a compendium of Christian Theology in three main sections which treat of God considered in himself, of God as the end of man, and of man's return to God in Christ.

THE IMPLICATIONS OF THE HYPOSTATIC UNION[6]

Third Part, Question 16: Statements relating to Christ as existing and as coming into existence

Article I: Is this statement true, "God is a man"?

THE FIRST POINT: 1. The statement,

[6] C. E. O'Neill (tr.), *St. Thomas Aquinas: Summa Theologiae*, Vol. 50 (New York: McGraw Hill Book Co., 1963), pp. 3–47 *passim*.

"God is a man," seems to be false. For every affirmative statement in remote matter is false. And the statement, "God is a man," is in remote matter since the natures signified by the Subject and the Predicate are infinitely diverse. Since the statement is affirmative, it seems, therefore, that it is false.

2. Moreover, there is more in common to the three divine persons than there is to human and divine nature. Yet in our statements about the mys-

tery of the Trinity one person is not predicated of another; we do not say that the Father is the Son, or vice versa. Consequently it seems that neither may we predicate human nature of God, saying that God is a man.

3. Moreover, Athanasius says, *As soul and flesh are one man, so God and man are one Christ.* Now it is false to say, "The soul is the body." It is equally false, then, to say, "God is a man."

4. Moreover, it has already been shown that in statements about God terms signifying absolute perfections, not relations, are to be predicated of the whole Trinity and hence of each person.[7] But the term "a man" signifies something absolute. If then it may be truly predicated of God, it follows that the whole Trinity and each person is a man. And this is patently false.

ON THE OTHER HAND we read, *Who being in the form of God, emptied himself, taking the form of a servant, being made in the likeness of men and in habit found as a man* (Phl 2:6–7). That is to say, he who is in the form or nature of God is a man. But he who is in the nature of God is God. God is therefore a man.

REPLY: The truth of the statement, "God is a man," is admitted by all Christians; not all, however, understand it in the same way. As some admit it the terms no longer stand for what they signify literally.

So the Manichees affirm that the Word of God is a man, not, however, a true man but an apparent one; for they hold that the Son of God assumed only what seemed to be a body.

From this it would follow that God is said to be a man in the same way as a bronze casting is so termed simply because it bears the likeness of a man.

Similarly, those for whom soul and body in Christ were not united did not hold that God is a true man, but rather that he is called a man metaphorically, being in possession of these parts. — The falsity of both these opinions has already been demonstrated.[8]

At the other extreme there are those who preserve the literal meaning of the term "man" but not that of the term "God." In this view Christ, the God-man, is God, not by nature, but by participation. It is by reason of grace, therefore, that he and all other holy men are said to be gods; he however, excels the others because of his fullness of grace. According to this opinion, in the statement, "God is a man," the term "God" does not stand for the true God by nature. This is the heresy of Photinus which has already been shown to be false.[9]

Others again admit this statement with both terms standing for what they signify literally; they affirm that Christ is both true God and true man; yet they do not preserve the truth of the predication. For they maintain that "a man" is predicated of "God" on the grounds of some form of association, whether it be one of dignity, or authority, or simply of affection or indwelling. It was in this fashion that Nestorius granted that God is a man; by this he meant nothing more than that God is united to a man in such wise that the man has God dwelling in him and that he is united to God by affection and by participation in divine authority and honor.

Those also who postulate two hypos-

---

[7] Cf. *S.T.*, I, 39, 4.

[8] *Ibid.*, III, 2, 5; also cf. *Ibid.*, III, 5, 1.
[9] *Ibid.*, III, 2, 10 and 11.

tases or two ontological subjects in Christ fall into a like error. For it is impossible to conceive, given two which are distinct as hypostases or as ontological subjects, that one should be literally predicated of the other. The only form of predication admissible here involves some type of metaphor based on something common to the two. So we might, for example, say that Peter is John because the two have a common interest. — These opinions too have already been shown to be false.[10]

Consequently, assuming, as the Catholic faith requires, that the true divine nature is united with a true human nature, not simply in the person but also in the ontological subject or hypostasis, we affirm that the statement, "God is a man," is both true and literal. This is not only because the terms stand for what they signify literally, Christ being both true God and true man, but also because of the truth of the predication. For a concrete term signifying a common nature can stand for every individual contained in that common nature. Thus the term "man" can stand for every individual man; and the term "God," already by reason of its mode of signification, can stand for the person of the Son, as has been explained.[11] Now a concrete term signifying a nature may truly and literally be predicated of any subject subsisting in that nature; so, for example, "a man" may be literally and truly predicated of Socrates and Plato. Since, therefore, the person of the Son of God, for whom the term "God" here stands, is a subject subsisting in human nature, the term "a man" may truly

and literally be predicated of the term "God" when the latter stands for the person of the Son of God.

Hence: 1. When it is impossible that diverse natures should belong to one ontological subject then a statement, the Subject of which signifies one of these natures and the Predicate of which signifies the other, is necessarily a statement in remote matter. When, on the contrary, two natures can belong to one ontological subject it is no longer a question of remote matter, but of matter which is either necessary or — as when I say, "The white man is a musician" — contingent. Now divine and human nature, though infinitely diverse, are nevertheless brought together in the mystery of the Incarnation in one ontological subject; and neither of them pertains to this subject in an accidental way, but rather substantially. Consequently, the statement, "God is a man," is neither diverse nor in contingent matter, but in necessary matter. And "a man" is predicated of God, not in the fashion of an accident but substantially, since it is question of its own ontological subject. The justification for such predication is not, of course the nature signified by the term "God," but the ontological subject which is the subject subsisting in the human nature.

2. The three divine Persons have in common their nature but are distinct as subjects subsisting in that nature. This latter forbids their being predicated one of the other. In the mystery of the Incarnation, on the contrary, the natures are distinct and so, when signified by abstract terms, are not predicated of each other; the divine nature is not the human nature. But because they have a common ontological subject they are predicated

---

[10] *Ibid.*, III, 2, 2 and 6.
[11] *Ibid.*, I, 39, 4.

of each other when signified by concrete terms.

3. The terms "soul" and "flesh" signify in abstract fashion, as do the terms "divinity" and "humanity." The corresponding concrete terms are "an animated being" and "fleshly" or "corporeal being"; or, in our other case, "God" and "a man." As regards both pairs, an abstract is not predicated of an abstract term, but only a concrete term of a concrete term.

4. The term "a man" is predicated of God on the basis of union in person. Now such union connotes a relation. Consequently, this term does not follow the rule governing use of those terms which are predicated of God absolutely and eternally.

Article 2. Is this statement true, "A man is God"?

THE SECOND POINT: 1. It seems that the statement, "A man is God," is false. For the name "God" is incommunicable. Idolators are reproved because they *gave the incommunicable name* of God *to stones and wood* (Wis 13:10; 14:21). For a like reason, then, it appears illegitimate to predicate the term *God* of a man.

2. Moreover, whatever may be predicated of the Predicate may also be predicated of the Subject. Now the following are true statements, "God is the Father," and "God is the Trinity." If, then, the statement, "A man is God," were true, it would seem to follow that the following statements would also be true, "A man is the Father," and "A man is the Trinity." But it is evident that these are false; so too, consequently, is the first.

3. Moreover, we read, *There shall be no new god in thee* (Ps 90:10). But the man we are talking about is something new; for Christ was not always a man. Consequently, the statement, "A man is God," is false.

ON THE OTHER HAND *Romans* states, *of whom is Christ, according to the flesh, who is over all things, God blessed for ever* (9:5). Now Christ, according to the flesh, is a man. Therefore the statement, "A man is God," is true.

REPLY: Assuming the reality of each nature, the divine and the human, and assuming their union in person and ontological subject, the statement, "A man is God," is both true and literal, just as much as the statement, "God is a man." For the term "a man" can stand for every subject subsisting in human nature; consequently it can stand for the person of the Son which we hold to be a subject subsisting in human nature. And it is of course evident that the term "God" is predicated truly and literally of the person of the Son of God.[12] From this it results that the statement, "A man is God," is both true and literal.

HENCE: 1. Idolators gave the name of deity to stones and wood in the belief that these things contained in their own natures something of the divine being. We, on the contrary, give the name of God to a man, not because of his human nature, but because of the eternal person, this being, through the union, a subject subsisting also in human nature.

2. The term "Father" is predicated of the term "God" only when the latter stands for the person of the Father. As long as the term has this supposition it is not predicated of the person of the Son, since the person of the Son is not the person of the Father. Consequently the term "Father" may not be predicated of the

---

[12] Cf. *Ibid.,* I, 39, 4.

term "a man" on the grounds that the term "God" is predicated of the latter. The reason is that "a man" here stands for the person of the Son.

3. While the human nature in Christ is admittedly something new, nevertheless the subject subsisting in this human nature is not new; it is eternal. And since the term "God" is predicated of a man, not because of his human nature, but because of the subsisting subject, we cannot be accused of positing a new God. — The objection would be valid if we were to hold that the term "a man" stands for a created subsisting subject, as those who posit two subsisting subjects in Christ must hold.

Article 4. May we predicate of God what is attributed to the human nature?

THE FOURTH POINT: 1. It seems that what is attributed to the human nature may not be predicated of God. For it is impossible that opposites should be predicated of the same subject. But the attributes of human nature are incompatible with those which belong to God. For God is uncreated, unchangeable and eternal, while human nature is created and subject to time and change. Consequently, what is attributed to the human nature may not be predicated of God.

2. Moreover, to attribute to God anything that implies imperfection would appear to be blasphemous, taking away from his divine honor. Yet what is attributed to human nature implies imperfection: death, suffering and the like. Therefore it seems that what is attributed to the human nature should in no way be predicated of God.

3. Moreover, one of the attributes of the human nature is that it is as-

sumed. But this cannot be applied to God. Consequently, what is attributed to the human nature cannot be predicated of God.

ON THE OTHER HAND we have Damascene saying, *God took upon himself the attributes* (idiomata) *of flesh, so that now he is named a God of suffering and now the God of glory is crucified.*[13]

REPLY: On this question there was a difference between Nestorians and Catholics. For the Nestorians wished to make a distinction between terms predicated of Christ: those referring to the human nature were not to be predicated of God; and those referring to the divine nature were not to be predicated of the man. So Nestorius said, *The attribution of sufferings to the Word of God is to be condemned.* In the case of those terms which can refer to either nature, the Nestorians predicated of them attributes of either nature; such are terms like "Christ" or "Lord." Accordingly, they admitted that Christ was born of the Virgin and that he existed from eternity; they did not, however, admit that God was born of the Virgin or that the man existed from eternity.

Catholics, in opposition to this, held that whatever is predicated of Christ, in virtue either of his divine nature or of his human nature, may be predicated both of God and of the man. So Cyril said, *If anyone should distribute between two persons or two substances,* that is, subsisting subjects, *the terms which appear in the Gospels or Apostolic Epistles, or those terms used to describe Christ by the saints or by Christ himself; and if he should believe that some of these terms are to be applied to the man, whilst others*

[13] *De Fide Orthodoxa,* III, 4.

he assigns to the Word alone: he is worthy of condemnation. The explanation is that, since there is a single subject subsisting in the two natures, concrete terms signifying either of the natures stand for the same subject. Whether, therefore, we speak of "the man" or of "God," the terms stand for the one subject subsisting in both divine and human nature. Consequently, we may predicate of the man what is attributed to the divine nature; and we may predicate of God what is attributed to the human nature.

It must, however, be observed that in a statement where one thing is predicated of another attention must be paid not only to the identity of the subject to which the Predicate is attributed, but also to the particular aspect of the subject which justifies such attribution. While, accordingly, no distinction is to be made between the various Predicates attributed to Christ, it is necessary to distinguish the two aspects of the subject which justify the predication. For attributes of the divine nature are predicated of Christ in virtue of his divine nature, while attributes of the human nature are predicated of him in virtue of his human nature. In this sense Augustine says, *We should distinguish in Scripture what refers to the form of God and what to the form of the servant;*[14] and further on, *The prudent, careful and devout reader will understand the reason and the ground for each attribution.*[15]

HENCE: I. It is impossible that opposites should be predicated of the same subject under the same aspect; but there is no difficulty when there is question of diverse aspects. And it is in this latter fashion that opposites are predicated of Christ, for they

refer, not to the same aspect, but to the diverse natures.

2. If imperfections were to be attributed to God in virtue of his divine nature, this would indeed be blasphemous since it would take away the honor which is his due; but no wrong is done God if they are attributed to him in virtue of his assumed nature. So in one of the speeches at the Council of Ephesus it was said, *God considers nothing a wrong to himself that is the occasion of man's salvation. None of the indignities which he elected for our sake can bring hurt to that nature which is subject to no hurt; he made his own what is lowly that he might have our nature. If then what is unworthy and what is defiled bring no hurt to the divine nature but rather bring about the salvation of men, how can you suggest that what was the cause of our salvation was the occasion of wrong to God?*

3. The fact of being assumed affects the human nature, not as personalized, but as it is in itself. Consequently, this does not affect God.

Article 5. May we predicate of the divine nature what is attributed to the human nature?

THE FIFTH POINT: I. It seems that we may predicate of the divine nature what is attributed to the human nature. For the attributes of the human nature are predicated of the Son of God and of God. Now God is identified with his nature. Consequently, what is attributed to the human nature may be predicated of the divine nature.

2. Moreover, flesh is an attribute of human nature. But, according to Damascene[16] *we say that the nature of*

---

[14] *De Trinitate,* I, 11.   [15] *Ibid.,* 13.

[16] *De Fide Orthodoxa,* III, 6.

the Word was enfleshed, following in this Saints Athanasius and Cyril. Equally well, then, what is attributed to the human nature may be predicated of the divine nature.

3. Moreover, attributes of the divine nature belong to Christ's human nature: knowledge of the future, for example, and the possession of healing power. Equally well, then, it seems that what is attributed to the human nature may be predicated of the divine nature.

ON THE OTHER HAND, Damascene says, *When we speak of the divinity we do not predicate of it the properties (idiomata) of the humanity; thus we do not say that the divinity is subject to suffering or the term of creation.*[17] Since the divinity is the divine nature, it follows from this that what is attributed to the human nature cannot be predicated of the divine nature.

REPLY: The attributes of a thing may be truly predicated only of a subject identified with the thing; "a being with a sense of humor," for example, may be predicated only of that thing which is a man. Now, in the mystery of the Incarnation the divine and the human natures are not identical; what is identical is the subject subsisting in both natures. Accordingly, attributes of one nature may not, when signified by an abstract term, be predicated of the other.

On the contrary, concrete terms stand for a subject subsisting in a certain nature. In consequence, attributes of either nature may be predicated without distinction of concrete terms; and here it makes no difference whether the term of which they are predicated signifies both natures (as does the term "Christ" by which are

to be understood both *anointing divinity* and *anointed humanity*) or whether it signifies the divine nature alone (as does the term "God" or "Son of God") or the human nature alone (as does the term "the man" or "Jesus"). We accordingly find Pope Leo writing, *It is irrelevant from which nature Christ is denominated; since, given the unity of person, it is the same being who is the whole Son of Man in virtue of the flesh and who is the whole Son of God in virtue of the unique divinity held with the Father.*[18]

HENCE: 1. In the Trinity person and nature are really identified; and in virtue of this identity the divine nature is predicated of the Son of God. But the concrete term "person" and the abstract term "nature" signify two distinct concepts which we must use when thinking about a divine person. For this reason certain predicates are attributed to the Son of God which are not attributed to the divine nature; we say, for example, that the Son of God is generated, but not that the divine nature is generated.[19] Similarly with the mystery of the Incarnation, we say that the Son of God suffered, but we do not say that the divine nature suffered.

2. The Incarnation or enfleshment implies not so much attribution of the flesh to the divine nature as union with the flesh. In Christ each of the natures is united to the other in the person; and it is in virtue of this union, as has already been explained,[20] that the divine nature is said to be "incarnate" and the human nature is to be "deified."

---

[17] *Ibid.*, III, 4.

[18] *Ep. ad Palaest.*, 124.
[19] *S.T.*, I, 39, 5.
[20] *Ibid.*, III, 2, 1, ad 3.

3. Attributes of the divine nature are predicated of the human nature, not in the way that they pertain essentially to the divine, but in so far as they are communicated in limited fashion to the human nature. Consequently, whatever attributes cannot be communicated in this way to human nature, as, for example, uncreatedness or omnipotence, may in no fashion be predicated of the human nature. The divine nature, on the contrary, receives nothing by way of communication from the human nature. Consequently, attributes of the human nature may in no fashion be predicated of the divine nature.

Article 6. Is this statement true, "God was made a man"?

THE SIXTH POINT: 1. It seems that the statement, "God was made a man," is false. For since "a man" signifies an independently existing subject, to be made a man implies an absolute beginning of existence. But it is false to attribute an absolute beginning of existence to God. It is, then, false to say, "God was made a man."

2. Moreover, to be made a man is to undergo change. Yet God cannot be the subject of change, *I am the Lord and I change not* (Mal 3:6). Consequently, it appears that the statement, God *was made a man,* is false.

3. Moreover, the term *a man,* when predicated of Christ, stands for the person of the Son of God. Now it is false to say, *God has been made the person of the Son of God;* hence it is also false to say, *God was made a man.*

ON THE OTHER HAND, *The word was made flesh* (Jn 1:14). And Athanasius comments, *To say, "The Word was made flesh" is equivalent to saying, "was made a man."*[21]

[21] *Epistola ad Epictetum.*

REPLY: Whenever a new predicate is attributed to a subject we speak of the subject's being made whatever it is that the predicate signifies. Now it has already been pointed out that "to be a man" is truly predicated of God;[22] at the same time this is not an eternal attribute of God but one that arises in time, with the assumption of a human nature. Consequently, the statement, "God was made a man" is a true one. Nevertheless, different teachers understand it in different ways, as has already been noted regarding the statement, "God is a man."

HENCE: 1. To be made a man implies an absolute beginning of existence wherever a human nature begins to exist in a newly created subject. But when we say that God was made a man, we are referring to the fact that a human nature began to exist in a subject already subsisting from eternity in the divine nature. Consequently, that God was made a man does not imply an absolute beginning of existence in God.

2. It has already been stated that use of the term "to be made" implies that something is newly predicated of another. Whenever such new predication is accompanied by change in the subject, then "to be made" is equivalent to undergoing change. This is the case with predicates signifying attributes which intrinsically modify the subject. So, for example, whiteness or quantity cannot newly affect a subject without its newly undergoing change in respect of whiteness or quantity.

In the case, however, of predicates signifying relationships, it can happen that these are newly predicated of a subject without its being intrinsically changed. A man, for example, can be

[22] Cf. above, *S.T.* III, 16, 1.

made to stand on the right-hand side without any change occurring in himself, simply because someone else moves to his left. Accordingly, when there is question of such predicates as these, not everything which is said "to be made" necessarily undergoes change; it can happen that the same effect is produced in virtue of a change in something else. It is in this sense that we say, to God, *Thou O Lord, hast been made our refuge.* (Ps 89:1).

Now, "to be a man" is attributed to God in virtue of the union; and this union is a form of relation. Accordingly, without any change in God being implied, we newly predicate of him that he is a man by reason of the change occurring in the human nature which is assumed to the divine person. Similarly, when we say, "God was made a man," there is no question of attributing any change to God, but exclusively to the human nature.

3. The term "a man" does not stand for the bare person of the Son of God but for that person as in a human nature. While, therefore, the statement, "God was made the person of the Son," is false, this other is true, "God was made a man," because he was united to a human nature.[23]

Article 7. Is this statement true, "A man was made God"?

THE SEVENTH POINT: 1. It seems that this statement is true, "A man was made God." For we read, *This he had promised before, by his prophets, in the holy Scriptures, concerning his* Son, who was made to him of the seed of David according to the flesh (Rom 1:2–3). But it is as man that Christ is of the seed of David according to the flesh. Therefore a man was made the Son of God.

2. Moreover, Augustine says, *This assumption was such that it made God a man and made a man God.*[24] Now, in virtue of this assumption, the statement, "God was made a man," is true. Similarly then this also is true, "A man was made God."

3. Moreover, Gregory of Nazianzen says, *God was humanized while a man was deified (whether this or another term should be used).*[25] Now God is said to be humanized because he was made a man. Consequently, a man is said to be deified because he was made God. Therefore this statement is true, "A man was made God."

4. Moreover, when we say, "God was made a man," the subject affected by the making or the uniting is not God but the human nature signified by the term "man." Now the subject affected by the making appears to be the subject of which making should be predicated. Consequently, it is even more true to say, "A man was made God," than to say, "God was made a man."

ON THE OTHER HAND, Damascene says, *We do not speak of a man being deified, but of God being humanized.*[26] But "to be made God" and "to be deified" are equivalent terms. Consequently, this statement is false, "A man was made God."

REPLY: The statement, "A man was made God" may be understood in three ways. First, the participle "made" may

---

[23] Thus the statement, "God was made a man," is equivalent to, "the Son of God was made the Son of God subsisting in a human nature." Similarly, when a wall is painted white, we can say, "The wall has been made a white wall" (Cajetan, Commentary on this article, n. III).

[24] *De Trinitate,* I, 13.
[25] *Ep. ad Celid,* 161.
[26] *De Fide Orthodoxa,* III, 2.

be taken as a determination affecting unrestrictedly the Subject or the Predicate. In this reading the statement is false, for neither that man who is subject of the predication was made, nor was God made, as will be explained below.[27] Read in this way, the statement, "God was made a man" is equally false. But such a reading is excluded from our present consideration of these statements.

The statement may be understood in a second way as a modal statement, in such wise that "made" determines the composition of Subject and Predicate; then the reading would be, "A man was made God," that is, "it has been made" or "brought about that a man is God." In this sense both statements are true, "A man was made God" and "God was made a man." But this is not the natural sense of these expressions, — unless perhaps the Latin term "homo" were to be translated, not as "a man," but as "man" and thus were to be taken as standing, not for a person, but for the human race. For although this man was not made God, since this subsisting subject, the person of the Son of God, was God from eternity, nevertheless man, speaking universally, was not always God.

The third is the strict way of understanding the statement, namely, taking the participle "made" as attributing "being made" to the man in respect of God as term of the making. In this reading, granted what has already been shown,[28] namely, that in Christ there is one person, hypostasis and subsisting subject common to God and to the man, the statement in question is false. For when we say, "A man was made God" the term "man" stands

[27] S.T., III, 16, 8–9.
[28] Ibid, III, 2, 2–3.

for a person; for "to be God" is verified of the man, not in virtue of his human nature, but in virtue of his subsisting subject. And the subject subsisting in human nature of which "being God" is verified is identical with the hypostasis or person of the Son of God which was always God. Consequently, it is not permissible to say that "this man began to be God" or that he "becomes God" or that he "was made God."

If, however, as the Nestorians held, the person or hypostasis of God were distinct from that of the man, so that "being God" would be predicated of the man (and vice versa) in virtue of some association between the subsisting subjects — one of personal dignity, affection or indwelling — then it would be equally legitimate to say, "The man was made God," that is, "was associated with God," or to say, "God was made a man," that is, "was associated with a man."

HENCE: 1. In the quotation from St. Paul the relative pronoun "who" referring to the Son of God, must not be taken, as it is in the objection, as a Predicate, as though someone *existing of the seed of David according to the flesh*, were made Son of God. It must be taken as a Subject so that the sense is, "The Son of God was made to him" (that is, *to the honor of the Father,* as the Gloss notes) *existing of the seed of David according to the flesh;* in other words, "[the Son of God was made] the Son of God possessing flesh of the seed of David, to the honor of God."

2. The quotation from Augustine is to be understood in the sense that, in virtue of the assumption, in the Incarnation it has been brought about that a man is God and God is a man.

In this sense, as has already been remarked, both statements are true.

3. A similar interpretation is required; for "being deified" is equivalent to "being made God."

4. A term put as Subject of a statement is taken materially, that is, for a subsisting subject; but put as Predicate it is taken formally, that is, for the nature signified. Accordingly, when we say, "A man was made God," the being made is attributed, not to the human nature, but to the subject subsisting in human nature; and this subject is God from eternity and consequently cannot be made God. When on the contrary, we say, "God was made a man," the making is understood to terminate in the human nature alone. Consequently, according to the demands of logic, the statement, "God was made a man" is true, and the statement, "A man was made God" is false. Something similar occurs when Socrates, already a man, is afterwards made white; then, with reference to Socrates, this statement is true, "This man was today made white," whereas this other statement is false, "This white being was made a man."

If, however, as Subject of a statement should be placed an abstract term signifying human nature, then the nature could be signified as the subject of the making; so, for example, we might say, "Human nature was made the nature of the Son of God."

Article 11. Is this statement true, "Christ, as man, is God"?

THE ELEVENTH POINT: 1. It seems that this statement is true, "Christ, as man, is God." For Christ is God by the grace of union. But Christ, as man, possesses the grace of union. Conse-

quently, Christ, as man, is God.

2. Moreover, to forgive sins is a prerogative of God, *I am he that blots out thy iniquities for my own sake* (Is 43:25). But Christ, as man, forgives sins, *That you may know that the Son of Man has power on earth to forgive sins,* etc. (Mt 9:6.) Therefore Christ, as man, is God.

3. Moreover, Christ is not universal man but this particular man. Now Christ, as he is this man, is God; for the term "this man" stands for the eternally subsisting subject which is by nature God. Consequently, Christ, as man, is God.

ON THE OTHER HAND whatever pertains to Christ as man pertains to all men. If, then, Christ, as man, is God, it follows that every man is God. This is evidently false.

REPLY: The term "man" when placed in reduplication may be taken in two ways. Firstly, as referring to the nature. And in this way it is not true that Christ, as man, is God, since there is a difference of nature between human and divine nature.

Secondly, it may be taken as referring to the subsisting subject. And in this way, since the subject subsisting in human nature in Christ is the person of the Son of God to whom it belongs essentially to be God, it is true that Christ, as man, is God.

Taking into consideration, however, that a term placed in reduplication is more naturally taken for the nature than for the subsisting subject, as has already been said,[29] then the following statement should rather be denied than affirmed, "Christ, as man, is God."

HENCE: 1. It is under two different

[29] Cf. *S. T.,* III, 16, 10.

aspects that a thing is first moved towards a new mode of being and then actually exists according to this mode. For movement affects the thing inasmuch as the latter is potential or submissive; actual being, on the contrary, affects the thing inasmuch as it is perfected by some form. Similarly, it is under two different aspects that Christ is, on the one hand, ordered towards being God by the grace of union and, on the other hand, is actually God. The first belongs to him according to his human nature, the second according to his divine nature. Consequently, this statement is true, "Christ, as man, possesses the grace of Union"; but this one is false, "Christ, as man, is God."

2. The Son of God has power on earth to forgive sins, in virtue, not of his human, but of his divine nature. It is in his divine nature that the power of forgiving sins resides as a personal prerogative; while in his human nature this power resides instrumentally and ministerially. So Chrysostom, commenting on this passage, says, *Pointedly he spoke of forgiveness as being "on earth," thus indicating that he has united his divine power to his human nature in an indissoluble union. For, although he was made a man, he still remained the Word of God.*[30]

3. In the expression "this man" the demonstrative adjective makes the term "man" refer to the subsisting subject. Consequently, the statement, "Christ, as this man, is God" is true rather than, "Christ, as man, is God."

Article 12. Is this statement true, "Christ, as man, is an independent subject or person"?

THE TWELFTH POINT: 1. It seems that

[30] *Hom. 30 in Matthaeum.*

this statement is true, "Christ, as man, is an independent subject or person." For what is attributed to any man is to be attributed to Christ as man; because he is like other men, *in habit found as a man.* But every man is a persons. Consequently, Christ, as man, is a person.

2. Moreover, Christ, as man, is a substance in rational nature. He is not universal substance. Therefore he is an individual substance. Now a person, according to Boëthius' definition, is nothing other than *an individual substance in rational nature.*[31] Consequently, Christ, as man, is a person.

3. Moreover, Christ, as man, is a realized human nature; he is hypostasis and subject subsisting in that nature. But every hypostasis and subject subsisting in human nature, every realized human nature, is a person. Consequently, Christ, as man, is a person.

ON THE OTHER HAND, Christ, as man, is not an eternal person. If, consequently, as man he were a person, it would follow that in Christ there were two persons, one temporal, the other eternal. And this is false.

REPLY: . . . the term "man," when placed in reduplication, may be taken as referring either to the subsisting subject or to the nature. Accordingly, in the statement, "Christ, as man, is a person," if "man" is taken as referring to the subsisting subject, then it is evident that Christ, as man, is a person; for the subject subsisting in the human nature is none other than the person of the Son of God.

If, on the contrary, "man" is taken as referring to the nature, then two interpretations are possible.

Firstly, it could be meant that hu-

[31] *De Duabus Naturis.*

man nature can exist only in a person. This also is true, for whatever subsists in human nature is a person.

Secondly, it could be meant that the human nature in Christ ought to have its own personality, having its causal origin in the human nature. In this sense, Christ, as man, is not a person; for his human nature does not exist by itself apart from the divine nature, as would be required if it were to have its own personality.

HENCE: 1. It belongs to every man to be a person inasmuch as every subject in human nature is a person. But what is exclusive to the man Christ is that the person subsisting in his human nature has not got its causal origin in the human nature but is eternal. Consequently . . . Christ, as man, in one sense is a person, in another sense he is not.

2. The words "individual substance" appearing in the definition of person signify a complete substance, subsisting in its own right, and separately from others. Otherwise, a man's hand could be called a person, since it is an individual substance; but because it is an individual substance only as it exists in something else, it may not be called a person. A like reasoning applies to Christ's human nature; though it may be said to be an individual or singular reality.

3. The term "person" signifies something complete, subsisting in its own right, in rational nature; likewise, the terms "hypostasis," "subsisting subject" and "realized nature" (granted that the nature is in the category of substance) signify a thing subsisting in its own right. Now Christ's human nature does not exist in its own right and apart from the person of the Son; neither is it in its own right a hypos-tasis or a subsisting subject or a realized nature. Consequently, in the same sense in which we must deny the statement, "Christ, as man, is a person," we must also deny statements predicating the other terms of him.

Question 17. The Unity of Christ's existence

Article 1. Is Christ one or two?

THE FIRST POINT: 1. It seems that Christ is not one but two. For Augustine says, *The form of God received the form of a servant; hence each of the two is God by reason of the God who receives, each of the two is man by reason of the man received.*[32] But we cannot speak of "each of two" except where there are two. Consequently, Christ is two.

2. Moreover, wherever there is question of distinct things there are two, But Christ is distinct things, for Augustine says, *When he was in the form of God he received the form of a servant; one person is both, yet he is one thing in virtue of the Word, another thing in virtue of the man.*[33] Christ is, consequently, two.

3. Moreover, Christ is not only a man; for if he were nothing more than a man he would not be God. Therefore he is something distinct from a man. There are, then, in Christ distinct things. Consequently, Christ is two.

4. Moreover, Christ is something that the Father is, and he is something that the Father is not. Therefore Christ is distinct things. Consequently, he is two.

5. Moreover, in the mystery of the Trinity there are three persons in one nature; and in the mystery of the Incarnation there are two natures in

---

[32] *De Trinitate* I, 7.
[33] *Enchiridion,* 35.

one person. Now because of their unity of nature, and in spite of their personal distinction, Father and Son are one thing: *I and the Father are one* (Jn 10:30). Consequently, in spite of his personal unity, Christ is two because of his two natures.

6. Moreover, Aristotle states that "one" and "two" are predicated as descriptive terms.[34] But Christ has a duality of natures. Therefore Christ is two.

7. Moreover, Porphyry remarks that, while an accidental nature makes its subject *other*, a substantial nature makes its subject a *distinct thing*. Now in Christ there are two substantial natures, the human and the divine. Consequently Christ is distinct things. Therefore Christ is two.

ON THE OTHER HAND there is Boëthius, teaching, *Whatever exists, inasmuch as it exists, is one*.[35] Now we admit that Christ exists. Therefore Christ is one.

REPLY: A nature, considered as such, and signified by an abstract term, may not be truly predicated of a subsisting subject or person except in the case of God in whom the being which exists is not distinct from the nature, as has been explained.[36]

Now in the case of Christ, where there are two natures, the divine and the human, one of these, the divine, may be predicated of him either by means of an abstract term or by means of a concrete term. So we say that "the Son of God," for whom the term "Christ" stands, "is the divine nature" and "he is God." His human nature, on the contrary, may not be predicated of Christ by itself, by

means of an abstract term; a concrete term must be used signifying the nature as subsisting in a subject. So the statement, "Christ is his human nature," is not true because human nature is not suitable for being predicated of its subject. We say rather, "Christ is a man," which is parallel to "Christ is God." Here the term "God" signifies "one possessing divinity"; and the term "a man" signifies "one possessing humanity."

One possessing humanity may be signified, though in different ways, by the term "a man" and by the term "Jesus" or "Peter." The term "a man" refers to an indeterminate subject possessing humanity; likewise the word "God" refers to an indeterminate subject possessing divinity. On the contrary, the term "Peter" or "Jesus" refers to a determinate subject possessing it with determinate, individual characteristics; likewise the term "the Son of God" refers to a subject possessing divinity with a determinate personal property.

Now, duality is attributed to Christ by reason of the natures considered in themselves. Consequently, if both natures were predicated of Christ by means of abstract terms, it would follow that Christ was two. But since the two natures are predicated of Christ only by means of a term signifying them as in a subject, it is necessarily with respect to this subsisting subject that "one" or "two" be predicated of Christ.

Some theologians did indeed hold that in Christ there are two subsisting subjects but one person; the latter appears to have been considered in this opinion as a subsisting subject brought to a state of final completion. Having attributed to Christ two subsisting subjects, they logically declared

---

[34] *Physics*, III.
[35] *De Duabus Naturis.*
[36] *S.T.*, I, 29, ad 11.

that Christ is two things; but since they attributed to him only one person they declared him to be one individual. The term "thing" is here taken to signify something indeterminate and incomplete, while "individual" is taken to signify something determinate and complete.

The Nestorians, on the other hand, since they attributed to Christ two persons, declared that he is not simply two things, but also two persons.

Since we, on the contrary, as is clear from what has gone before,[37] attribute to Christ one person and one subsisting subject, we logically affirm that Christ is not only one individual but also one thing.

HENCE: 1. The quotation from Augustine should not be understood as though the term "each of two" were a Predicate, when the sense would be, "Christ is each of two"; it is to be taken as a Subject. This means that the term "each of two" stands, not for two subsisting subjects, but for two terms signifying the two natures in concrete fashion. For I may legitimately say, "Each of the two," that is, God and man, "is God, by reason of the God who receives," and, "each of the two," that is, God and the man, "is a man by reason of the man received."

2. If we find it said, "Christ is distinct things," the statement should be explained as follows, "He has distinct natures." So, in fact, Augustine explains it. He first writes, *In the mediator of God and men, the Son of God is one thing and the son of man is another thing.* Further on, he adds, *I use the term "another thing" to signify the distinction of substantial natures; I do not speak of "another individual"* because of the unity of person.[38] And Gregory Nazianzen says, *In brief, distinct elements enter into the being of the Savior; for the invisible is not the same as the visible, the eternal is not the same as the temporal. But this certainly does not mean that he is distinct individuals. In him both elements form one.*[39]

3. The statement, "Christ is only man," is false, not because it excludes a second subsisting subject, but because it excludes a second nature. For terms placed in the predicate are taken formally. If, however, an addition were to be made to this statement, making the Predicate to be taken instead for the subsisting subject, then it would be true; so, for example, "Christ is only that which is a man." But though we thus deny, with the objector, the first proposition, it does not follow that Christ is "something distinct from a man." For the term "distinct" is a relative implying diversity of substance and thus refers to a subsisting subject, as do all terms which establish a relation between persons. All that follows from our denial is, "Therefore he has another nature."

4. In the statement, "Christ is something that the Father is," the term "something" is taken for the divine nature which, even when signified by an abstract term, may be predicated of both the Father and the Son. On the contrary, in the statement, "Christ is something that the Father is not," the term "something" is taken for Christ's human nature signified, not in abstract fashion, but concretely, that is, as pertaining to a subsisting subject — not to a determinate, but to an indeterminate subject, one, that is, con-

---

[37] Cf. S.T., III, 2, 2 and 3.

[38] *Contra Felic.*, II.
[39] *Epistula ad Celid.*, 101.

ceived as subsisting in the nature but without individuating features. Consequently, it does not follow (from the conjunction of these two statements) that Christ is "distinct things" or that he is "two." For in Christ the subject subsisting in human nature — in other words, the person of the Son of God — is not numerically distinct from the divine nature which is predicated of Father and Son.[40]

5. When we are speaking about the mystery of the divine Trinity we predicate the divine nature, signified by an abstract term, of the three Persons. This permits us to say without qualification, "The three Persons are one thing." But when we are speaking about the mystery of the Incarnation we do not predicate the two natures, signified by abstract terms, of Christ. Consequently, it may not be said without qualification that Christ is two.

6. The term "two" signifies "possessing duality"; and this is evidently placed, not in something else, but in that reality of which the two are predicated. Now here predication is made of the subsisting subject for which the term "Christ" stands. Granted, therefore, that Christ possesses duality of nature, this still does not mean that he may be said to be two, for he does not possess duality of subsisting subject.

7. The term "other" indicates accidental variation and, consequently, accidental variation suffices for a thing to be said without qualification to be

"other." The term "distinct," on the contrary, indicates diversity of substance. Now, not only a nature, but also a subsisting subject is said to be a substance.[41] Consequently, if we are to say without qualification that a thing is distinct, it is not sufficient that it possess diverse natures; there must also be diversity of subsisting subject. However, even should there be no diversity of subsisting subject, possession of diverse natures will make a thing distinct in a restricted sense, namely, as regards its natures.

Question 19. The Unity of Christ's Activity

Article I. Is the activity of Christ's divinity and of his humanity one only?

THE FIRST POINT: 1. It seems that the activity of Christ's divinity and of his humanity was one only. For Denis states, *The merciful action of God in our regard is revealed in this that the Word who is above every creature became like us, came from among us, truly and integrally humanizing himself; and he performed and suffered whatever befitted his divine and human action.*[42] It is question here of a single activity at once human and divine for which the term derived from Greek is "theandric," that is, "of the God-man." There seems, then, to be a single, composite activity in Christ.

2. Moreover, a principal agent and its instrument possess a single activity. Now Christ's human nature was the instrument of the divinity. . . . Consequently there is a single activity belonging to both the divine and the human nature in Christ.

3. Moreover, the two natures in Christ being united in a single sub-

---

[40] The two statements have been reduced to the following forms, "Christ is the divine nature; as is the Father," and, "Christ is the person of the Son (subsisting in human nature); therefore distinct from the Father." No duality ensues in Christ, for divine person and divine nature are identified. We are left with the mystery of the Trinity.

[41] Aristotle, *Metaphysics*, V.
[42] *De Divinis Nominibus*, 2.

sisting subject or person, it necessarily follows that whatever belongs to his subject or person is one and the same being. Now, action belongs to the subject or person, for only a subsisting subject is capable of action, so that Aristotle says, *It is the individual that acts*.[43] Consequently, the activity of Christ's divinity and of his humanity is one and the same reality.

4. Moreover, action, like existence, belongs to the subsisting subject. It has already been shown that the unity of subject in Christ implies that his existence is one.[44] For the same reason, therefore, Christ's activity is one.

5. Moreover, where the effect is one the action responsible for the effect is also one. Now Christ's divinity and humanity were responsible for common effects such as the healing of a leper or the raising of the dead. It seems, consequently, that the activity of Christ's divinity and of his humanity is only one.

ON THE OTHER HAND, Ambrose says, *How can the same action derive from distinct faculties? Can a lower faculty act in the same fashion as a higher? Or can there be a single activity where there are distinct natures?*[45]

REPLY: . . . those heretics who attributed only one will to Christ attributed to him also only one activity. In order to understand how they were led into this false position it should be observed that wherever there is given an ordered series of agents, the lower is moved by the higher. In man, for example, the body is moved by the soul, the less perfect faculties by the mind. From this point of view the actions and movement of the lower faculty

are effects even more than they are activities; and the title of activity in the strict sense will thus be reserved to the motion of the highest agent. We can take an example. We might say that walking, an action of the feet, and touching, an action of the hands, are effects produced by the man, one of which the soul produces by means of the feet, the other by means of the hands. And since it is the same soul which is active through both, there is as far as the agent or primary moving principle is concerned, just one, undifferentiated action; any differences are located in the effects.

In an ordinary man, then, the body is moved by the soul and the sense impulses are moved by the will. In somewhat similar fashion the humanity of our Lord Jesus Christ was moved and controlled by his divine nature. On this basis the heretics whom we are discussing affirmed that there is a single, undifferentiated action deriving from the activity of his divinity. They admitted, however, that diversity may be found in the effects of this action; for Christ's divine nature produced one kind of effect when acting by itself — Christ *upheld all things by the word of his power* — and another kind of effect when acting through the human nature — for example, the bodily action of walking. In this sense the Sixth General Council [Third Council of Constantinople] quotes Severus, one of these heretics, *The actions and works of the one Christ differ considerably among themselves. Some of them are to be attributed to God; others were human. For example, the bodily action of walking on earth is clearly human; but to heal crippled limbs deprived of the power of walking, this is a gift only God can give. Nevertheless, one and*

---

[43] *Metaphysics* I, I. 981a16.
[44] Cf. S.T., III, 17, 2.
[45] *De Fide*, II, 8.

*the same being, the incarnate Word,
did both of these things; and it is not
the case that one of them derives
from one of his natures, the other from
the other. From the fact that diverse
effects were produced we are not entitled to assert that there were two
natures or forms operating.*[46]

But there is faulty reasoning here.
In fact the action of a being which
is moved by another is two-fold: one
it has in virtue of its own nature; the
other originates in the movement received from the mover. So the action
of an adze in virtue of its own nature
is cutting; but in virtue of the movement imparted to it by the workman
its action is to shape a plank. Accordingly, the action belonging to a thing
in virtue of its nature is native to it;
it does not belong to the mover except
insofar as he employs the thing in
question for his own activity. Heating, for example, is the native action
of fire; it is the action of the smith
only because he uses fire for heating
iron. On the contrary, the action belonging to a thing only because it is
being moved by another is not distinct from the action of the mover;
shaping a plank is not an activity of
the adze distinct from the activity of
the workman. Accordingly, wherever
mover and thing moved have diverse
natures or sources of action there will
always be distinct activities, one native
to the mover, the other native to the
thing moved; at the same time the
thing moved will participate in the
activity of the mover and the mover
will employ the activity of the thing
moved; in other words, each of the
two acts in communion with the other.

In Christ, accordingly, his human
nature has its own form and possibility
of action; and the same is true of his

divine nature. Consequently the human nature has its native activity, distinct from the divine activity, and
vice versa. Yet at the same time the
divine nature employs the activity of
the human nature as the activity of an
instrument. Similarly, the human nature participates in the activity of the
divine nature as an instrument participates in the activity of its user.
This is what Pope Leo refers to when
he says, *Each form* — that is both divine and human nature in Christ —
*acts in its native fashion in communion
with the other; the Word performs
what pertains to the Word, and the
flesh carries out what pertains to the
flesh.*[47]

If there were only one activity proceeding from the divinity and the humanity of Christ, then it would have
to be said that the human nature possessed no form or operative power of
its own — since it is clear that no such
assertion could possibly be made of the
divine nature; from this it would follow that Christ had only divine activity. The alternative would be to say
that Christ's divine and human powers came together to form a single
power. Each of these conclusions is
untenable. The first implies that
Christ's human nature is imperfect;
the second implies mingling of the
natures.

It was, consequently, with justice
that the Sixth General Council condemned the opinion we have been considering. In its decree we read, *We
honor in the one Lord Jesus Christ,
our true God, two native activities,
which are undivided, not interchangeable, not intermingled, inseparable,*[48]
this referring to the divine and human
activity.

[46] Art. 10.

[47] *Epistola ad Flavianum,* 28.
[48] Art. 18.

Hence: 1. Denis's attribution to Christ of *theandric* or *divino-human activity,* does not imply any intermingling of the activities or powers of the two natures. It refers rather to the fact that the divine activity employs the human, while the human activity participates in the efficacy of the divine. Denis himself writes, *He did in superhuman fashion the things that men do; as may be seen in the Virgin conceiving him supernaturally and in the waters which sustained the weight of his earthly feet.*[49] Evidently, to be conceived and to walk both belong to human nature; but each is realized in Christ in a supernatural way. And similarly Christ performed divine works through human means, as when he healed a leper by touching him. Denis accordingly adds later in the same letter, *God being made man, his was a new form of activity, belonging at once to God and man.*

That Denis understood there to be two activities in Christ, one from his divine nature, the other from the human, is quite clear from what he says elsewhere. He states, *The Father and the Holy Spirit have no part in Christ's human action, unless it be through their loving, merciful will,*[50] inasmuch, that is, as Father and Holy Spirit willed in their mercy that Christ should perform and bear what is human. But then he adds, *or unless it be through each of those sublime and ineffable actions which Christ as God performed when, being in our nature, he yet remained the unchanging God and Word of God.*[51] It clearly emerges from this that there are two activities in Christ. One is human, and in this the Father and the Holy Spirit have

no part except through their merciful assent.[52] The other is his activity as Word of God in which the Father and the Holy Spirit communicate.[53]

2. A thing is termed an instrument because it is moved by a principal agent; but apart from this it may possess a native activity corresponding to its own form, as in the example already used of fire. Accordingly, the action of an instrument precisely as instrument is not distinct from the action of the principal agent. Yet, as a reality with its own nature, it may also possess another activity. Applying this to the case of Christ: the activity of his human nature, insofar as that nature is the instrument of the divinity, is not distinct from the activity of the divinity; for it is one and the same saving action by which his humanity and his divinity save us. At the same time Christ's human nature, as a nature, possessed its own activity distinct from the divine activity.

3. While activity is to be attributed to the subsisting subject, it is nevertheless determined by the form and nature, in the sense that it is from this that the activity receives its determinate character. Consequently, diversity of forms or natures results in diverse kinds of activity; the unity of the subsisting subject, on the other hand, ensures the numerical unity of the specifically determinate action. Fire, for example, has two specifically distinct activities, giving light and giving heat, corresponding to the distinction between light and heat; yet when it is giving light its activity of lighting

---

[49] *Ad Caium,* 4.
[50] *De Divinis Nominibus,* **II.**
[51] *Ibid.*

[52] Christ's human actions, like those of other men, are subject to divine Providence; cf. I, 22; III, 24.
[53] It is a question of divine activity with respect to creatures which is common to the three persons of the Blessed Trinity; cf. I, 45, 6.

is numerically one. In the same fashion there must be two specifically distinct activities in Christ, corresponding to his two natures; yet each of these activities, on being exercised, is numerically one so that, for example, Christ had a single act of walking and a single act of healing.

4. Both existence and activity belong to the person and derive from the nature, but in different ways. Existence is an element in the actual realization of the person; under this aspect, therefore, it is to be considered as the ultimate perfection. Consequently, unity of the person depends on unity of the complete, personal existence. On the contrary, activity is an effect of the person, proceeding according to a form or nature. For this reason diverse kinds of activity do not prejudice the unity of the person.

5. The distinctive effect of Christ's divine activity and that of his human activity are quite distinct. Healing a leper is a distinctive effect of his divine activity; touching him is a distinctive effect of his human nature. And yet the two activities cooperate in producing a single effect for . . . one nature acts in communion with the other.

Article 2. Is there only one act of existence in Christ?

THE SECOND POINT: 1. It seems that in Christ there is not only one act of existence but two. For Damascene states that whatever follows upon nature is in Christ two-fold. But the act of existence follows upon nature since it is a consequence of form. Therefore in Christ there are two acts of existence.

2. Moreover, the act of existence of the Son of God is identified with the divine nature and is eternal. On the contrary, the existence of the man Christ is not identified with the divine nature and is a temporal existence. Consequently there is not only one act of existence in Christ.

3. Moreover, in the Trinity, although there are three persons, there is only one act of existence by reason of the unity of nature. Now in Christ, while there is one person, there are two natures. Consequently, in Christ there is not only one act of existence but two.

4. Moreover, Christ's soul, inasmuch as it is the form, communicates to his body an act of existence. But it does not communicate the divine existence, since this is uncreated. Consequently, there is in Christ another act of existence in addition to the divine existence. So there is not only one act of existence in Christ.

ON THE OTHER HAND a thing is one to the extent that it is a being; for 'that which is one' and 'that which is a being' are convertible terms. If, then, there were two acts of existence in Christ and not only one, he would be two and not one.

REPLY: Since in Christ there are two natures and one subsisting subject, it necessarily follows that what pertains to nature is in Christ two-fold, while what pertains to the subsisting subject is one only. Now the act of existence pertains both to nature and to the subsisting subject. It pertains to the subject as to *that which* possesses existence. It pertains to the nature as to that *by which* something has existence; thus the nature is considered as a form which belongs to the order of existence inasmuch as by it something exists. It is, for example, by whiteness that something is white, and by humanity that someone is a man.

It is, however, to be observed that if there is any form or nature which does not pertain to the personal existence of a subsisting subject, this form's existence is attributed to the person, not purely and simply, but only under a certain aspect. So, white existence is an existence of Socrates, not as he is Socrates, but as he is white. Nothing forbids existence of this kind being multiplied in a subsisting subject or person; so Socrates has one existence by which he is white and another by which he is musical. But it is impossible that the existence which belongs to the subsisting subject or person as such should be multiplied in the same subject or person. For it is impossible that one thing should not have one act of existence.

If, then, as some have suggested, human nature pertained to the Son of God, not hypostatically, or personally, but accidentally, then it would be necessary to attribute to Christ two acts of existence, by one of which he would be God, by the other, man. It is in this way that one existence is attributed to Socrates as white, another to Socrates as man; for to be white does not belong to the personal existence of Socrates.

On the contrary, to be provided with a head or a body or a soul, all this belongs to the single person of Socrates; and consequently from all of these derives no more than one existence in Socrates. And should it happen, after the appearance of Socrates as a person, that he should acquire hands or feet or eyes (as might happen if he were born blind), then from none of these would he acquire a new existence. There would be added simply a relation to these new parts inasmuch as Socrates would now be said to exist not merely in respect of what he formerly possessed, but also in respect of his new acquisitions.

Now, as has been said, a human nature is united to the Son of God hypostatically or personally, and not accidentally. Consequently, with his human nature he does not acquire a new personal existence, but simply a new relation of his already existing personal existence to the human nature. Accordingly, this person is now said to subsist not only in divine nature but also in human nature.

Hence: 1. Existence follows on nature, not as on that which possesses existence, but as on that by which something exists. On the contrary, it follows on the person or subsisting subject as on that which possesses existence. As a consequence Christ rather preserves unity in virtue of the unity of the subsisting subject than acquires duality in virtue of the duality of natures.

2. The eternal existence of the Son of God which is identified with the divine nature becomes the existence of the man inasmuch as the human nature is assumed by the Son of God into the unity of his person.

3. As has already been explained, the fact that each of the divine Persons is identified with the nature means that in the divine Persons the existence of the Person is not distinct from the existence of the nature. Consequently the three Persons have only one existence. They would have a three-fold existence if in them the existence of the Person were distinct from the existence of the nature.

4. Christ's soul communicates existence to his body in the sense that it makes it actually animated; and this is to complete its nature and kind. But if we represent to ourselves a body completed by a soul yet with no sub-

sisting subject possessing the two, then this whole, composed of body and soul, which is signified by the term "humanity," is understood to be, not that which exists, but that by which something exists. Consequently actual existence belongs to the subsisting person inasmuch as the latter bears a relation to such a nature; and the soul is the cause of this relation insofar as it completes human nature by animating the body.

V. DUNS SCOTUS*

Commentary on the Sentences of Peter Lombard

* Duns Scotus (c. 1264–1308) was a Franciscan theologian who greatly deemphasized rational methods which involved ascribing necessary connections between revealed truths or necessary conclusions drawn from them as premises. He highly favored appeal to the divine will as the ultimate reason or explanation for anything. This theological posture sets him off sharply from St. Thomas. For the latter, natural law depends on God's intellect, for Scotus it depends on God's will, and as such is not immutable. The former asserts that beatitude consists formally in the act of intellect of the blessed, for Scotus it consists in their act of will. In philosophy he argued against St. Thomas that the principle of individuation is not matter, but a third principle, *haecceitas*, which is superimposed on matter and form. For Scotus the Incarnation would have taken place even if man had not fallen, because God's decision had predestined the Incarnation before the sin of Adam. His Christology is in the line of the *asumptus homo* tradition of Antioch, which stressed the complete humanity of the Redeemer.

On the Nature of the Union of the Two Persons in Christ

Just as the Doctor [Lombard] says that there cannot be two masculines, because if there were two masculines there would of necessity be two persons, so also if one masculine is spoken of concerning the human nature [of Christ] and according to the divine nature another masculine is spoken of, then there would be two persons subsisting in two natures. If so, this union of the human nature to the divine would not result in one person, because we speak of the divine nature and the human nature as united in the Word in a unity of person. — *Opus Oxon.* In Lib. III, dist. 6, q. 2.

It is not necessary that everything which comes into being change in order to become such and such, but only inasmuch as it happens in those things which were previously in potency to this thing, just as something comes into act by the imposition of form. It was not in this manner that the Word became man, but rather through a personal union. If we look for any kind of change, this could be located in the human nature, but then only if the human nature had been in existence before the uniting. Change does not take place except between two terminals, one of which precedes the other in time. — *Opus Oxon.,* In Lib. III, dist. 7, q. 2.

One view says that the soul and body of Christ were united together first in the order of nature to form man and, as thus constituted, this was assumed by the Word. Also, because man is the name of the supposit, this vicar therefore maintains that in Christ there are two supposits, one created, which is man subsisting in human nature, and the other uncreated, which is the Word subsisting in the divine nature. Further, it postulates that in Christ there was only one person, although two supposits, and that this person is the divine supposit as far as dignity is concerned. Since, therefore the created supposit in Christ is united to the more worthy divine supposit, the *ratio* of the person must be determined by the more worthy supposit.

I cannot hold this view, because that which assumes is not that which is assumed. For if the assumed manhood is truly a supposit, then the uncreated supposit is a created supposit, and this is impossible, because one supposit cannot rightly be predicated of another. . . .

Another theory holds that the body and soul of Christ were first by nature, but in relation to time were not united to constitute a human nature, and thus were assumed simultaneously by the Word. Thence it holds that the person of the Word was made composite after the incarnation because previously it was simple, understanding by this that the person of the Word, which before the incarnation subsisted solely in one nature, subsisted after the incarnation in two natures. I would hold to the first part of this contention, but not to the second because such a composition means an imperfection.

A third opinion proposes that the soul of Christ and the body of Christ, divided from each other without any composition, were united together by the Word or assumed by the Word. Thus when it is said that the Word assumed human nature, we ought to understand that it assumed the parts of human nature, just as the parts of a house are called a house. Another says that the soul and body were united to the Word only accidentally or extrinsically, as a coat is united to a body. This position is untenable. — *Opus Oxon.* In Lib. III, dist. 6, q. 2.

Duns Scotus Disagrees With Anselm As to the Necessity of Christ's Passion

Was it necessary that the human race be restored through Christ's passion? . . . To answer this question we must first consider with Anselm, who devoted his entire *Cur Deus Homo?* to the problem, the need there was for redemption, that the redemption could not have taken place without satisfaction, and what manner of satisfaction had to be made by the God-man, namely his passion. With Anselm we hold that neither God nor nature do anything uselessly; but a rational creature would have been made in vain, he maintains, unless it was able to love the greatest good on account of itself and cling to it through knowledge and love. God either leads man to this accomplished end or he does not. If not, in vain did he make man; if so, then when man fell through sin, it was necessary that he restore him. . . .

(Anselm) also maintains that a (fallen) man ought not to be declared unjust, because he can be excused on the grounds of his impotence. . . . I answer that man could be excused on account of his inability to make amends, only if he had not sinned of his own free will. Because he put himself in such an impotent state the impotence itself is sinful because he ought not to be in such a state. He should be able to render to God that honor which he withheld, and if through sin he rendered himself unable to do so, his inability is not to be excused, it is to be censured.

(Anselm) concludes that God had to become man because no one was able to repair the debt except God, and the debt was truly man's. . . . But Anselm seems to be mistaken when he holds that redemption was impossible except through the death of Christ. I maintain that man could have been redeemed otherwise than by the death of Christ. Augustine says, "Another manner of redeeming man was not lacking to God, to whose power all things are subject" (de Trin. Ch. X). Further, it was not necessary that Christ redeem man by means of death. If it is seen as necessary, it is only in the sense that it was necessary after the fact, with a consequent, not an antecedent necessity. . . . Further, it was not necessary at all that the human race be redeemed. Thus neither was it necessary that Christ had to suffer. Men, indeed were predestined to glory, but this predestination was contingent and not necessary. . . . Just as there was no absolute necessity for God to predestine man to beatitude, so also there was no absolute necessity for his redemption. — Opus Oxon. In Lib. III, q. unica.

CHAPTER 5. DEVELOPMENTS DURING THE REFORMATION PERIOD

INTRODUCTION[1]

One of the notable elements in Luther's religious thought was his conception of God as a loving Father, who graciously and freely forgives sin, and saves men without any merit on their part. But this did not mean that he broke away from the idea of God as a stern and angry Judge — the avenger of sin who will let no guilty man escape. On the contrary, it was his vivid sense of God's wrath that drove him to despair, and God's wrath constituted, not simply the precondition, but the permanent background of his doctrine of divine forgiveness. It is only in Christ, and only to the Christian believer, that God discloses himself as a gracious Father; outside of Christ there is only wrath and vengeance. The explanation Luther found in the atoning work of Christ. It is true that in his impatience with the Catholic theory of penance, and with the interpretation of Christ's work in its light, he used words on one occasion which have been taken to mean the rejection of the doctrine of the atonement. "Therefore this word satisfaction ought to be used no longer in our churches and theology, but should be commended to the judges and lawyers to whom it belongs, and from whom it was taken by the Papists."[2] But quite apart from the isolated character of this utterance, to interpret it thus is to misunderstand Luther. The doctrine of the atonement was absolutely fundamental with him. That

---

[1] A. C. McGiffert, *Protestant Thought before Kant* (New York: Harper and Brothers, 1962), pp. 48–53, 87–93.

[2] *Works,* Vol. XI, p. 280.

God was gracious to the Christian and forgave his sins freely was due to the fact that Christ had suffered the penalty of human sin, and had moreover lived a life of perfect obedience, so that His merit could be imputed to the believer. "In the first place, do not doubt that you have a gracious God and Father who has forgiven all your sins, and saved you in baptism. In the second place, know, in addition, that all this has happened not for nothing, or without the satisfaction of His righteousness. For there is no room for mercy and grace to work over us and in us, or to help us to eternal blessings, and to salvation, unless enough has been done to satisfy righteousness perfectly; as Christ says: 'Not one jot or tittle of the law shall pass away.' "[3] The traditional scheme of redemption thus retained its place in Luther's thinking, and the Anselmic theory of the atonement, modified and supplemented in ways that need not be further indicated here, acquired a prominence hitherto unknown. Had Luther's experience been of another type — the fruit of a more modern estimate of man — he might have repudiated altogether the mediaeval notion of God as an avenger of sin, and with it the doctrine of the atoning work of Christ. As it was, only that doctrine made it possible for him to justify his faith in the forgiving love of God, and hence it became more central and important then ever.

With the doctrine of the atonement is connected the dogma of the Deity of Christ. Unless He possesses the divine nature, the work which He does has finite value only, and cannot avail to atone for human sin. And so the Deity of Christ also constituted an essential element in Luther's faith.

It was retained, not out of mere conservatism, or respect for the traditional system, but because it was necessary to his fundamental belief in God's forgiving love. An added emphasis was given to the Deity of Christ by the fact that only in Him is God apprehended as a gracious Father. Were it not for His revelation God would be known only as a God of wrath. It is significant that the contrast which Luther drew between the Christian God and the God of natural theology was not the traditional contrast between a personal father and the abstract absolute, but between a gracious and an angry God. The latter alone is known apart from Christ, and as the former is the object of the Christian's faith, the Deity of Christ is made more vitally essential than ever.

The belief in the Deity of Christ is the central element in the historic doctrine of the Trinity; and so again it is no accident and no mere sign of conservatism that Luther retained that doctrine. It is true that in his insistence upon the fact that all knowledge of God outside of Christ is "empty fancy and mere idolatry," he was led at times to oppose all speculation about the divine nature. It is therefore not surprising that all Trinitarian formulae are entirely wanting in his *Little Catechism,* and that on more than one occasion he criticized the doctrine of the Trinity, declaring that "the words Trinity and Unity are mathematical words,"[4] and that "the expression Trinity is not in the Scriptures, and sounds cold, and we shall do much better to speak of God, and not of Trinity."[5]

But, on the other hand, although

---

[3] *Ibid.,* Vol. VII, p. 175.

[4] *Ibid.,* Vol. IV, p. 168.

[5] *Ibid.,* Vol. XII, p. 378. Cf. Vol. VI, p. 230 ff.

his interest, like that of Athanasius himself, was always more in the Deity of Christ than in the distinction of persons within the Godhead, he yet commonly emphasized the doctrine of the Trinity, and gave it a prominent place in his preaching and writing.[6] Moreover the doctrine was not merely a traditional form of words to him. He knew how to make it practically useful, and to give it a vital place in the experience of the Christian.

Christ's Deity meant to Luther, as to the Catholic theologians, the possession of a dual nature, the divine and the human. He thought in terms of the traditional ontology, and drew the same distinction between the nature of God and the nature of man that the Fathers and schoolmen had drawn. As a consequence, though in his interest in Christ's redemptive work he always laid emphasis rather upon the unity than upon the distinction of His natures, he yet found the historic Christological formulae entirely congenial, and his faith expressed itself naturally through them. It is therefore not surprising that the Nicene and Athanasian Creeds, as well as the Apostles', which was interpreted as a Trinitarian formula, were accepted by him and handed down to his followers as expressions of the truth which every Christian must accept. In the dogmas of the Trinity and the Person of Christ he found his gospel of the forgiving love of God confirmed and guaranteed. Where they are believed and properly interpreted there exists ample assurance that God is a gracious Father through Jesus Christ; where they are doubted or denied all ground of assurance is gone. He thus read into them a significance which they had not before possessed, and

[6] Cf. e.g., ibid., Vol. IX.

gave them a reality and vitality lacking since the days that gave them birth. During the Middles Ages they had been largely matter of tradition. Now they became again in Luther's hands expressions of practical Christian faith. It may thus be fairly said, with Harnack, that they were not simply preserved, but rehabilitated.

While Luther denied that salvation depends in any way upon a man's own efforts, and so destroyed the traditional incentive to virtue, his conception of faith, as has already been said, was such as to guarantee the Christlike character of the believer's life.[7] But unfortunately he was not always true to his own convictions in this matter. Sure as he was that the Christian believer cannot do otherwise than live as Christ would have him live, the influence of Catholic tradition was so strong, and his distrust of men so ingrained, that it proved impossible for him to maintain his belief that faith alone is sufficient for holiness, and he was obliged to add the sanctifying influence of the Holy Spirit. In spite of what he says about the ethical power of faith, he yet fre-

---

[7] "Whenever Luther refers to the incarnation, he always thinks of the humanity in terms of its frailest and weakest. He speaks of the babe at the breast and the child in the manger, of the man forsaken and his dying on the cross. He thinks of the humanity in its hour of impotence and in its hour of utter humility. The natural man thinks of Christ as the flower and perfection of humanity, but Luther knows that this is a false starting point for man to understand God's redemptive work in the incarnation. The incarnation reveals God but also veils God. Luther does not see the incarnation as a demonstration or proof of God's presence. God cannot be demonstrated or pointed out; he can only be believed. . . ." J. Atkinson, Luther: Early Theological Work (Philadelphia: Westminster Press, 1962), p. 109, n. 2.

quently declares that even the Christian man is weak and frail, and cannot live as he ought without the presence and power of the Spirit. This mystical idea was evidently due largely to the influence of the Apostle Paul. But while Paul made the presence of the Spirit, transforming man from a corrupt to a holy being, the ground of salvation, Luther conceived salvation in an entirely different way, in such a way as to make the Spirit quite unnecessary. The two points of view were wholly distinct, and only ambiguity and inconsistency resulted from their combination.

Intimately bound up with the Pauline idea of the presence of the Spirit was the mystical conception of faith as uniting the believer to Christ in such a way that he ceases to be himself, and becomes one person with Christ. This idea also, inconsistent as it was with his controlling way of looking at things, and with his general view of faith, Luther took over from Paul. His doctrine of salvation was not in the least mystical; it moved wholly in the sphere of personal relationships. The adoption of mystical conceptions and forms of speech, whether due to the influence of Paul or of Catholic tradition, worked only confusion, and prevented his gospel from being fully understood and appreciated by those who came after him. . . .

Calvin's doctrine of God occupied the same central place in his system as in Zwingli's. But while it resembled closely the earlier reformer's doctrine, it was less profound and was worked out with less consistency. To the Genevan reformer God is a strictly personal Being whose will controls the universe; to Zwingli He is the only real Being, the all-pervading energy and the immanent cause of all things. The practical effects are the same, but the philosophical basis is different, or rather it should be said that while Zwingli's is a philosophical theory, Calvin's is theological only. The younger reformer had apparently no philosophical interest, and Zwingli's ontological speculations did not appeal to him in the least. He blamed the older man for them, and claimed that he himself followed Scripture only, and allowed human reason no place in the formation of his views. He was mistaken in this. His ideas touching God's character and activities were in no small part the result of logical deduction from a preconceived theory of deity. Scripture, though continually appealed to and ostensibly made the sole source, really did no more than supply some of the data upon which a logical theory was constructed. These data harmonized with his own temperament and experience, and so were made use of to the exclusion of all others.

Calvin's appeal to the Bible rather than to philosophy in support of his teaching did much to establish the doctrine of absolute predestination in the reformed church. The philosophical considerations of Zwingli carried little weight except among philosophers. The Biblical argument, which both Zwingli and Bucer had employed, but which Calvin presented with new emphasis and in greater fulness, was much more convincing.

Calvin's claim that the Scriptures alone were to be followed, and that no one was to go beyond what was written, made it possible for him frequently to avoid drawing the obvious conclusions of his own theory. He contrasts his moderation in this respect with Zwingli's greater consistency, and criticises the latter for his extreme statements.[8] As a matter of fact, Calvin's theory led exactly where Zwingli's did, and his customary reticence was less creditable than the outspokenness of the older reformer.[9] But it undoubtedly served to obscure some of the most obnoxious features of the doctrine, and thus made it more acceptable to the church.

Correlative with his conception of God was Calvin's idea of man and his duty. No one can understand and estimate himself aright unless he knows God. "For such is the inborn pride of us all that we invariably esteem ourselves righteous, innocent, wise, and holy, until we are convinced by clear proofs of our unrighteousness, turpitude, folly, and impurity. But we are never thus convinced while we confine our attention to ourselves and regard not the Lord who is the only standard by which judgment ought to be formed."[10] "Man is utterly corrupt and depraved, and humility alone becomes him in the presence of God, who is all that he is not. To know God is to be struck with horror and amazement, for then and only then does one realize his own character."[11] Man exists for the sake of God's glory, and his supreme duty is to promote it. There is no true virtue where concern for God's glory is not present, and the worst of all sins is giving to oneself the glory due

to God.[12] Man can best promote the divine glory by reverencing, fearing, and worshipping God, and by rendering perfect obedience to His will. Pure and genuine religion consists "in faith united with a serious fear of God — such a fear as comprehends willing reverence and results in legitimate worship agreeable to the injunctions of the law."[13] It is all-important, therefore, that man shall know God and His will. This knowledge is written upon the pages of nature and the tables of the heart, but man has been blinded by sin, and so a clearer revelation is given in the Bible, which is God's highest and final communication of His will. Like Zwingli, Calvin recognized God's general revelation of Himself, and he even declared that the knowledge of God in Himself precedes the knowledge of Christ, but he denied its efficacy and sufficiency. The only adequate and trustworthy declaration of God's will is found in the Scriptures. The Bible is conceived, as by Zwingli, not primarily as a means of grace, but as a revelation of the divine will. From beginning to end it is the word of God, and is equally authoritative in all its parts.

Man needs, not only a revelation of God's will, but also power to obey it, and forgiveness for disobedience. This he gets through Christ, whose work is pictured in the same traditional way as by the other reformers. Faith in Christ justifies man and frees him from the divine condemnation; salvation is by faith alone. But this is not enough, for he is utterly corrupt, and can do nothing good unless regenerated by the power of the Spirit. He is predestinated, not simply to salvation, but to holiness. He is called to

---

[8] See his letter to Bullinger, *Opera*, Vol. XIV, p. 253; on the other side his response in the *Process of Bolsec*, VIII, 182.

[9] In his *Institutes*, edition of 1559, Bk. I, Chap. XVIII, Calvin declares in full agreement with Zwingli that God is Himself the cause of man's evil deeds.

[10] *Institutes*, edition of 1559, Bk. I, Chap. I, § 2.

[11] *Ibid.*, § 3.

[12] *Ibid.*, Bk. II, Chap. III, § 4.

[13] *Ibid.*, Bk. I, Chap. II, § 2.

do God's will, and for this end he was created. The Christian life consists simply in keeping God's commands, and that not because they are good, but because they are commanded. It is not the free and spontaneous expression of the character of the child of God, but faithful obedience to the divine will laid down in the Scriptures. As is said in Book IV, Chap. X, § 7: "Everything pertaining to the perfect rule of a good life the Lord has so comprehended in His law that there remains nothing for man to add to that summary. And He has done this, first, that since all rectitude of life consists in the conformity of all our actions to His will as their standard, we might consider Him as the sole master and director of our life; and secondly, to show that He requires of us nothing more than obedience."[14] Calvin has a section on Christian Liberty in all the editions of his *Institutes*, but it is a very different kind of liberty from that which Luther taught. Not liberty, but bondage was dear to Calvin. He distrusted, not only the natural man, but the Christian man as well, and believed that he must be held strictly to the observance of the divine law, or he would go astray and fall into sin. By Christian liberty he meant freedom from dependence upon the works of the law for justification — how could any man justify himself in the sight of God? — and also freedom from the obligation to obey the commandments of men, particularly the oppressive regulations of the ecclesiastical authorities. . . .

[14] This is a genuinely Catholic position. With it might be compared the definition of the essence of Christianity in the [now old] *Catholic Encyclopaedia*: 'Obedience of the mind and will to the Supreme Power, *i.e.*, faith and works' (Vol. VI, p. 529).

In his conception of God and of man's relation to Him, Calvin agreed with Zwingli, but he was ethically more rigorous, and conceived the Christian life in a much more Puritanic fashion. Zwingli was engaged chiefly in breaking the control of Rome, and in securing a foothold for the new faith. Calvin devoted himself very largely to strengthening, consolidating, and purifying a Protestantism already established before he began his work. We call Calvin one of the Reformers, but he belonged to the second generation, and his task was to conserve rather than to create. This is illustrated both in his theology and in his practical work.

It was a mark of Calvin's greater conservatism that he made more than Zwingli did of the means of grace. He saw, as Luther did, in Zwingli's liberal attitude toward the non-Christian world a dangerous error. No one has ever been saved or can possibly be saved except through Christ. It is true that God elects whom He pleases, and that His election is the ultimate ground of salvation, but He saves no one apart from Christ. Although Calvin recognized the possibility that the Spirit of God might act independently of the ordinary means of grace in certain special cases, as, for instance, in the case of infants and idiots, he yet made much more of those means that Zwingli, and attached salvation, as Luther did, to the word and the sacraments. His view of the Lord's Supper he took from Bucer, teaching the spiritual presence of Christ in the elements and the nourishment of the regenerated life by Him. The idea is more Catholic than the controlling idea of Luther, even though it substitutes a spiritual for a material presence, for Luther laid emphasis on the testimony borne by the sacrament, while with Calvin the important thing was feeding upon Christ. Calvin's adoption of the doctrine gave it a permanent and indisputable place in reformed theology.

I. MARTIN LUTHER*

The Incarnation[15]

---

* Martin Luther (1483–1546), German Reformer, Augustinian priest, was lecturer in moral philosophy and later professor of Scripture at the University of Wittenberg. Personally the victim of extreme and scrupulous anxiety, intellectually influenced by the prevalent philosophical Nominalism, Luther underwent a deep and sudden revelation at about the age of thirty-two. It left him convinced that man finds his justification by faith alone without concomitant works. Luther's writings on Christ in his Small and Large Catechisms reflects his strong conviction that Redemption results from trust in Christ alone. Since justification resulted, not from grace and merit but from God's attribution of righteousness, he stressed the soteriological aspects of Christianity in his writings.

[Like other articles of the Christian faith, the divinity of Christ is to be ap-prehended, not com-prehended, Luther advises at the beginning of his exposition of John 17:3]:

Stop Reasoning; Simply Believe: Let him who would fare safely by all means beware of the criticism of reason and human thoughts concerning this article. And let him know that there is no way of withstanding the seduction of the devil except to cling to the bare, bright Word of Scripture, to think or speculate no farther but simply to close the eyes and to say: Whatever Christ says should and must be true, though neither I nor any other human being can understand and comprehend or know how it can possibly be true. Christ well knows what He is and what and how He should speak of Himself. He who does not so act is bound to run into trouble and to err and fall. For it is simply impossible for the human mind or reason to comprehend even the least important article of faith.

[Nor is it possible for the Spirit of God Himself to speak of the divinity of our Lord so plainly that refractory reason cannot cavil. Luther develops this thought in his exposition of John 14:13–14, delivered in 1537 and published in the following year.]

No Language Plain Enough for Captious Criticism. What good would it have done if the Holy Spirit had everywhere used words such as these: Christ is true God and man, as indeed He has often done? The heretics would only have had more occasions to blaspheme: It is not clear enough, for although these words, God and man, were spoken of Christ, yet we could not conclude with certainty that He truly has both the divine and the human nature. Since the mere names stand there and no further description is given of Him to prove that He had a truly human being and activity, and divine majesty and power as well,

---

[15] *What Luther Says*, Vol. I (St. Louis: Concordia Publishing House, 1959), pp. 168–178 *passim*.

He is God or man in name only. This is precisely what the heretics have done when people held under their noses texts and passages in which Christ is called the Virgin's Son or the Son of Man. Oh, well, said they: "Man" at this place does not mean a true man, the flesh and blood of his mother. Rather it means the specter or semblance of a man, who passed through the body of the Virgin as the sun throws his beam or light through a painted glass against the wall. . . . Just so the Arians. Although people showed them the words which Scriptures use of Christ, "God" and "God's Son," they said in rebuttal that He is not God by nature and essence but in name, and that the name "God's Son" at that place meant no more than a lord or prince or a creature glorious above all other creatures. But come now, who could not say this? If twisting and turning of this sort is to be allowed so that wood is to mean stone, a man but a monster; again, if "God" and "God's Son" are not to mean what they mean but what men desire to make of them, what would remain clear and certain in all Scripture, nay, in all languages? Then I could also say if a gulden were placed before me: That is not a gulden but a counter, or: That is not a groat but a piece of tin.

For this reason the Holy Spirit has kept frivolous spirits from explaining and juggling these words, "God" and "man," in either direction in accordance with their desire. He has compelled them to give them the proper meaning and explanation, which they are intended to have in all languages: the word "God" meaning God and the word "man" meaning man. For He has not only applied the names of God and man to Christ but has also sup-

plied a definition of them, that is, has properly and clearly stated how these words are to be explained and understood, so that everybody may not put his own comment upon them and make of them whatever he pleases. Therefore He describes Him in both ways: with the name and with the work or deed He performed, so that in case the name were not sufficient, we would nonetheless be obliged to say in view of the works ascribed to Him: This is God even though He were nowhere called God.

[Few, if any, theologians have, on the basis of Scripture, pointed out more clearly than Martin Luther the many implications of the essential divinity of our Lord. In 1515–16 the Doctor lectured on St. Paul's Letter to the Romans. Commenting on Rom. 1:3–4, he points out that the historic Person Jesus Christ was the God-man from the moment of His conception.]

Personal Union at Conception. From the moment of Christ's conception it was right to say, because of the union of both natures: This God is the Son of David, and this man is the Son of God. The first statement is true because the Godhead voluntarily restrained (*exinanita*) and hid itself in the flesh of Christ. The second is true because His human nature was filled and permeated by the Godhead.

[In 1527 Luther, writing against the fanatical spirits (*Schwärmgeister*) who, because of their misunderstanding of Christ's Person, denied the Real Presence in the Lord's Supper, tells how we are to envision the personal union of God and man in Jesus Christ and how we are not to picture it to ourselves.]

The Personal Union of God and Man in Christ. When Christ, God's Son, was to be conceived in the body of His mother and become man, He must have been already present essentially and personally in the body of the Virgin and there assumed humanity. For the Deity is immovable in itself and cannot move from one place to another as the creature does. At His incarnation the Son of God, therefore, did not climb down from heaven as on a ladder or slide down as on a rope; but even before His incarnation He was essentially and personally present in the Virgin's body, as in all other places, according to His divine nature, manner, and might. Now if He is present essentially and personally at one place, as in the body of the Virgin, and at the same time is with the Father, as our Creed obliges us to believe, then He is certainly also present everywhere in this way. For there is no reason why He should be present in the body of the Virgin and may not also be present in this way everywhere. But in Christ there is something different, something higher and greater than God's presence in all other creatures. For in Him God is not only essentially present, as in all other creatures; but He dwells in Him bodily in such a way that man and God are one Person. And although I may say of all creatures: There is God, or God is in it, I may not say: That Person is God Himself. But of Christ faith not only says that God is in Him, but it also affirms that Christ is God Himself. Whoever murders a human being may well be called a murderer of someone who is God's and in whom God is present. But he who murders Christ has murdered God's Son, nay, God and the Lord of Glory Himself.

[Since the controversy concerning the Lord's Supper continued to agitate Christendom, Luther, in 1528, published what became known as his large confession concerning this Sacrament. Here he again points out that the false doctrine to which his adversaries held was rooted in a wrong conception of the Person of Christ.]

A Union of Natures, Not of Persons. They denounce us and cry out that we mingle the two natures into one essence. This is not true. We do not say that divinity is humanity or that the divine nature is the human nature, which would be mixing the two natures into one essence. But we do merge the two distinct natures into one Person and say: God is man, and man is God. We, however, denounce them for dissolving the Person of Christ, as though it were two persons. For if the *alloeosis*[16] is to stand as Zwingli teaches it, Christ will have to be two persons, a divine one and a human one; for he applies all passages treating of suffering to the human nature alone and disassociates them in all respects from Christ's divinity. For if the works are parted and separated, then also the Person must be parted, because all works or sufferings are ascribed, not to natures, but to persons. For it is the Person which does and suffers everything, now according to this nature, then according to that nature. All this the learned well know. Therefore we hold our Lord Christ to be God and man in one Person in such a way *non confundendo naturas nec dividendo personam,* that we do not mix the natures nor separate the Person.

[If this were not the case, says Luther, in the same incisive publication, if the suffering of Jesus Christ were not the suffering of the Person who is God, then we would have no divine Redeemer; in fact, then we would have no Redeemer at all.]

God Suffered for Our Sins. Be-

---

16 Ἀλλοίωσις means as much as substitution, a sort of *quid pro quo.*

ware, beware, say I, of the *alloeosis!*
It is a mask of the devil; for in the
end it manufactures a Christ after
whom I should not relish being a
Christian, a Christ who would be no
more and do no more with His suffering and life than any other, ordinary
saint. For if I believe that only the
human nature has suffered for me,
then this Christ is a poor Savior to me;
in fact, then He Himself needs a Savior. In short, it is unspeakable what
the devil seeks to achieve by this
alloeosis. . . .

Now if that old weather witch,
Madam Reason, the grandmother of
this *alloeosis,* were to say: Divinity
can assuredly not suffer or die, you
should reply: That is true; yet because divinity and humanity are one
Person in Christ, Scripture, because
of this personal union, ascribes also
to divinity everything that happens to
humanity, and vice versa. And so it
is in reality. For you must certainly
say that the Person (meaning Christ)
suffers and dies. Now the Person is
true God; therefore it is correctly said:
The Son of God suffers. For although
the one part (to put it that way),
namely, the divinity, does not suffer,
yet the Person, who is God, suffers in
the other part, namely, in His humanity. Even as we say: The king's
son is wounded, although only his leg
is wounded; Solomon is wise, although
only his soul is wise; Peter is gray,
although only his head is gray. For
since body and soul are one person,
everything that happens to body or
soul, nay, to the smallest member of
the body, is correctly and properly
ascribed to the entire person. This is
the way people speak throughout the
world, not only in Scripture; and it expresses the truth, too. For, in truth,
God's Son has been crucified for us,
that is, the Person who is God;
for it, *it,* say I, the PERSON, is crucified according to His humanity.

[Naturally, says Luther, we believe
this solely on the basis of Scripture. Yet
illustrations may be adduced which show
that somewhat analogous relations exist
elsewhere. (From a sermon on John 3:13
in 1538.)]

**Human and Divine Natures in
Christ Like Body and Soul in Man.**
Since two natures are in the undivided
Person of Christ, that which pertains
to the human nature and is characteristic of it is ascribed also to the divine
nature. For this reason it is not wrong
to say: God and Mary's Son descended
into hell, suffered, and died; again:
God and Mary's Son ascended into
heaven and sits at the right hand of
His heavenly Father.

Now since so much depends on it,
I should like to impress this article
by means of illustrations if I can do so.
But we shall have to draw them from
wherever we can. You observe that a
man has a body and a soul joined together. Now the nature of the body is
very different from that of the soul,
and that the nature of the soul is very
different from that of the body. Yet
the body without the soul is no man.
The soul without the body is also no
man. But body and soul together are
one human being, not two human beings; and these two are united in such
a way that whoever touches a hair on
a person must be said to have touched
the entire person. Again, whoever
strikes an arm or a leg is said to have
struck the entire person, body and
soul. . . . But you may not separate
the body from the soul if a man is to
be a living person.

Furthermore, when a woman has
given birth to a child and the child is
alive and perfect, it has a body and

a soul. Yet the mother does not say that she has given birth to two sons, to two children or two persons, but to only one child. The child has two natures and yet is one human being, in which one nature is not like the other.

[There are other illustrations. A number of these Luther introduces into a Christmas sermon of 1541 on his favorite text (John 1:1–14).]

Similar Illustrations. Note well the word of the evangelist. He will not let the natures be separated in the Person who is true God and man, of whom he has said: "In the beginning was the Word" (Jn 1:1), and 1 John 1:1; The Word of Life was from the beginning; and a little later he says: "The Word was made flesh" (Jn 1:14). This same Word, says he, we have not only glanced at but we have observed very carefully with the bodily eyes in our head and have also touched with our hands. But, (you object) this same Word existed, as you say, before any eye had been created. How, then, can you say that you have seen Him? I reply: Do you not hear that John wants the Person undivided, so that Mary gave birth not only to a mere man but also and at the same time to the true, natural Son of God?

When she saw her bodily son, she also saw the true Son of God, the Lord over all. Although her eyes do not rise to a view of the Godhead, they do rise to a view of the Person in whom two natures, the divine and the human, are indissolubly united. For instance, when I see a person covered by a garment and wrapped in it, I see nothing but the garment, although the person is actually and really present. Again, you give someone a purse full of gulden. You see only the purse and

not the gulden, and yet the gulden are in it. This is far more truly the case in the instance before us, in which God and man are one Person. Origen compares this union of the divine and human natures with a glowing iron. As fire is wont to heat an iron through and through and to permeate it completely, so the eternal Word has assumed a human nature and has completely filled it with divine light and life. This human nature is as completely united with the Word as heat penetrates an iron when exposed to fire or beaten upon with a hammer.

[Once the union of the two natures into one Person has taken place, Luther points out in his exposition of John 6:57 (1531), these natures are henceforth inseparable.]

The Two Natures Inseparable in Christ. To be sure, humanity and divinity are not naturally one Being. Yet they exist in the one and indivisible Person in such a way that one cannot separate them from each other. Just so sugar water is water; but it is so mixed with sugar that no one can now separate the sugar and the water from each other, although they really have different natures by themselves. The illustration is not perfect; yet in a way it shows that Christ, our true Savior, is a Person who is God and man, so that when you grasp the humanity of Christ, you have also grasped the Godhead in its entirety, just as you find pure sugar in the sugar water.

[However intimate the union of body and soul in man, death temporarily disrupts it; but, says Luther, death did not break the union of the human and divine natures in Christ.]

Their Union Permanent and For-

ever. The two natures are so united in Christ that God and man cannot now be separated and divorced from each other. I may not say: At this point Christ is God; here Christ is man. Rather I must say: Where Christ is God, there Christ is man; and, again, Where Christ is man, there Christ is God; whatever Christ the man does, the Christ who is God also does; and, conversely, whatever the Christ who is God does, Christ the man also does.

Such a Redeemer and Savior we have in Christ. He is the Image of the invisible God, through whom all was made. He it is who has redeemed us through His blood. His blood is the blood of God, the Almighty Creator, the blood of the Lord of Glory, the blood of the Son of God. So the apostles speak of it, and to this they forcefully testify. For the two natures in Christ are far more intimately united than body and soul are united in man. Body and soul constitute one person until a man dies; then the soul leaves the body. But here in Christ God and man have become united and form one Person in such a way that the Godhead can eternally not be separated or divorced from humanity; and though Christ dies on the cross, yet God and man remain one Person, one Christ.

[In consequence, when Christ died, God died. That this momentous fact must necessarily follow Luther points out in a little *discursus* in his explanation of the last words of David (2 Sam 23:1–7) in 1543.]

Christ's Death, Then, Is the Death of God. If you say, as did Nestorius, that not God, or Jesus, God's Son, was born of Mary and crucified by the Jews, but only the man, Mary's son, then you are separating the one Person and are making two. Then one person was born and crucified, and another Person was not born and crucified, and each nature becomes a distinct person by itself, and there are two sons, distinct from each other. This amounts to saying that God did not become man but that God remains a Person by Himself, apart from the man Jesus, and this man remains a person by himself, apart from God. This separation will not do. It does not agree with Scripture.

[As one would expect, the effects of this personal union are profound and far-reaching. From it results what is known as the communication of attributes. According to it, the one Person of Christ possesses the attributes of both the human and the divine nature, deriving His human characteristics from the human nature, His divine characteristics from the divine nature. (From an exposition of John 14:16 in 1537–38.)]

The Communication of Attributes. Indeed, everything Scripture says of Christ it expresses in such a way that it embraces the entire Person, as if both, God and man, were one Being (*Wesen*); and it often so interchanges the words that both are attributed to each nature because of the personal union. This they call *communicationem idiomatum* (communication of attributes). Thus one may say: The man Christ is God's eternal son, through whom all creatures were created, and Lord of heaven and earth. On the other hand, this, too, may be said: Christ, God's Son (that is, the Person who is true God), was conceived and born by the Virgin Mary, suffered under Pontius Pilate, was crucified, and died. Again, God's Son sits at the table with publicans and sinners, washes the feet of His disciples. This He does not do according to the divine nature; but because the same Person does this, we correctly say that God's Son does it. Thus St. Paul says: "Had they known it, they would not have crucified the Lord of Glory" (1 Cor 2:8); and Christ Himself says: "What and if ye shall see the Son of Man ascend up where He was before?" (Jn 6:62). This is properly said of the divine nature, which was with the Father from eternity; and yet it is also said of the Person who is true man.

[In one (June 1538) of his many expositions of John 3:16 Luther points out that we may, therefore, justly consider Mary the mother of God and God the Son of Mary.]

Christ Is the Son Both of God and of Mary. The Fathers have said that we must ascribe and credit the attributes of both natures to the entire Person of Christ *in concreto* (in the concrete, as He actually exists) and have recognized a *communicationem idiomatum,* a common possession, according to which the attributes of one nature are communicated to the other nature. For each nature has its own characteristics. For instance, an attribute of the human nature is that Christ should be born of the virgin Mary, yet the divine nature has other attributes. But since we are not to divide the Person, a common possession is formed, so that we say: The Child Christ, lying in the manger and nursing at the breasts of Mary the virgin, has created heaven and earth. Again, God's Son, who from eternity is with the Father, hangs on His mother's breast, is crucified, and dies. *Nam communicatio naturarum adducit etiam communicationem idiomatum* (for the communication of natures also brings on a communica-

tion of attributes). The ancient fathers diligently taught and wrote about this matter.

Divine Attributes Communicated to the Human Nature of Christ. Christ is a man who in a supernatural manner is one Person with God. Aside from this man there is no God. It must follow that this Person is, and in a supernatural manner can be, present wherever God is; and everything is filled with Christ, through and through, also according to his humanity; not according to the first, bodily, comprehensible manner (of being present) but according to the supernatural, divine manner. . . . If you were to point to a place where God is present, but not the man Christ, the Person would already be separated, because in that case I could truly say: Here is God who is not man nor ever became man. But I want no such God! (*Mir aber des Gottes nicht!*). . . . This would leave me a poor sort of Christ, a Christ who could not be a divine and a human Person at the same time at more than one place and must at all other places be only a separated God and a divine Person, without His humanity. No, my friend, where you put down God for me, you must also put down humanity for me. They allow no separation or divorce. They have become one Person; and this Person does not separate His humanity from Himself, as Master Henry does his coat when he takes it off and lays it aside on going to bed.

[This accession of power makes it more than possible for the human nature of our Lord to be present everywhere in the strength of these communicated attributes. Therefore Christ, even according to His human nature, is not locally circumscribed.]

Communicated Omnipresence of

Christ's Human Nature. Christ is outside space (*extra locum*). This I say in opposition to those who confine Christ to one place when in fact He is present everywhere (*ubique sit*). For the Word of God is not separated from the flesh: where God is, there the flesh of Christ is; but God is everywhere, therefore Christ also is everywhere.

[It appears, then, that Luther believed that the Bible clearly teaches various modes of presence so far as the God-man Christ is concerned. He discusses this matter at some length in his writing on the Lord's Supper (1528), to which we referred above.]

Various Modes of the Presence of Christ. The one body of Christ has a threefold manner, or all three manners, of being present at a place. First, the comprehensible, bodily manner. This He used when He went about bodily on earth, when, according to His size, He occupied and vacated space. This manner He can still use whenever He pleases, as He did after the resurrection and will do on the Last Day, as Paul says (1 Tim 6:15): "Which [Christ] in His time He [God the Father] shall show who is the blessed and only Potentate," and (Col 3:4): "When Christ, who is our Life, shall appear," etc. In this manner He is not in God or with the Father, neither in heaven, as the mad spirits dream; for God is not a bodily space or place. And to this manner of being present refer the passages about Christ's leaving the world and going to the Father, which the "enthusiasters" (*die Geistler*) quote.

Secondly, there is the incomprehensible, spiritual manner of being present. According to this, He neither occupies nor vacates space but penetrates all creatures, wherever He pleases, just as, to offer a crude illustration, my sight penetrates and is in air, light, or water and does not occupy or vacate space; as a sound or tone penetrates and is in air, water, board, or wall and also does not occupy or vacate space; again, as light and heat penetrate and are in air, water, glass, crystal, and the like, and also do not occupy space. Many similar illustrations could be presented. This manner He used when He left the closed sepulcher and when He came to His disciples through closed doors, when He is present in the bread and wine in the Lord's Supper and also, as people believe, when He was born of His mother.

Thirdly, there is the divine, heavenly manner. Since He is one Person with God, all creatures must, of course, be far more penetrable and present to Him according to this manner of being present than according to the second manner. For if, according to this second manner, He can be in and with creatures in such a way that they do not feel, touch, circumscribe, or comprehend Him, how much more marvelously will He be in all creatures according to this sublime third manner of presence, so that they do not circumscribe nor comprehend Him, but that He rather has them present before Him, circumscribes and comprehends them. For you must place this Being of Christ, who is one with God, far, very far indeed, outside the creatures — as far as God is outside them; again, as deeply into, and as near to, all creatures as God is within them. For He is inseparably one Person with God. Where God is, He, too, must be, or our faith is false.

II. ULRICH ZWINGLI*

On the Lord's Supper[17]

* Ulrich Zwingli (1484–1531), Swiss Reformer, was ordained priest in 1506 and devoted his time to various humanistic studies. From 1519 onwards this devout disciple of Luther championed the main tenets of Reform Theology.

For note well, good Christian, that in Christ there are two different natures, the divine and the human: and yet the two are only the one Christ.

According to his divine nature Christ never left the right hand of the Father, for he is one God with the Father, and that is why he says: "I and the Father are one" (Jn 10), and again, "No man hath ascended up to heaven: but the Son of man which is in heaven" (Jn 3). According to his divine nature he did not need to ascend up to heaven: for he is omnipresent. Even where two or three gather together in his name, he is there in the midst (Mt 18). Again, according to his nature he is always at the right hand of the Father, for he says that he is in heaven even when in the body he is upon earth (Jn 3). That was possible only according to his divine nature. The other nature is Christ's human nature. For our sakes he took this upon him in the pure body of Mary by the receiving and fructifying of the Holy Spirit, and he carried it truly in this present time. According to this nature he increased and grew both in wisdom and stature. According to it he suffered hunger and thirst and cold and heat and all other infirmities, sin only excepted. According to it he was lifted up on the cross, and with it he ascended up into heaven. This nature was a guest in heaven, for no flesh had ever previously ascended up into it. Therefore when we read in Mark 16 that Christ was received up into heaven and sat on the right hand of God we have to refer this to his human nature, for according to his divine nature he is eternally omnipresent, etc. But the saying in Matthew 28: "Lo, I am with you alway, even unto the end of the world," can refer only to his divine nature, for it is according to that nature that he is everywhere present to believers with his special gifts and comfort. If without distinction we were to apply to his human nature everything that refers to the divine, and conversely, if without distinction we were to apply to the divine nature everything that refers to the human, we should overthrow all Scripture and indeed the whole of our faith. For what can we make of a saying like: "My God, my God, why hast thou forsaken me?" if we try to refer it to his divine nature? And the same is true of countless other Scriptures, although I know that by virtue of the fact that the two natures are one Christ, things which are said of only one nature are often ascribed to the other. Nevertheless, the proper character of each nature must be left intact and we ought to refer to it only those things which are proper to it. For instance, it is often said that God suffered on our behalf. This saying is tolerated by Christians and I myself

---

[17] *Zwingli and Bullinger* (Philadelphia: Westminster Press, 1953), pp. 213–214.

do not object to it: not that the God-head can suffer, but because he who suffered according to his human nature is very God as well as very man. Yet strictly speaking, the suffering appertains only to the humanity. Similarly the Ascension can be ascribed properly only to his humanity. And do not make of this a matter for jest, for according to his divine nature he no more needed to ascend up into heaven than he was capable of suffering, for John says in John 1: "The only begotten Son, which is in the bosom of the Father" — and yet in the flesh he was at that time on the earth and not at the right hand of the Father. Therefore in respect of his divine nature he did not need to ascend up into heaven, although we are not at fault but speak quite rightly if we say: The Son of God ascended up into heaven, for he who ascended up is God. Strictly speaking, however, the Ascension is proper only to his human nature. Let the ordinary reader hold fast to that truth and not puff himself up with mischievous subtleties, for much contention has arisen in relation to this question and it all comes back ultimately to what I have briefly set out concerning the two natures.

Hence the content of the two groups of texts must not be confused. That which is said concerning the Ascension must be referred specifically to the human nature, as, for example, in Mark 16: "He was received up into heaven, and sat on the right hand of God." And that which is proper to his divine nature must be referred specifically to that nature, as for example, his omnipresence, his abiding fellowship with us, his presence in all our hearts, and that all things consist in him, etc. In our reading of the Scripture this distinction must always be made. But if Christ is now seated at the right hand of God, and will sit there until he comes at the last day, how can he be literally eaten in the sacrament? You say: He is God. He can be everywhere. But note with what circumspection you say this. First you say: He is God. You give it to be understood that it is the property of God to be everywhere. But it is not the property of the body. I will elucidate. In John 16 Christ says: "I came forth from the Father, and am come into the world: again, I leave the world, and go to the Father." Note that these words contradict his saying: "Lo, I am with you always, even unto the end of the world," for here he says: "Again, I leave the world." How then does he leave the world? with his divine presence and protection and grace and goodness and loving kindness? God forbid: it is not for any creature to say that. But necessarily he has left us, for he said so himself, and he cannot lie. It follows then, that he has departed from us at any rate in the body, he has left us in the body. And there is nothing singular in that, for in Matthew 26 he said even more plainly: "Ye have the poor always with you; but me ye have not always." Now if the saying: "Lo, I am with you always, even unto the end of the world," refers to the body of Christ, it follows that he is with us in the body, but not with divine grace and power, for he said: "Me ye have not always." But that saying is incredible and misleading if we refer it to his divine nature. Therefore we have conclusive proof that the two sayings: "Again, I leave the world," and: "Me ye have not always," both refer to the departure and absence of his human nature. But if he has gone away, if he has left the world, if he is no longer with us, then either the Creed is unfaithful to the words of Christ, which is impossible, or else the body and blood of Christ cannot be present in the sacrament. The flesh may fume, but the words of Christ stand firm: he sits at the right hand of the Father, he has left the world, he is no longer present with us. And if these words are true, it is impossible to maintain that his flesh and blood are present in the sacrament.

An Exposition of the Faith[18]

We believe and teach that this Son of God, who is God, so took to himself the nature of man that his divine nature was not destroyed or changed into that of a man: but that each nature is present truly, properly and naturally: his divine nature has not in any way been diminished so as not to be truly, properly and naturally God. Nor has his human nature passed into the divine so that he is not truly, properly and naturally man, except insofar as he is without the propensity to sin. According to his divine nature, in every respect he is God with the Father and the Holy Spirit, not forfeiting any of the divine attributes by the assumption of human weakness. And according to his human nature he is in every way man, having all the properties which belong to the true and proper nature of man save only the propensity of sin, and not lacking any of them by reason of union with the divine nature.

Hence the attitudes and properties of both natures are reflected in all his works, so that the pious mind is able to see without difficulty which is to be accredited to each, although everything is rightly ascribed to the one Christ. It is quite correct to say that Christ hungered, for he is both God and man: yet he did not hunger according to his divine nature. It is quite correct to say that Christ healed all manner of sickness and all manner of disease: yet if you consider it more closely, this is something which concerns the divine power and not the human. But the difference of natures does not involve a division of the person any more than when we say that a man thinks and yet also sleeps. For although the power of thought belongs only to the mind and the need of sleep to the body, yet the man does not consist of two persons, but one. For the unity of the person continues in spite of the diversity of the natures.

And everywhere we confess that God and Man are one Christ, just as man subsists of a reasonable soul and an earthly body, as St. Athanasius taught. But Christ assumed the nature of man into the hypostasis or person of the Son of God. It is not as though the humanity taken by him was one person and his eternal deity another, but the person of the eternal Son of God assumed humanity in and by its own power, as holy men of God have truly and clearly shown.

We believe that this human nature was received when the Holy Spirit quickened the Virgin, being manifested without any violation of her virginity, that the redeemer and healer of souls might be born into the world of a virgin-mother, he who from all eternity was Lord and God begotten

[18] *Ibid.*, pp. 252–253.

of the Father without mother, to be a holy and spotless sacrifice, to whom the smoke of beast-laden altars ascended in vain. And on his account men should cease from offering up beasts and be moved to offer spiritual sacrifices, seeing that God has himself prepared and offered up for them the sacrifice of his own Son.

We believe that Christ suffered, being nailed to the cross under Pilate the governor. But it was only the man who felt the pangs of suffering, and not God, for God is invisible, and therefore is not subject to any pain, that is, suffering or passion. The cry of pain is this: "My God, my God, why hast thou forsaken me?" But, "Forgive them, for they know not what they do," that is the voice of inviolable deity. To make atonement for our sins he suffered the most ignominious form of execution, so that there is no humiliation which he has not experienced and borne.

If he had not died and been buried, who would believe that he is very Man? And for the same reason the apostolic Fathers added to the Creed the words, "He descended into hell." They used this expression periphrastically, to signify the reality of his death — for to be numbered amongst those who have descended into hell means to have died — and also to make it clear that the power of his atonement penetrates even to the underworld. This is confirmed by St.

Peter when he says that the Gospel was preached to the dead, that is, to those in Hades who from the beginning of the world had believed the divine warnings, like Noah, even when the wicked had despised them. On the other hand, if he had not risen again to newness of life, who would have believed that he is very God, having been put to death and being without life or power? Therefore we believe that according to his human nature the very Son of God truly died to give us assurance of the expiation of our sins. But we also believe that he truly rose again from the dead, to give us the assurance of eternal life. For all that Christ is is ours and all that he does is ours. For God so loved the world that he gave his only begotten Son that he might give us life. If he rose again, he rose again for us, thereby initiating our resurrection. Hence Paul describes him as the first-fruits of them that slept, that is, of the dead. For if he lives who was dead, he makes it plain that we shall live though we die. In Hebrew the word "to rise again" strictly means "to remain," "continue," or "endure." Therefore Paul's argument has a double bearing. Even when he was thought to be dead Christ rose again, that is, he lived, and again assumed his body. And if that is the case, then undoubtedly there is a resurrection of the dead.

III. JOHN CALVIN*

Institutes of the Christian Religion[19]

---

* John Calvin (1509–1564), French Reformer, abandoned early intentions of ordination and devoted himself to the study of law. In 1533 he underwent a mystical experience which led him to believe that it was his manifest mission to restore the Church to its primitive purity. He became a preacher and professor of theology at Geneva. Later he established a theocratic city-state at Geneva. His *Institutes*, published first in 1536 and periodically revised, contains his theological doctrine. Basically his teachings followed Luther, to which he added doctrines on the infallible efficacy of grace and his position on absolute predestination.

---

1. *Proof of Christ's true manhood*: The divinity of Christ has been proved elsewhere by clear and firm testimonies. Hence, unless I am mistaken, it would be superfluous to discuss it again here. It remains, then, for us to see how, clothed with our flesh, he fulfilled the office of Mediator. Indeed, the genuineness of his human nature was impugned long ago by both the Manichees and the Marcionites. The Marcionites fancied Christ's body a mere appearance, while the Manichees dreamed that he was endowed with heavenly flesh. But many strong testimonies of Scripture stand against both. For the blessing is promised neither in heavenly seed nor in a phantom of a man, but in the seed of Abraham and Jacob [Gen 12:3; 17:2, 7; 18:18; 22:18; 26:4]. Nor is an eternal throne promised to a man of air, but to the Son of David and the fruit of his loins [Ps 45:6; 132:11]. Hence, when he was manifested in the flesh, he was called "the Son of David and of Abraham" [Mt 1:1]. This is not only because he was born of the virgin's womb, although created in the air, but because, according to Paul's interpretation, he "was made of the seed of David ac-

[19] *Calvin's Institutes* (Philadelphia: Westminster Press, 1960), pp. 475–479.

cording to the flesh" [Rom 1:3 p.]. Similarly, the same apostle in another passage teaches that he descended from the Jews [Rom 9:5]. For this reason the Lord himself, not content with the name "man," frequently calls himself also "Son of man," meaning thereby to explain more clearly that he is a man truly begotten of human seed. Since the Holy Spirit has often declared this plain fact by many instruments and with very great diligence and simplicity, who would have supposed that any would be so shameless as to dare besmirch it with deceptions? Yet we have other testimonies ready at hand, if we should want to amass more of them. One of these is Paul's statement: "God sent forth his Son, born of woman" [Gal 4:4]. And there are innumerable other evidences that show him to have been subject to hunger, thirst, cold, and other infirmities of our nature. From these numerous testimonies we must choose those particular ones which serve to edify our minds in true confidence. Such are these: when it is said that he did not so concern himself with angels [Heb 2:16] as to take their nature, but took ours, that "in flesh and blood . . . he might through death destroy him who had the power of death" [Heb 2:14]. Another: we are reckoned his brethren by the benefit of association with him [Cf. Heb 2:11]. Again: "He had to be made like his brethren . . . so that he might be a merciful and faithful intercessor" [Heb 2:17 f.] "We have not a high priest who is unable to sympathize with our infirmities" [Heb 4:15]. And like passages. What we touched on a little while ago pertains to this same point: the sins of the world had to be expiated in our flesh, as Paul clearly declares [Rom 8:3]. Surely, for this reason, whatever the Father bestowed upon Christ pertains to us because he is the Head "from whom the whole body, knit together through joints," grows into one [Eph 4:16]. Yes, otherwise this statement will not fit. "The Spirit was given to him [Christ] without measure" [Jn 3:34 f.] so that "we should all receive from his fullness" [Jn 1:16 f.]. Nothing is more absurd than that God should be enriched in his essence by some accidental gift! For this reason, also, Christ himself says in another place, "For their sake I sanctify myself" [Jn 17:19].

2. *Against the opponents of Christ's true manhood*

They grossly distort the passages that they put forward to confirm their error. And they accomplish nothing with the trifling subtleties by which they try to do away with what I have already adduced. Marcion imagines that Christ put on a phantasm instead of a body because Paul elsewhere says that Christ was "made in the likeness of man, . . . being found in fashion as a man" [Phil 2:7–8, KJV/RV]. But he wholly overlooks Paul's intention there: Paul does not mean to teach what sort of body Christ assumes. Rather, although Christ could justly have shown forth his divinity, he manifested himself as but a lowly and despised man. For, to exhort us to submission by his example, he showed that although he was God and could have set forth his glory directly to the world he gave up his right and voluntarily "emptied himself." He took the image of a servant, and content with such lowness, allowed his divinity to be hidden by a "veil of flesh" [cf. Phil 2:5–7]. Here Paul is really teaching not what Christ was, but how he conducted himself. From the whole context we may easily infer that Christ emptied himself in a nature truly human. For what does "being found in fashion as a man" mean [Phil 2:8], save that for a time the divine glory did not shine, but only human likeness was manifest in a lowly and abased condition. Peter's statement that "Christ was put to death in the flesh, but made alive in the spirit" [1 Pet 3:18 f.] would not otherwise make sense unless the Son of God in human nature had been weak. Paul explains this more clearly, declaring that Christ suffered according to the infirmity of the flesh [2 Cor 13:4]. Christ is expressly said to have obtained new glory after he had humbled himself. Herein lies his exaltation. This could not very well apply except to a man endowed with human body and soul.

Mani forged him a body of air, because Christ is called "the Second Adam of heaven, heavenly" [1 Cor 15:47]. But in this passage the apostle is introducing no heavenly essence of Christ's body, but a spiritual force that, poured out by Christ, quickens us. Now, as we have seen, Peter and Paul separate that force from Christ's flesh. Rather, the doctrine concerning Christ's flesh that flourishes among the orthodox is remarkably buttressed by this passage. For unless Christ had one bodily nature with us, the reasoning that Paul pursues with such vehemence would be meaningless: "If Christ arose, we also shall arise from the dead; if we do not arise, neither did Christ arise" [1 Cor 15:12–20]. Whatever the subtleties with which the ancient Manichees or their modern disciples try to evade [this proof], they do not succeed.

Their nonsense, that Christ is called "Son of Man" insofar as he was promised to men,[20] is a base evasion. For it is plain that in Hebrew idiom true man is called "son of man." Now, Christ undoubtedly retained this phrase of his own language. Also, the commonly accepted understanding of "Son of Adam" ought to be beyond controversy. Not to go too far afield, the Eighth Psalm, which the apostles apply to Christ, will amply suffice: "What is man that thou art mindful of him, and the son of man that thou visitest him?" [Ps 8:4; Heb 2:6]. Christ's true humanity is expressed by this figure. For even though he was not immediately begotten of a mortal father, his origin derived from Adam. Otherwise the passage that I have already cited would not stand: "Christ shared in flesh and blood" that he might gather his children unto himself to obey God [Heb 2:14]. In these words Christ is clearly declared to be comrade and partner in the same nature with us. In this sense he also says that "the Author of sanctification and those who are sanctified have all one origin" [Heb 2:11]. The context shows that this expression refers to the fellowship of nature, for he immediately adds: "That is why he is not ashamed to call them brethren" [Heb 2:11]. For if he had previously said that believers are of God, in such

great dignity what reason would there have been for shame? But because Christ of his boundless grace joins himself to base and ignoble men, it is said that "he is not ashamed" [Heb 2:11]. Moreover, baseless is their objection that in this way the impious would be Christ's brethren. For we know that the children of God are not born of flesh and blood [cf. Jn 1:13] but of the Spirit through faith. Hence flesh alone does not make the bond of brotherhood. Even though the apostle assigns to believers alone the honor of being one with Christ, it does not follow that unbelievers cannot be born of the same source. For example, when we say that Christ was made man that he might make us children of God, this expression does not extend to all men. For faith intervenes, to engraft us spiritually into the body of Christ.

They also bunglingly stir up contention over the expression "first-born." They allege that Christ should have been born of Adam at the very beginning, to "be the first-born among the brethren" [Rom 8:29]. "First-born" here refers not to age but to degree of honor and loftiness of power!

Even less plausible is their babbling that Christ assumed human, not angelic, nature [Heb 2:16], meaning that he received humankind into grace. To enhance the honor that Christ deigned to give us, Paul compares us with the angels, to whom in this respect we were preferred. If we carefully weigh Moses' testimony — where he says that the seed of the woman will crush the serpent's head [Gen 3:15] — the controversy will be completely resolved. For the statement there concerns not only Christ but the whole of mankind. Since we must acquire victory through Christ, God

---

[20] Cf. Augustine, *Against Faustus*, ii, 4; v. 4 (MPL 42, 211, 222).

declares in general terms that the woman's offspring is to prevail over the devil. Hence it follows that Christ was begotten of mankind, for in addressing Eve it was God's intention to raise her hope that she should not be overwhelmed with despair.

3. Christ's descent through the Virgin Mary: an absurdity exposed

Our opponents both foolishly and wickedly entangle in allegories those testimonies wherein Christ is called the seed of Abraham and the fruit of David's loins. For if the term "seed" had been allegorically intended, Paul surely would not have remained silent about this when he affirmed, clearly and unfiguratively, that there are not many redeemers among the children of Abraham, but only one, Christ [Gal 3:16]. Of the same stuff is their pretense that Christ was called "son of David" only because he had been promised and at last was revealed in his own time [Rom 1:3]. For when Paul named him "Son of David," and then immediately added "according to the flesh," he surely designates his human nature by this. Thus in the ninth chapter, after calling Christ "blessed God," he asserts separately that he descended from the Jews "according to the flesh" [Rom 9:5]. Now, if he had not truly been begotten of the seed of David, what will be the point of this expression that he is "the fruit of her womb" [cf. Lk 1:42]? What is this promise, "From your loins will descend one who will remain upon your throne" [cf. Ps 132:11; also 2 Sam 7:12; Acts 2:30]?

Now they sophistically disport themselves over Matthew's version of the geneology of Christ. Matthew does not list Mary's ancestors, but Joseph's [Mt 1:16]. Still, because he is mentioning something well known at the time, he considers it sufficient to show that Joseph sprang from the seed of David, since it was clear enough that Mary came from the same family. Luke emphasizes this even more, teaching that the salvation provided by Christ is common to all mankind. For Christ, the Author of salvation, was begotten of Adam, the common father of us all [Lk 3:38]. I admit that one can gather from the geneology that Christ was the son of David solely insofar as he was begotten of the virgin. But in order to disguise their error — to prove that Christ took his body out of nothing — the new Marcionites too haughtily contend that women are "without seed." Thus they overturn the principles of nature.

But this is not a theological issue, and such is the futility of the reasons they bring forward that these can be refuted without trouble. Accordingly, I shall not touch upon matters that belong to philosophy and medicine. It will be enough to refute the objections that they derive from Scripture, namely: Aaron and Jehoiada took wives from the tribes of Judah [Ex 6:23; 2 Chr 22:11], and so the distinction of tribes would then have been confused if women possessed the seed of generation. But it is sufficiently well known that descent is reckoned by the male line as far as the political order is concerned; yet this preferential position of the male sex does not gainsay the fact that the woman's seed must share in the act of generation.

CHAPTER 6. MODERN DEVELOPMENTS IN PROTESTANT THOUGHT

INTRODUCTION

The Image of Christ in Non-Catholic Theology[1]

by Karl Adam

In its attempts to grasp Christ's essence more deeply, Catholic theology had looked for guidance to the faith and doctrine of the Church. At first Protestant theology took over this image of the Christ of faith, but ever since the Enlightenment of the eighteenth century, it has fallen victim to the far-reaching and destructive analytical tendency of rationalistic thinking. These rationalistic circles sought many ways to tear the belief in the divinity of Jesus out of the Christian creed. Some would have Christ be the ideal man; for others, his

[1] K. Adam, *The Christ of Faith* (London: Burns, Oates, 1957; New York: Pantheon, 1957), pp. 45–49 *passim.*

figure vanished completely into myth. The question whether Christ was in truth God's Son was no longer asked; the only important thing was to explain how this (impossible) faith could have arisen in the Christian communities. In particular they attempted to find a solution to the eschatological problem raised by certain statements of Jesus. But they no longer looked for it in the tension of the relationship between the human and divine nature in Jesus, and in his peculiar consciousness that he was the Messias. They sought their solution in contemporary errors, to which he too was bound, or in the arguments of modern Existentialism, which in reality make of Christ's message an empty thing.

The questions posed by modern non-Catholic theology are based on the rationalistic assumption that the divinity of the Lord, the figure of God made man, is *a priori* impossible and therefore unhistorical, because it contradicts every comparison with experience and destroys the sequence of cause and effect — new, disrupting, miraculous. So the question as to whether Christ was God could from the start never be an object of historical investigation. It belongs, they would maintain, rather to the realm of subjective belief. The only genuine object of scholarly probing was to *explain* historically how the belief in Christ's divinity came to be held among men. What are the historical roots of the belief in Christ?

It was D. F. Strauss who, influenced by Hegel and following Reimarus, the author of the Wolfenbüttel fragments, contested the tenet that the Christ of faith was the Jesus of history. In his *Leben Jesu* (1835) he took great pains to prove the Christ of faith to be a product of myth fashioned by the credulous. This axe was laid at the root. From now on the true Christological problem was: How is the belief in Christ to be historically explained? Is it possible to accept unquestioningly the testimonies of Paul and John and the Synoptic Gospels as sober historical documents? Or are these testimonies themselves already secondary, produced by the faith of the community, and not original historical truth? In the crude light of this most radical of questions, the questions of the Monarchians, Arians, Apollinarians, Nestorians, Monophysites, Monotheletists, and the rest seem tame and harmless.

THE IMAGE OF CHRIST OF THE MYTHOLOGICAL SCHOOL

Three judgments on Jesus derive from Strauss. The first is represented by the mythological school. It is inspired by certain fundamental ideas of Hegel, according to which the seminal creative force in history is not historical personalities but ideas. So Christianity too arose not from the act of a single personality but under the impetus of ideas, be they religious or literary, economic, political, or social. These ideas embodied themselves in myth. Thus the Christian faith can be explained without reference to Christ. Christianity is an anonymous movement. Even then Bruno Bauer, at that time a lecturer at Bonn University, called this kind of Gospel criticism of Strauss' reactionary and apologetic. He himself described the oldest portrayal of Christ as a free literary creation from the pen of the first Evangelist Mark. So in the last analysis, Christianity was a literary production. Its existence had been brought about by ideas that had been spread abroad solely by means of literature. Certain ideals, such as love of mankind, equality and fraternity, which at that time had been put forward by individual Platonic, Neo-Platonic, and in particular Stoic writers, had gradually merged to form a movement among the people, and found their expression in Christianity. Kalthoff, of Bremen, regarded the entire content of the Gospels merely as the personification of such collective social ideals. It was the social distress of the dying ancient world that found liberating expression in the figure of him who was killed on the cross and yet rose again the third day. This was also related to Nietzsche's conception that Christianity was in essentials a movement of resentment on the part of the repressed plebeian instinct of the mass to assert itself against the high heroic instincts of the superman.

THE IMAGE OF CHRIST OF THE LIBERAL SCHOOL

The second trend proceeding from Strauss is the so-called liberal study of Jesus. In contrast to Hegel, it emphasizes that history is made not by ideas but by personalities. So for them the major factor in explaining Christianity is the personality of Jesus. But they are disposed to think that the personality of Jesus must submit to being grasped with the means of historical method — i.e., the tools of secular history, a thorough analysis of sources, and the laws of correlation and analogy. They hold that those things in Jesus that go beyond similar historical situations and parallels, and transcend historical correlation — i.e., demonstrably go beyond the historical chain of cause and effect — are unhistorical and must be removed from the picture. The liberal school aims on principle at proving everything that is mysterious and supernatural in the life of our Lord to be unhistorical, and merely the product of the faith of the community — what they call the dogma of the community. . . .

THE IMAGE OF CHRIST OF THE ESCHATOLOGICAL SCHOOL

The third trend proceeding from Strauss, which we know as the eschatological school, rejects both the mythological and the liberal trends in the study of Christ. It rightly perceives in them a dogmatic *a priori*, a compulsion based upon unproven assumptions, which has made their criticism the slave of an ideology. So, independent of these schools, it sets out once again to cull the image of our Lord quite factually from the sources. The eschatological school regards itself as the sole critical historical school. Among its adherents are numbered, *inter alia*, W. Bousset, Albert Schweitzer, J. Wellhausen, R. Bultmann, and M. Werner. With the help of a thorny textual criticism, they attempt to lay the original stones bare, and free them from all the secondary and tertiary strata. But indeed, pathetically little turns up by way of original stones.

THE IMAGE OF CHRIST OF THE DIALECTICAL SCHOOL

Even this image of Christ could not be upheld in historical criticism as soon as it became clear that these eschatological texts were not at the center, but rather on the periphery, of Jesus' teaching, and that Jesus had striven to realize the kingdom of God in the present rather than intended that it should come about in the future.

All these images of Christ were withdrawn from circulation almost overnight, and replaced by the so-called "dialectic" theology of Karl Barth, Emil Brunner, Gogarten, and others. They follow the reformers, especially Calvin, in confirming anew the divine in Christianity, the absoluteness of its manifestation, in face of all the humanized versions of the liberals, tailored to meet the taste of the time. With incomparable passion, Barth in particular has condemned the modern ideological Jesus. His school seems to have reconquered the theological field. However, the school itself can hardly be regarded as a unity. On the one hand Karl Barth and Emil

Brunner have drawn ever nearer to the traditional image of Christ. But on the other hand Rudolf Bultmann has combined his attempt to rehabilitate Christian teaching with a radical rejection of all those events in the life of Jesus that imply the break-through of transcendence into this world; he denies the incarnation, Christ's miracles, his expiatory death, his resurrection and second coming at the Last Judgment, and so on and so forth. He is of the opinion that only by stripping the Christian message bare of all traces of myth can it be salvaged to have any significance for modern man; for Bultmann the essence of the Christian faith lies in man's realization, as he apprehends the teaching of Christ, of his complete surrender to the world of the senses; by accepting the message of Christ's death and resurrection, man succeeds in conquering the world and redeeming himself. In spite of Bultmann's protestations to the contrary, his doctrine has abandoned Christ's teaching, which is centered precisely on the supernatural events of his life. Revelation becomes a mere philosophy of religion, which has its roots in Kierkegaard and in Heidegger's Existentialism. On the one hand Bultmann agrees with Barth in seeing in the faith in the cross the miracle of forgiveness wrought by divine Grace. But on the other hand it is equally clear that his systematic contestation of the possibility of a scholarly foundation for Christianity carries the line of liberal critical theology to its very end.

I.   FRIEDRICH SCHLEIERMACHER*

The Existence of God in Christ[2]

---

* Friedrich Schleiermacher (1768–1834), German theologian, was a reformed preacher in Berlin whose early writings showed influences of Spinoza, Leibniz, and Kant. In his *Religion, Speeches to its Cultured Despisers* (1799), he attempts to make religion palatable to the estranged educated class, defining religion as "a sense and taste for the infinite." Not dogma, but feeling and intuition are the basis of religion. The basic fact of human experience, man's feeling of absolute dependence, has brought about the many different religions of mankind. Christian monotheism is the most perfect of these, though not necessarily the only true one. For Schleiermacher the consciousness of God and man's total dependence upon him was realized to the highest degree and most typically in Jesus Christ, so that we can truly speak of "God's being in him." In Christ supernatural revelation has reached its highest level.

That the Redeemer should be entirely free from all sinfulness is no objection at all to the complete identity of human nature in Him and others, for we have already laid down that sin is so little an essential part of the being of man that we can never regard it as anything else than a disturbance of nature.

1. It follows that the possibility of a sinless development is in itself not incongruous with the idea of human nature; indeed, this possibility is involved, and recognized, in the consciousness of sin as guilt, as that is universally understood. This likeness, however, is to be

[2] *The Christian Faith* (Edinburgh: T. & T. Clark, 1960), pp. 385–395.

understood in such a general sense that even the first man before the first sin stood no nearer the Redeemer, and was like Him in no higher sense, than all other men. For if even in the life of the first man we must assume a time when sin had not yet appeared, yet every first appearance of sin leads back to a sinful preparation. But the Redeemer too shared in the same vicissitudes of life, without which we can hardly imagine the entrance of sin at a definite moment even in Adam, for they are essential to human nature. Furthermore, the first man was originally free from all the contagious influences of a sinful society, while the Redeemer had to enter into the corporate life when it had already advanced far in deterioration, so that it would hardly be possible to attribute His sinlessness to external protection — which we certainly must somehow admit in the case of the first man, if we would not involve ourselves in contradictions. Of the Redeemer, on the contrary, we must hold that the ground of His sinlessness was not external to Himself, but that it was a sinlessness essentially grounded in Himself, if He was to take away, through what he was in Himself, the sinfulness of the corporate life. Therefore, so far as sin is concerned, Christ differs no less from the first man than from all others.

The identity of human nature further involves this, that the manner in which Christ differs from all others also has its place in this identity. This would not be the case if it were not involved in human nature that individuals, so far as the measure of the different functions is concerned, are originally different from each other, so that to every separate corporate life (regarded in space as well as in time)

there belong those who are more and less gifted; and we only arrive at the truth of life when we thus correlate those who differ from each other. In the same way, therefore, all those who in any respect give character to an age or a district are bound up with those over whom (as being defective in that particular respect) they extend an educative influence, even as Christ is bound up with those whom His preponderatingly powerful God-consciousness links to the corporate life thus indicated. The greater the difference, and the more specific the activity, the more must these also have established themselves against the hindering influences of a worthless environment, and they can be understood only by reference to this self-differentiating quality of human nature, not by reference to the group in which they stand; although by divine right they belong to it, as the Redeemer does to the whole race.

2. But in admitting that what is peculiar in the Redeemer's kind of activity belongs to a general aspect of human nature, we by no means wish to reduce this activity, and the personal dignity by which it is conditioned, to the same measure as that of others. The simple fact that faith in Christ postulates a relation on His part to the whole race, while everything analogous is valid only for definite individual times and places, is sufficient to prove this. For no one has yet succeeded, in any sphere of science or art, and no one will ever succeed, in establishing himself as head, universally animating and sufficient for the whole human race.

For this peculiar dignity of Christ, however, in the sense in which we have already referred back to the ideality of His person to this spiritual

function of the God-consciousness im-
planted in the self-consciousness, the
terms of our proposition alone are adequate; for to ascribe to Christ an absolutely powerful God-consciousness,
and to attribute to Him an existence
of God in Him, are exactly the same
thing. The expression "the existence
of God in anyone," can only express
the relation of the omnipresence of
God to this one. Now since God's existence can only be apprehended as
pure activity, while every individualized existence is merely an intermingling of activity and passivity — the
activity being always found appor-
tioned to this passivity in every other
individualized existence — there is, so
far, no existence of God in any individual thing, but only an existence of
God in the world. And only if the
passive conditions are not purely passive, but mediated through vital receptivity, and this receptivity con-
fronts the totality of finite existence
(so far, *i.e.*, as we can say of the individual as a living creature that, in
virtue of the universal reciprocity, it
in itself represents the world), could
we suppose an existence of God in it.
Hence this clearly does not hold of
what is individualized as an unconscious thing; for since an unconscious
thing brings no living receptivity to
meet all the forces of consciousness it
cannot represent these forces in itself.
But just as little and for the same
reason can what is conscious but not
intelligent represent them, so that it
is only in the rational individual
that an existence of God can be admitted. How far this is also true similarly and without distinction if we
regard reason as functioning in objec-
tice consciousness lies outside our investigation. But so far as the rational
self-consciousness is concerned, it is certain that the God-consciousness which
(along with the self-consciousness)
belongs to human nature originally,
before the Redeemer and apart from
all connexion with Him, cannot fit-
tingly be called an existence of God
in us, not only because it was not
a pure God-consciousness (either in
polytheism or even in Jewish monotheism, which was everywhere tinc-
tured with materialistic conceptions,
whether crude or finer), but also because, such as it was, it did not assert
itself as activity, but in these religions
was always dominated by the sensuous self-consciousness. If, then, it was
able neither to portray God purely and
with real adequacy in thought, nor
yet to exhibit itself as pure activity,
it cannot be represented as an existence of God in us. But just as the
unconscious forces of nature and non-
rational life become a revelation of
God to us only so far as we bring that
conception with us, so also that dark-
ened and imperfect God-consciousness
by itself is not an existence of God in
human nature, but only insofar as we
bring Christ with us in thought and
relate it to Him. So that originally it
is found nowhere in Him, and He is
the only "other" in which there is an
existence of God in the proper sense,
so far, that is, as we posit the God-
consciousness in His self-consciousness as continually and exclusively
determining every moment, and consequently also this perfect indwelling
of the Supreme Being as His peculiar
being and His inmost self. Indeed,
working backwards we must now say,
if it is only through Him that the human God-consciousness becomes an
existence of God in human nature, and
only through the rational nature that
the totality of finite powers can become an existence of God in the

world, that in truth He alone mediates all existence of God in the world and all revelation of God through the world, insofar as he bears within Himself the whole new creation which contains and develops the potency of the God-consciousness.

3. But if a person of this kind, He needs to have the whole human development in common with us, so that even this existence of God must in Him have had a development in time, and as the most spiritual element in His personality could only emerge into manifestation after the lower functions; yet He cannot have entered life as one for whom the foundations of sin had already been laid before His being began to be manifested. We have envisaged this earlier establishment of sin for all of us, without entering upon natural-scientific investigations into the origin of the individual life, and the coming together in us (if we may use the phrase) of soul and body, but simply by holding to the general facts of experience; so here, too, we seek to combine with these facts only the relatively supernatural, which we have already admitted in general for the entrance of the Redeemer into the world.

The origin of every human life may be regarded in a twofold manner, as issuing from the narrow circle of descent and society to which it immediately belongs, and as a fact of human nature in general. The more definitely the weaknesses of that narrow circle repeat themselves in an individual, the more valid becomes the first point of view. The more the individual by the kind and degree of his gifts transcends that circle, and the more he exhibits what is new within it, the more we are thrown back upon the other explanation. This means that the beginning of Jesus' life cannot in any way be explained by the first factor, but only and exclusively by the second; so that from the beginning He must have been free from every influence from earlier generations which disseminated sin and disturbed the inner God-consciousness, and He can only be understood as an original act of human nature, *i.e.* as an act of human nature as not affected by sin. The beginning of His life was also a new implanting of the God-consciousness which creates receptivity in human nature; hence this content and that manner of origin are in such a close relation that they mutually condition and explain each other. That new implanting came to be through the beginning of His life, and therefore that beginning must have transcended every detrimental influence of His immediate circle; and because it was such an original and sin-free act of nature, a filling of His nature with God-consciousness became possible as its result. So that upon this relation too the fullest light is thrown if we regard the beginning of the life of Jesus as the completed creation of human nature. The appearance of the first man constituted at the same time the physical life of the human race; the appearance of the Second Adam constituted for this nature a new spiritual life, which communicates and develops itself by spiritual fecundation. And as in the former its originality (which is the condition of the appearance of human nature) and its having emerged from creative divine activity are the same thing, so also in the Redeemer both are the same — His spiritual originality, set free from every prejudicial influence of natural descent, and that existence of God in Him which also proves itself creative,

If the impartation of the Spirit to human nature which was made in the first Adam was insufficient, in that the spirit remained sunk in sensuousness and barely glanced forth clearly at moments as a presentiment of something better, and if the work of creation has only been completed through the second and equally original impartation to the Second Adam, yet both events go back to one undivided eternal divine decree and form, even in a higher sense, only one and the same natural system, though one unattainable by us. . . . for how can divine and human nature be thus brought together under any single conception, as if they could both be more exact determinations, coordinated to each other, of one and the same universal? Indeed, even divine spirit and human spirit could not without confusion be brought together in this way. But the word "nature" is particularly ill-adapted for such a common use, even if we leave Latin and Greek etymology completely out of account and simply take our stand on our own use of the word. For in one sense we actually oppose God and nature to one another, and hence in this sense cannot attribute a nature to God. Nature in this sense is for us the summary of all finite existence, or, as in the opposition of nature and history, the summary of all that is corporeal, and that goes back to what is elementary, in its various and discrete phenomena, in which all that we so describe is mutually conditioned. Over against this divided and conditioned we set God as the unconditioned and the absolutely simple. But just for this reason we cannot attribute a nature to God in the other sense. For always, whether we use the word generally, as when we speak of animal and vegetable nature, or of an individual, as when we say that a person has a noble or an ignoble nature, always we use it solely of a limited existence, standing in opposition to something else, an existence in which active and passive are bound up together, and which is revealed in a variety of appearances, in the latter case of individuals, in the former of vital factors. And upon closer consideration it is hardly to be denied that this expression, if we go back to the original Greek word, bears in itself traces of heathen influence, though possibly of unconscious influence. For in polytheism, which represents the Godhead as no less split up and divided than finite existence appears to us, the word "nature" has certainly the same meaning in the expression *divine nature* as it has elsewhere. The fact ought to have been a warning, that the heathen sages themselves had already risen above imperfect representation of God, and said of Him that He was to be thought of as beyond all existence and being.

It is no better with the relation which is here set forth between nature and person. For in utter contradiction to the use elsewhere, according to which the same nature belongs to many individuals or persons, here one person is to share in two quite different natures. Now if "person" indicates a constant unity of life, but "nature" a sum of ways of action or laws, according to which conditions of life vary and are included within a fixed range, how can the unity of life coexist with the duality of natures, unless the one gives way to the other, if the one exhibits a larger and the other a narrower range, or unless they melt into each other, both systems of ways of action and laws really becoming one in the one life? — if indeed we are speaking of a person, *i.e.* of an Ego which is the same in all the consecutive moments of its existence. The attempt to make clear this unity along with the duality naturally but seldom results in anything else than a demonstration of the possibility of a formula made up by combining indications out of which it is impossible to construct a figure. On the other hand, as soon as the same writer avoids this formula of two natures, he not seldom says something which one can follow, and of which the figure can be drawn (*nachzeichnen*). Hence all the results of the endeavor to achieve a living presentation of the unity of the divine and the human in Christ, ever since it was tied down to this expression, have always vacillated between the opposite errors of mixing the two natures to form a third which would be neither of them, neither divine nor human, or of keeping the two natures separate, but either neglecting the unity of the person in order to separate the two natures more distinctly, or, in order to keep firm hold of the unity of the person, disturbing the necessary balance, and making one nature less important than the other and limited by it. The same thing comes out even in the vacillation between the expressions "connexion" and "union" — in the latter there is a tendency to wipe out the difference of the natures, while the former makes the unity of the person doubtful. The utter fruitlessness of this way of presenting the matter becomes particularly clear in

the treatment of the question whether Christ as one person formed out of two natures had also two wills according to the number of the natures, or only one according to the number of the person. For if Christ had only one will, then the divine nature is incomplete if this is a human will; and the human nature, if it is a divine will. But if Christ has two wills, then the unity of the person is no more than apparent, even if we try to conserve it by saying that the two wills always will the same thing. For what this results in is only agreement, not unity; and, in fact, to answer the problem thus is to return to the division of Christ. And one or the other will is always simply a superfluous accompaniment of the other, whether it be the divine will that accompanies the human or *vice versa*. And manifestly, as we are accustomed to take reason and will together the same question may be raised with regard to the reason; then all that has just been said repeats itself, since each nature is incomplete without the reason that belongs to it, and a unity of the person is as little compatible with such a twofold reason as with a twofold will; and it is equally unthinkable that a divine reason, which as omniscient sees everything at once, should think the same as a human reason, which only knows separate things one after the other and as a result of the other, and that a human will, which always strives only for separate ends and one for the sake of the other, should will the same as a divine will, whose object can be nothing but the whole world in the totality of its development.

II. DAVID FRIEDRICH STRAUSS*

Life of Jesus[3]

---

* D. F. Strauss (1808–1874), German theologian, was greatly influenced by Schleiermacher and the dialectical idealism of Hegel. His *Life of Jesus* was the first attempt to explain the gospel writings as "mythical" constructions. The traditional view was severely criticized, to the extent that Strauss denied that there is any real historical foundation for gospel narratives and attributed them to creative legend.

PREFACE TO THE FIRST
GERMAN EDITION

It appeared to the author of the work . . . that it was time to substitute a new mode of considering the life of Jesus, in the place of the antiquated systems of supernaturalism and naturalism. This application of the term antiquated will in the present day be more readily admitted in relation to the latter system than to the former. For while the interest excited by the explanations of the miracles and the conjectural facts of the rationalists has long ago cooled, the commentaries now most read are those which aim to adapt the supernatural interpretation of the sacred history to modern taste. Nevertheless, in point of fact, the orthodox view of this history became superannuated earlier than the rationalistic, since it was only because the former had ceased to satisfy an advanced state of culture, that the latter was developed, while the recent attempts to recover, by the aid of a mystical philosophy, the supernatural point of view held by our forefathers, betray themselves, by the exaggerating spirit in which they are conceived, to be final, desperate efforts to render the past present, the inconceivable conceivable.

The new point of view, which must take the place of the above, is the

³ *The Life of Jesus* (New York: Macmillan & Co., 1893), xxix–xxxi.

mythical. This theory is not brought to bear on the evangelical history for the first time in the present work; it has long been applied to particular parts of that history, and is here only extended to its entire tenor. It is not by any means meant that the whole history of Jesus is to be represented as mythical, but only that every part of it is to be subjected to a critical examination, to ascertain whether it have not some admixture of the mythical. The exegesis of the ancient church set out from the double presupposition: first, that the gospels contained a history, and secondly, that this history was a supernatural one. Rationalism rejected the latter of these presuppositions, but only to cling the more tenaciously to the former, maintaining that these books present unadulterated, though only natural, history. Science cannot rest satisfied with this half-measure: the other presupposition also must be relinquished, and the inquiry must first be made whether in fact, and to what extent, the ground on which we stand in the gospels is historical. This is the natural course of things, and thus far the appearance of a work like the present is not only justifiable, but even necessary.

It is certainly not therefore evident that the author is precisely the individual whose vocation it is to appear in this position. He has a very vivid consciousness that many others would have been able to execute such a work with incomparably superior erudition. Yet on the other hand he believes himself to be at least possessed of one qualification which especially fitted him to undertake this task. The majority of the most learned and acute theologians of the present day fail in the main requirement for such a work, a requirement without which no amount of learning will suffice to achieve anything in the domain of criticism — namely, the internal liberation of the feelings and intellect from certain religious and dogmatical presuppositions; and this the author early attained by means of philosophical studies. If theologians regard this absence of presupposition from his work as unchristian he regards the believing presuppositions of theirs as unscientific. Widely as in this respect the tone of the present work may be contrasted with the edifying devoutness and enthusiastic mysticism of recent books on similar subjects; still it will nowhere depart from the seriousness of science, or sink into frivolity; and it seems a just demand in return, that the judgments which are passed upon it should also confine themselves to the domain of science, and keep aloof from bigotry and fanaticism.

The author is aware that the essence of the Christian faith is perfectly independent of his criticism. The supernatural birth of Christ, his miracles, his resurrection and ascension, remain eternal truths, whatever doubts may be cast on their reality as historical facts. The certainty of this can alone give calmness and dignity to our criticism, and distinguish it from the naturalistic criticism of the last century, the design of which was, with the historical fact, to subvert also the religious truth, and which thus necessarily became frivolous. A dissertation at the close of the work will show that the dogmatic significance of the life of Jesus remains inviolate: in the meantime let the calmness and insensibility with which, in the course of it, criticism undertakes apparently dangerous operations, be explained solely by the security of the author's conviction that no injury is threatened to the Christian faith. Investigations of this kind may, however, inflict a wound on the faith of individuals. Should this be the case with theologians, they have in their science the means of healing such wounds, from which, if they would not remain behind the development of their age, they cannot possibly be exempt. For the laity the subject is certainly not adequately prepared; and for this reason the present work is so framed, that at least the unlearned among them will quickly and often perceive that the book is not destined for them. If from curiosity or excessive zeal against heresy they persist in their perusal, they will then have, as Schleiermacher says on a similar occasion, to bear the punishment in their conscience, since their feelings directly urge on them the conviction that they understand not that of which they are ambitious to speak.

A new opinion, which aims to fill the place of an older one, ought fully to adjust its position with respect to the latter. Hence the way to the mythical view is here taken in each particular point through the supernaturalistic and rationalistic opinions and their respective refutations; but, as becomes a valid refutation, with an acknowledgment of what is true in the opinions combated, and an adoption of this truth into the new theory.

III. KARL BARTH*

The Humanity of God[4]

---

* Karl Barth (1886–   ), Swiss Protestant theologian, after years of pastoral duties before and during World War I, challenged current theological notions in his *Commentary on Romans* (1919). Later in Germany he attacked Nazism openly. Barth sought to purge theology of scientific, cultural and mystical influences and return to basic principles of Reformation theology.

He so emphasized the transcendence of God that he viewed any theology grounded in human reason or experience as impossible. Barth's *Church Dogmatics* is an attempt to develop a dogmatic theology based on the Word of God, He founds all created life and reality, even political, on Christ, in whom God becomes the object of human apprehension.

Who God is and what He is in His Deity He proves and reveals not in a vacuum as a divine being-for-Himself, but precisely and authentically in the fact that He exists, speaks, and acts as the *partner* of man, though, of course, as the absolutely superior partner. He who does *that* is the living God. And the freedom in which He does *that* is His deity. It is the deity which as such also has the character of humanity. In this and only in this form was — and still is — our view of the deity of God to be set in opposition to that earlier theology. There must be positive acceptance and not unconsidered rejection of the elements of truth, which one cannot possibly deny to it even if one sees all its weaknesses. It is precisely God's *deity* which, rightly understood, includes his *humanity*.

How do we come to know that? What permits and requires this statement? It is a *Christological* statement, or rather one grounded in and to be unfolded from Christology. A second change of direction after that first one would have been superfluous had we from the beginning possessed the presence of mind to venture the whole in-

evitable counterthrow from the Christological perspective and thus from the superior and more exact standpoint of the central and entire witness of Holy Scripture. Certainly in *Jesus Christ,* as He is attested in Holy Scripture, we are not dealing with man in the abstract: not with the man who is able with his modicum of religion and religious morality to be sufficient unto himself without God and thus himself to be God. But neither are we dealing with *God* in the abstract: not with one who in His deity exists only separated from man, distant and strange and thus a non-human if not indeed an inhuman God. In Jesus Christ there is no isolation of man from God or of God from man. Rather, in Him we encounter the history, the dialogue, in which God and man meet together and are together, the reality of the covenant *mutually* contracted, preserved, and fulfilled by them. Jesus Christ is in His one Person, as true God, *man's* loyal partner, and as true *man,* God's. He is the Lord humbled for communion with man and likewise the Servant exalted to communion with God. He is the Word spoken from the loftiest, most luminous transcendence and likewise the Word heard in the deepest, darkest immanence. He

[4] *The Humanity of God* (Richmond, Va.: John Knox Press, 1960), pp. 45–51.

is both, without their being confused but also without their being divided; He is wholly the one and wholly the other. Thus in this oneness Jesus Christ is the Mediator, the Reconciler, between God and man. Thus He comes forward to *man* on behalf of *God* calling for and awakening faith, love, and hope, and to *God* on behalf of *man*, representing man, making satisfaction and interceding. Thus He attests and guarantees to man God's free *grace* and at the same time attests and guarantees to God man's free *gratitude*. Thus He establishes in His Person the justice of God vis-à-vis man and also the justice of man before God. Thus He is in His Person the covenant in its fullness, the Kingdom of heaven which is at hand, in which God speaks and man hears, God gives and man receives, God commands and man obeys, God's glory shines in the highest and thence into the depths, and peace on earth comes to pass among men in whom He is well pleased. Moreover, exactly in this way Jesus Christ, as this Mediator and Reconciler between God and man, is also the *Revealer* of them both. We do not need to engage in a free-ranging investigation to seek out and construct who and what God truly is, and who and what man truly is, but only to read the truth about both where it resides, namely, in the fullness of their togetherness, their covenant which proclaims itself in Jesus Christ.

Who and what *God* is — this is what in particular we have to learn better and with more precision in the new change of direction in the thinking and speaking of evangelical theology, which has become necessary in the light of the earlier change. But the question must be, who and what is God *in Jesus Christ*, if we here today would push forward to a better answer.

Beyond doubt God's *deity* is the first and fundamental fact that strikes us when we look at the existence of Jesus Christ as attested in the Holy Scripture. And God's deity in Jesus Christ consists in the fact that God Himself in Him is the *subject* who speaks and acts with sovereignty. *He* is the free One in whom all freedom has its ground, its meaning, its prototype. *He* is the initiator, founder, preserver, and fulfiller of the covenant. *He* is the sovereign Lord of the amazing relationship in which He becomes and is not only different from man but also one with him. *He* is also the creator of him who is His partner. *He* it is through whose faithfulness the corresponding faithfulness of His partner is awakened and takes place. The old Reformed Christology worked that out especially clearly in its doctrine of the "hypostatic union": God is on the throne. In the existence of Jesus Christ, the fact that God speaks, gives, orders, comes absolutely first — that man hears, receives, obeys, can and must only follow this first act. In Jesus Christ man's freedom is wholly enclosed in the freedom of God. Without the condescension of God there would be no exaltation of man. As the Son of God and not otherwise, Jesus Christ is the Son of Man. This sequence is irreversible. God's independence, omnipotence, and eternity, God's holiness and justice and thus God's deity, in its original and proper form, is the power leading to this effective and visible sequence in the existence of Jesus Christ: superiority preceding subordination. Thus we have here no universal deity capable of being reached conceptually, but this concrete deity — real and recognizable in the *descent* grounded in that sequence and peculiar to the existence of Jesus Christ.

But here there is something even more concrete to be seen. God's high freedom in Jesus Christ is His freedom for *love*. The divine capacity which operates and exhibits itself in that superiority and subordination is manifestly also God's capacity to bend downwards, to attach Himself to another and this other to Himself, to be together with him. This takes place in that irreversible sequence, but in it is completely real. In that sequence there arises and continues in Jesus Christ the highest communion of God with man. God's deity is thus no prison in which He can exist only in and for Himself. It is rather His freedom to be in and for Himself but also with and for us, to assert but also to sacrifice Himself, to be wholly exalted but also completely humble, not only almighty but also almighty mercy, not only Lord but also servant, not only judge but also Himself the judged, not only man's eternal king but also his brother in time. And all that without in the slightest forfeiting His deity! All that, rather, in the highest proof and proclamation of His deity! He who *does* and manifestly *can* do all that, He and no other is the living God. So constituted is His deity, the deity of the God of Abraham, Isaac, and Jacob. In Jesus Christ it is in this way operative and recognizable. If He is the Word of Truth, then the truth of *God* is exactly this and nothing else.

It is when we look at Jesus Christ that we know decisively that God's deity does not exclude, but includes His *humanity*. Would that Calvin had energetically pushed ahead on this point in his Christology, his doctrine of God, his teaching about predestination, and then logically also in his ethics! His Geneva would then not have become such a gloomy affair. His letters would then not have contained so much bitterness. It would then not be so easy to play a Heinrich Pestalozzi and, among his contemporaries, a Sebastian Castellio off against him. How could God's deity exclude His humanity, since it is God's freedom for love and thus His capacity to be not only in the heights but also in the depths, not only great but also small, not only in and for Himself but also with another distinct from Him, and to offer Himself to him? In His deity there is enough room for communion with man. Moreover, God has and retains in His relation to this other one the unconditioned priority. It is His act. *His* is and remains the first and decisive Word, *His* the initiative, *His* the leadership. How could we see and say it otherwise when we look at Jesus Christ in whom we find man taken up into communion with God? No, God requires no exclusion of humanity, no non-humanity, not to speak of inhumanity, in order to be truly God. But we may and must, however, look further and recognize the fact that actually His deity *encloses humanity in itself*. This is not the fatal Lutheran doctrine of the two natures and their properties. On the contrary, the essential aim of this doctrine is not to be denied at this point but to be adopted. It would be the false deity of a false God if in His deity His humanity did not also immediately encounter us. Such false deities are by Jesus Christ once for all made a laughingstock. In Him the fact is once for all established that

God does not exist without man.

It is not as though God stands in need of another as His partner, and in particular of man, in order to be truly God. "What is man, that thou art mindful of him, and the son of man that thou dost care for him?" Why should God not also be able, as eternal Love, to be sufficient unto Himself? In His life as Father, Son, and Holy Spirit He would in truth be no lonesome, no egotistical God even without man, yes, even without the whole created universe. And He must more than ever be not *for* man; He *could* — one even thinks He *must* — rather be against him. But that is the mystery in which He meets us in the existence of Jesus Christ. He wants in His freedom actually not to be without man but *with* him and in the same freedom not against him but *for* him, and that apart from or even counter to what man deserves. He wants in fact to be man's partner, his almighty and compassionate Saviour. He chooses to give man the benefit of His power, which encompasses not only the high and the distant but also the deep and the near, in order to maintain communion with him in the realm guaranteed by His deity. He determines to love him, to be his God, his Lord, his compassionate Preserver and Saviour to eternal life, and to desire his praise and service.

In this divinely free volition and election, in this sovereign decision (the ancients said, in His decree), God is *human*. His free affirmation of man, His free concern for him, His free substitution for him — this is God's humanity. We recognize it exactly at the point where we also first recognize His deity. Is it not true that in Jesus Christ, as He is attested in the Holy Scripture, genuine deity includes in itself genuine humanity? There is the father who cares for his lost son, the king who does the same for his insolvent debtor, the Samaritan who takes pity on the one who fell among robbers and in his thoroughgoing act of compassion cares for him in a fashion as unexpected as it is liberal. And this is the act of compassion to which all these parables as parables of the Kingdom of heaven refer. The very One who speaks in these parables takes to His heart the weakness and the perversity, the helplessness and the misery, of the human race surrounding Him. He does not despise men, but in an inconceivable manner esteems them highly just as they are, takes them into His heart and sets Himself in their place. He perceives that the superior will of God, to which He wholly subordinates Himself, requires that He sacrifice Himself for the human race, and seeks His honor in doing this. In the mirror of this humanity of Jesus Christ the humanity of God enclosed in His deity reveals itself. Thus God is as He is. Thus He affirms man. Thus He is concerned about him. Thus He stands up for him. The God of Schleiermacher cannot show mercy. The God of Abraham, Isaac, and Jacob can and does. If Jesus Christ is the Word of Truth, the "mirror of the fatherly heart of God," [as Luther said] then Nietzsche's statement that man is something that must be overcome is an impudent lie. Then the truth of God is, as Titus 3:4 says, His lovingkindness and nothing else.

IV. RUDOLPH BULTMANN*

The New Testament and Mythology[5]

---

* Rudolph Bultmann (1884–   ), German New Testament scholar and theologian, was professor of New Testament studies at Marburg for thirty years. He espoused the cause of the Form Criticism of Dibelius and through his systematic application of its principles to the Gospels ended up in an almost total skepticism concerning their historical content. He introduced a chasm between history and faith, and later by "demythologizing" tried to bridge the gap somewhat. He has written *History of the Synoptic Tradition, Theology of the New Testament,* and *History and Eschatology.*

THE NATURE OF MYTH

The real purpose of myth is not to present an objective picture of the world as it is, but to express man's understanding of himself in the world in which he lives. Myth should be interpreted not cosmologically, but anthropologically, or better still, existentially. Myth speaks of the power or the powers which man supposes he experiences as the ground and limit of his world and of his own activity and suffering. He describes these powers in terms derived from the visible world, with its tangible objects and forces, and from human life, with its feelings, motives, and potentialities. He may, for instance, explain the origin of the world by speaking of a world egg or a world tree. Similarly he may account for the present state and order of the world by speaking of a primeval war between the gods. He speaks of the other world in terms of this world, and of the gods in terms derived from human life.[6]

Myth is an expression of man's conviction that the origin and purpose of the world in which he lives are to be sought not within it but beyond it — that is, beyond the realm of known and tangible reality — and that this realm is perpetually dominated and menaced by those mysterious powers which are its source and limit. Myth is also an expression of man's awareness that he is not lord of his own being. It expresses his sense of dependence not only within the visible world, but more especially on those forces which hold sway beyond the confines of the known. Finally, myth expresses man's belief that in this state of dependence he can be delivered from the forces within the visible world.

Thus myth contains elements which demand its own criticism — namely, its imagery with its apparent claim to objective validity. The real purpose of myth is to speak of a transcendent power which controls the world and man, but that purpose is impeded and

---

[5] *Kerygma and Myth* (New York: Harper and Bros., 1961), pp. 10–11, 34–44 *passim.*

[6] Myth is here used in the sense popularized by the "History of Religions" school. Mythology is the use of imagery to express the other worldly in terms of this world and the divine in terms of human life, the

other side in terms of this side. For instance, divine transcendence is expressed as spatial distance. It is a mode of expression which makes it easy to understand the cultus as an action in which material means are used to convey immaterial power. Myth is not used in that modern sense, according to which it is practically equivalent to ideology.

obscured by the terms in which it is expressed.

Hence the importance of the New Testament mythology lies not in its imagery but in the understanding of existence which it enshrines. The real question is whether this understanding of existence is true. Faith claims that it is, and faith ought not to be tied down to the imagery of New Testament mythology.

THE NEW TESTAMENT ITSELF

The New Testament itself invites this kind of criticism. Not only are there rough edges in its mythology, but some of its features are actually contradictory. For example, the death of Christ is sometimes a sacrifice and sometimes a cosmic event. Sometimes his person is interpreted as the Messiah and sometimes as the Second Adam. The kenosis of the pre-existent Son (Phil 2:6 ff) is incompatible with the miracle narratives as proofs of his messianic claims. The Virgin birth is inconsistent with the assertion of his pre-existence. The doctrine of the Creation is incompatible with the conception of the "rulers of this world" (1 Cor 2:6 ff), the "god of this world" (2 Cor 4:4) and the "elements of this world" (Gal 4:3). It is impossible to square the belief that the law was given by God with the theory that it comes from the angels (Gal 3:19 f).

But the principal demand for the criticism of mythology comes from a curious contradiction which runs right through the New Testament. Sometimes we are told that human life is determined by cosmic forces, at others we are challenged to a decision. Side by side with the Pauline indicative stands the Pauline imperative. In short, man is sometimes regarded as a cosmic being, sometimes as an inde-

pendent "I" for whom decision is a matter of life or death. Incidentally, this explains why so many sayings in the New Testament speak directly to modern man's condition while others remain enigmatic and obscure. Finally, attempts at demythologization are sometimes made even within the New Testament itself. . . .

THE EVENT OF JESUS CHRIST

Anyone who asserts that to speak of an act of God at all is mythological language is bound to regard the idea of an act of God in Christ as a myth. But let us ignore this question for a moment. Even Kamlah thinks it philosophically justifiable to use "the mythological language of an act of God." The issue for the moment is whether that particular event in which the New Testament sees the act of God and the revelation of his love — that is, the event of Jesus Christ — is essentially a mythical event.

(a) The Demythologizing of the Event of Jesus Christ

Now, it is beyond question that the New Testament presents the event of Jesus Christ in mythical terms. The problem is whether that is the only possible presentation. Or does the New Testament itself demand a restatement of the event of Jesus Christ in non-mythological terms? Now, it is clear from the outset that the event of Christ is of a wholly different order from the cult-myths of Greek or Hellenistic religion. Jesus Christ is certainly presented as the Son of God, a pre-existent divine being, and therefore to that extent a mythical figure. But he is also a concrete figure of history — Jesus of Nazareth. His life is more than a mythical event; it is a human life which ended in the tragedy of crucifixion. We have here a unique combination of history and myth. The New Testament claims that this Jesus of history, whose father and mother were well known to his contemporaries (Jn 6:42) is at the same time the pre-existent Son of God, and side by side with the historical event of the crucifixion it sets the definitely non-historical event of the resurrection. This combination of myth and history presents a number of difficulties, as can be seen from certain inconsistencies in the New Testament material. The doctrine of Christ's pre-existence as given by St. Paul and St. John is difficult to reconcile with the legend of the Virgin birth in St. Matthew and St. Luke. On the one hand we hear that "he emptied himself, taking the form of a servant, being made in the likeness of men: and being found in fashion as a man . . ." (Phil 2:7), and on the other hand we have the gospel portraits of a Jesus who manifests his divinity in his miracles, omniscience, and mysterious elusiveness, and the similar description of him in Acts as "Jesus of Nazareth, a man approved of God unto you by mighty works and wonders and signs" (Acts 2:22). On the one hand we have the resurrection as the exaltation of Jesus from the cross or grave, and on the other the legends of the empty tomb and the ascension.

We are compelled to ask whether all this mythological language is not simply an attempt to express the meaning of the historical figure of Jesus and the events of his life; in other words, significance of these as a figure and event of salvation. If that be so, we can dispense with the objective form in which they are cast.

It is easy enough to deal with the doctrine of Christ's pre-existence and the legend of the Virgin birth in this way. They are clearly attempts to explain the meaning of the Person of Jesus for faith. The facts which historical criticism can verify cannot exhaust, indeed they cannot adequately indicate, all that Jesus means to me. How he actually originated matters little, indeed we can appreciate his significance only when we cease to worry about such questions. Our interest in the events of his life, and above all in the cross, is more than an academic concern with the history of the past. We can see meaning in them only when we ask what God is trying to say to each one of us through them. Again, the figure of Jesus cannot be understood simply from his inner-worldly context. In mythological language, this means that he stems from eternity, his origin is not a human and natural one.

We shall not, however, pursue the examination of the particular incidents of his life any further. In the end the crux of the matter lies in the cross and resurrection. . . .

(b) The Resurrection

But what of the resurrection? Is it not a mythical event pure and simple? Obviously it is not an event of past history with a self-evident meaning. Can the resurrection narratives and every other mention of the resurrection in the New Testament be understood simply as an attempt to convey the meaning of the cross? Does the New Testament, in asserting that Jesus is risen from the dead, mean that his death is not just an ordinary human death, but the judgment and salvation of the world, depriving death of its power? Does it not express this truth in the affirmation that the Crucified was not holden of death, but rose from the dead?

Yes indeed: the cross and the resurrection form a single, indivisible cosmic event. "He was delivered up for our trespasses, and was raised for our justification" (Rom 4:25). The cross is not an isolated event, as though it were the end of Jesus, which needed the resurrection subsequently to reverse it. . . . When he suffered death, Jesus was already the Son of God, and his death by itself was the victory over the power of death. St. John brings this out most clearly by describing the passion of Jesus as the "hour" in which he is glorified, and by the double meaning he gives to the phrase "lifted up," applying it both to the cross and to Christ's exaltation into glory.

Cross and resurrection form a single, indivisible cosmic event which brings judgment to the world and opens up for men the possibility of authentic life. But if that be so, the resurrection cannot be a miraculous proof capable of demonstration and sufficient to convince the sceptic that the cross really has the cosmic and eschatological significance ascribed to it.

Yet it cannot be denied that the resurrection of Jesus is often used in the New Testament as a miraculous proof. Take for instance Acts 17:31. Here we are actually told that God substantiated the claims of Christ by raising him from the dead. Then again the resurrection narratives: both the legend of the empty tomb and the appearances insist on the physical reality of the risen body of the Lord (see especially Lk 24:39–43). But these are most certainly later embellishments of the primitive tradition. St. Paul knows

nothing about them. There is however one passage where St. Paul tries to prove the miracle of the resurrection by adducing a list of eye-witnesses (1 Cor 15:3–8). But this is a dangerous procedure, as Karl Barth has involuntarily shown. Barth seeks to explain away the real meaning of 1 Cor 15 by contending that the list of eye-witnesses was put in not to prove the fact of the resurrection, but to prove that the preaching of the apostle was, like the preaching of the first Christians, the preaching of Jesus as the risen Lord. The eyewitnesses therefore guarantee St. Paul's preaching, not the fact of the resurrection. An historical fact which involves a resurrection from the dead is utterly inconceivable!

. . . The real Easter faith is faith in the word of preaching which brings illumination. If the event of Easter Day is in any sense an historical event additional to the event of the cross, it is nothing else than the rise of faith in the risen Lord, since it was this faith which led to the apostolic preaching. The resurrection itself is not an event of past history. All that historical criticism can establish is the fact that the first disciples came to believe in the resurrection. The historian can perhaps to some extent account for that faith from the personal intimacy which the disciples had enjoyed with Jesus during his earthly life, and so reduce the resurrection appearances to a series of subjective visions. But the historical problem is not of interest to Christian belief in the resurrection. For the historical event of the rise of the Easter faith means for us what it meant for the first disciples — namely, the self-attestation of the risen Lord, the act of God in which the redemptive event of the cross is completed.

We cannot buttress our own faith in the resurrection by that of the first disciples and so eliminate the element of risk which faith in the resurrection always involves. For the first disciples' faith in the resurrection is itself part and parcel of the eschatological event which is the article of faith. . . .

We have now outlined a program for the demythologizing of the New Testament. Are there still any surviving traces of mythology? There certainly are for those who regard all language about an act of God or of a decisive, eschatological event as mythological. But this is not mythology in the traditional sense, not the kind of mythology which has become antiquated with the decay of the mythical world view. For the redemption of which we have spoken is not a miraculous supernatural event, but an historical event wrought out in time and space. We are convinced that this restatement does better justice to the real meaning of the New Testament and to the paradox of the kerygma. For the kerygma maintains that the eschatological emissary of God is a concrete figure of a particular historical past, that his eschatological activity was wrought out in a human fate. And that therefore it is an event whose eschatological character does not admit of a secular proof. Here we have the paradox of Phil 2:7: "He emptied himself"; of 2 Cor 8:9: ". . . though he was rich, yet for your sakes he became poor"; of Rom 8:3: "God, sending his Son in the likeness of sinful flesh"; of Tim 3:16: "He was manifested in the flesh"; and above all of the classic formula of Jn 1:14: "The Word became flesh."

The agent of God's presence and activity, the mediator of his reconciliation of the world unto himself, is a real figure of history. Similarly the word of God is not some mysterious oracle, but a sober, factual account of a human life, of Jesus of Nazareth, possessing saving efficacy for man. Of course the kerygma may be regarded as part of the story of man's spiritual evolution and used as a basis for a tenable *Weltanschauung*. Yet this proclamation claims to be the eschatological word of God.

The apostles who proclaim the word may be regarded merely as figures of past history, and the Church as a sociological and historical phenomenon, part of the history of man's spiritual evolution. Yet both are eschatological phenomena and eschatological events.

All these assertions are an offense, which will not be removed by philosophical discussion, but only by faith and obedience. All these are phenomena subject to historical, sociological and psychological observation, yet for faith they are all of them eschatological phenomena. It is precisely its immunity from proof which secures the Christian proclamation against the charge of being mythological. The transcendence of God is not as in myth reduced to immanence. Instead, we have the paradox of a transcendent God present and active in history: "The Word became flesh."

V. PAUL TILLICH*

The Reality of the Christ[7]

* Paul Tillich (1886–1965), German Protestant theologian, who, compelled to leave Germany in 1933, came to the U.S. where he was appointed professor of philosophical theology at Union Theological Seminary, New York. He was later a professor at Harvard Divinity School and at the University of Chicago. Influenced by Barth and existentialism, Tillich is essentially a great synthesizer who by "correlation" attempted to relate traditional doctrines to varying emerging human situations. In his *Systematic Theology* he develops his basic theological standpoint, namely, that Jesus Christ, the one whose life is but a transparency of the divine, is the standard and acme of revelation.

THE NAME "JESUS CHRIST"

Christianity is what it is through the affirmation that Jesus of Nazareth, who has been called "the Christ," is actually the Christ, namely, he who brings the new state of things, the New Being. Wherever the assertion that Jesus is the Christ is maintained, there is the Christian message; wherever this assertion is denied, the Christian message is not affirmed. Christianity was born, not with the birth of the man who is called "Jesus," but in the moment in which one of his followers was driven to say to him, "Thou art the Christ." And Christianity will live as long as there are people who repeat this assertion. For the event on which Christianity is based has two sides: the fact which is called "Jesus of Nazareth" and the reception of this fact by those who received him as the Christ. The first of those who received him as the Christ in the early tradition was named Simon Peter. This event is reported in a story in the center of the Gospel of Mark; it takes place near Caesarea Philippi and marks the turning point in the narrative. The mo-

[7] *Systematic Theology II* (Chicago: University of Chicago Press, 1957), pp. 97–103, 142–155 passim.

ment of the disciples' acceptance of Jesus as the Christ is also the moment of his rejection by the powers of history. This gives the story its tremendous symbolic power. He who is the Christ has to die for his acceptance of the title "Christ." And those who continue to call him the Christ must assert the paradox that he who is supposed to overcome existential estrangement must participate in it and its self-destructive consequences. This is the central story of the Gospel. Reduced to its simplest form, it is the statement that the man Jesus of Nazareth is the Christ.

The first step demanded of christological thought is an interpretation of the name "Jesus Christ," preferably in the light of the Caesarea Philippi story. One must clearly see that Jesus Christ is not an individual name, consisting of a first and a second name, but that it is the combination of an individual name — the name of a certain man who lived in Nazareth between the years 1 and 30 — with the title "the Christ," expressing in the mythological tradition a special figure with a special function. The Messiah — in Greek, *Christos* — is the "anointed one" who has received an unction from God enabling him to establish the reign of God in Israel and in the world. Therefore, the name Jesus Christ must be understood as "Jesus who is called the Christ," or "Jesus who is the Christ," or "Jesus as the Christ," or "Jesus the Christ." The context determines which of these interpretative phrases should be used; but one of them should be used in order to keep the original meaning of the name "Jesus Christ" alive, not only in theological thought but also in ecclesiastical practice. Christian preaching and teaching must continually re-emphasize the paradox that the man Jesus is called the Christ — a paradox which is often drowned in the liturgical and homiletic use of "Jesus Christ" as a proper name. "Jesus Christ" means — originally, essentially, and permanently — "Jesus who is the Christ."

EVENT, FACT, AND RECEPTION

Jesus as the Christ is both a historical fact and a subject of believing reception. One cannot speak the truth about the event on which Christianity is based without asserting both sides. Many theological mistakes could have been avoided if these two sides of the "Christian event" had been emphasized with equal strength. And Christian theology as a whole is undercut if one of them is completely ignored. If theology ignores the fact to which the name of Jesus of Nazareth points, it ignores the basic Christian assertion that Essential God-Manhood has appeared within existence and subjected itself to the conditions of existence without being conquered by them. If there were no personal life in which existential estrangement had been overcome, the New Being would have remained a quest and an expectation and would not be a reality in time

and space. Only if the existence is conquered in *one* point — a personal life, representing existence as a whole — is it conquered in principle, which means "in beginning and in power." This is the reason that Christian theology must insist on the actual fact to which the name Jesus of Nazareth refers. It is why the church prevailed against competing groups in the religious movements of the first centuries. This is the reason that the church had to fight a vehement struggle with the gnostic-docetic elements within itself — elements which entered Christianity as early as the New Testament. And this is the reason that anyone who takes seriously the historical approach to the New Testament and its critical methods becomes suspect of docetic ideas, however strongly he may emphasize the factual side of the message of Jesus the Christ.

Nevertheless, the other side, the believing reception of Jesus *as* the Christ, calls for equal emphasis. Without this reception the Christ would not have been the Christ, namely, the manifestation of the New Being in time and space. If Jesus had not impressed himself as the Christ on his disciples and through them upon all following generations, the man who is called Jesus of Nazareth would perhaps be remembered as a historically and religiously important person. As such, he would belong to the preliminary revelation, perhaps to the preparatory segment of the history of revelation. He could then have been a prophetic anticipation of the New Being, but not the final manifestation of the New Being itself. He would not have been the Christ even if he had claimed to be the Christ. The receptive side of the Christian event is as important as the factual side. And only their unity creates the event upon which Christianity is based. According to later symbolism, the Christ is the head of the church, which is his body. As such, they are necessarily interdependent. . . .

THE RESEARCH FOR THE HISTORICAL JESUS AND ITS FAILURE

From the moment that the scientific method of historical research was applied to biblical literature, theological problems which were never completely absent became intensified in a way unknown to former periods of church history. The historical method unites analytical-critical and constructive-conjectural elements. For the average Christian consciousness shaped by the orthodox doctrine of verbal inspiration, the first element was much more impressive than the second. One felt only the negative element in the term "criticism" and called the whole enterprise "historical criticism" or "higher criticism" or, with reference to a recent method, "form criticism." In itself, the term "historical criticism" means nothing more than historical research. Every historical research criticizes its sources, separating what has more probability from that which has less or is altogether improbable. Nobody doubts the validity of this method, since it is confirmed continuously by its success; and nobody seriously protests if it destroys beautiful legends and deeply rooted prejudices. But biblical research became suspect from its very beginning. It seemed to criticize not only the historical sources but the revelation contained in these sources. Historical research and rejection of biblical authority were identified. Revelation, it was implied, covered not only the revelatory content

but also the historical form in which it had appeared. This seemed to be especially true of the facts concerning the "historical Jesus." Since the biblical revelation is essentially historical, it appeared to be impossible to separate the revelatory content from the historical reports as they are given in the biblical records. Historical criticism seemed to undercut faith itself.

But the critical part of historical research into biblical literature is the less important part. More important is the constructive-conjectural part, which was the driving force in the whole enterprise. The facts behind the records, especially the facts about Jesus, were sought. There was an urgent desire to discover the reality of this man, Jesus of Nazareth, behind the coloring and covering traditions which are almost as old as the reality itself. So the research for the so-called "historical Jesus" started. Its motives were religious and scientific at the same time. The attempt was courageous, noble, and extremely significant in many respects. Its theological consequences are numerous and rather important. But, seen in the light of its basic intention, the attempt of historical criticism to find the empirical truth about Jesus of Nazareth was a failure. The historical Jesus, namely, the Jesus behind the symbols of his reception as the Christ, not only did not appear but receded farther and farther with every new step. The history of the attempts to write a "life of Jesus," elaborated by Albert Schweitzer in his early work, *The Quest of the Historical Jesus,* is still valid. His own constructive attempt has been corrected. Scholars, whether conservative or radical, have become more cautious, but the methodological situation has not changed. This became manifest when

R. Bultmann's bold program of a "demythologization of the New Testament" aroused a storm in all theological camps and the slumber of Barthianism with respect to the historical problem was followed by an astonished awakening. But the result of the new (and very old) questioning is not a picture of the so-called historical Jesus but the insight that there is no picture behind the biblical one which could be made scientifically probable.

This situation is not a matter of a preliminary shortcoming of historical research which will some day be overcome. It is caused by the nature of the sources itself. The reports about Jesus of Nazareth are those of Jesus as the Christ, given by persons who had received him as the Christ. Therefore, if one tries to find the real Jesus behind the picture of Jesus as the Christ, it is necessary critically to separate the elements which belong to the factual side of the event from the elements which belong to the receiving side. In doing so, one sketches a "Life of Jesus"; and innumerable such sketches have been made. In many of them scientific honesty, loving devotion, and theological interest have worked together. In others critical detachment and even malevolent rejection are visible. But none can claim to be a probable picture which is the result of the tremendous scientific toil dedicated to this task for two hundred years. At best, they are more or less probable results, able to be the basis neither of an acceptance nor of a rejection of the Christian faith.

In view of this situation, there have been attempts to reduce the picture of the historical Jesus to the "essentials," to elaborate a *Gestalt* while leaving the particulars open to doubt. But this is not a way out. Historical research cannot paint an essential picture after all the particular traits have been eliminated because they are questionable. It remains dependent on the particulars. Consequently, the pictures of the historical Jesus in which the form of a "Life of Jesus" is wisely avoided still differ from one another as much as those in which such self-restriction is not applied.

The dependence of the *Gestalt* on the valuation of the particulars is evident in an example taken from the complex of what Jesus thought about himself. In order to elaborate this point, one must know, besides many other things, whether he applied the title "Son of Man" to himself and, if so, in what sense. Every answer given to this question is a more or less probable hypothesis, but the character of the "essential" picture of the historical Jesus depends decisively on this hypothesis. Such an example clearly shows the impossibility of replacing the attempt to portray a "Life of Jesus" by trying to paint the *"Gestalt* of Jesus.". . .

DANGERS AND DECISIONS IN THE
DEVELOPMENT OF THE
CHRISTOLOGICAL DOGMA

The two dangers which threaten every christological statement are immediate consequences of the assertion that Jesus is the Christ. The attempt to interpret this assertion conceptually can lead to an actual denial of the Christ-character of Jesus as the Christ; or it can lead to an actual denial of the Jesus-character of Jesus as the Christ. Christology must always find its way on the ridge between these two chasms, and it must know that it will never completely succeed, inasmuch as it touches the divine mystery, which remains mystery even in its manifestation.

In traditional terms the problem has been discussed as the relation of the divine to the human "nature" in Jesus. Any diminution of the human nature would deprive the Christ of his total participation in the conditions of existence. And any diminution of the divine nature would deprive the Christ of his total victory over existential estrangement. In both cases he could not have created the New Being. His being would have been less than the New Being. Therefore, the problem was how to think the unity of a completely human with a completely divine nature. This problem never has been solved adequately, even within the limits of human possibilities. The doctrine of the two natures in the Christ raises the right question but uses wrong conceptual tools. The basic inadequacy lies in the term "nature." When applied to man, it is ambiguous; when applied to God, it is wrong. This explains the inescapable definitive failure of the councils, e.g., of Nicaea and Chalcedon, in spite of their substantial truth and their historical significance.

The decision of Nicaea, defended by Athanasius as a matter of life and death for the church, made it inadmissible to deny the divine power of the Christ in revelation and salvation. In the terminology of the Nicaean controversy, the power of the Christ is the power of the divine Logos, the principle of divine self-manifestation. This leads to the question of whether the Logos is equal in divine power with the Father or less than he. If the first answer is given, the distinction between the Father and the Son seems to disappear, as in the Sabellian heresy. If the second answer is given,

the Logos, even if called the greatest of all creatures, is a creature nevertheless and therefore unable to save the creation, as in the Arian heresy. Only the God who is really God can create the New Being, not a half-god. It was the term *homo-ousios*, "of equal essence," which was supposed to express this idea. But in that case, the semi-Arians asked, how could a difference exist between the Father and the Son, and does not the picture of the Jesus of history become completely ununderstandable? It was hard for Athanasius and his most intimate followers (e.g., Marcellus) to answer such questions.

The Nicaean formula has often been considered the basic Trinitarian statement of the church. It has been distinguished from the christological decisions of the fifth century, but that is misleading. The doctrine of the Trinity has independent roots in the encounter with God in all his manifestations. We have tried to show that the idea of the "living God" requires a distinction between the abysmal element of the divine, the form element, and their spiritual unity. This explains the manifold forms in which Trinitarian symbolism appears in the history of religion. The Christian doctrine of the Trinity systematizes the idea and adds the decisive element of the relation of the Christ to the Logos. It was this latter point which led to a systematically developed Trinitarian dogma. The decision of Nicaea is a christological one, although it also made the basic contribution to the Trinitarian dogma. In the same way the restatement and enlargement of Nicaea in Constantinople (381) was a christological statement, although it added the divinity of the Holy Spirit to the divinity of the Logos. If the being of Jesus as the Christ is the New Being, the human spirit of the man Jesus cannot make him into the Christ; then it must be the divine Spirit, which, like the Logos, cannot be inferior to God. Although the final discussion of the Trinitarian doctrine must await the development of the idea of the Spirit (Part IV), it can be stated here that the Trinitarian symbols become empty if they are separated from their two experiential roots — the experience of the living God and the experience of the New Being in the Christ. Both Augustine and Luther had a feeling for this situation. Augustine found that the distinction among the three *personae* (*not* persons) in the Trinity is without any content and is used, "not in order to say something, but in order not to remain silent." And, indeed, terms like "non-generated," "eternally generated," "proceeding," even if understood as symbols — which they certainly are — do not say anything which could be meaningful for symbolic imagination. Luther found that a word like "Trinity" is strange and almost ridiculous but that here, as in other instances, there was no better one. Since he was aware of the two existential roots of the Trinitarian idea, he rejected a theology which makes the Trinitarian dialectic into a play with meaningless number combinations. The Trinitarian dogma is a supporting part of the christological dogma; and the decision of Nicaea saved Christianity from a relapse to a cult of half-gods. It rejected interpretations of Jesus as the Christ which would have deprived him of his power to create the New Being.

The decision at Nicaea that God himself and not a half-god is present in the man Jesus of Nazareth was open to the loss of the Jesus-character of Jesus as the Christ or, in traditional terminology, to the denial of his full human nature. And this danger, as we have indicated several times, was real. Popular and monastic piety was not satisfied with the message of the eternal unity of God and man appearing under the conditions of estrangement. These pieties wanted "more." They wanted a God, walking on earth, participating in history, but not involved in the conflicts of existence and the ambiguities of life. Popular piety did not want a paradox but a "miracle." It desired an event in analogy with all other events in time and space, an "objective" happening in the supranatural sense. By this kind of piety the way for every possible superstition was opened. Christianity was in danger of being swallowed up in the tidal wave of a "secondary religion," for which monophysitism provided the theological justification. This danger soon became real in countries like Egypt, which, partly for this reason, became an easy prey to iconoclastic Islam. The danger would have been more easily overcome if it had not been for the support that such popular piety found in the intensive and developing ascetic-monastic movements and their direct influence on the deciding synods. The hostility of the monks toward the natural, not only in its existential distortion, but also in its essential goodness, made them fanatical enemies of a theology which emphasized the total participation of the Christ in man's existential predicament. In the great Bishop of Alexandria, Cyril, the alliance of popular and monastic piety found a theologically cautious and politically skillful defender. The monophysitic tendency would have prevailed in the whole church in a sophisticated form if there had not been a partly victorious opposition.

The opposition came from theologians who took seriously the participation of Jesus in man's existential predicament. It also came from church leaders like Pope Leo of Rome, who, in the line of his Western tradition, emphasized the historical-dynamic character of the New Being in the Christ over against its static-hierarchical character in the East. This opposition was largely victorious in the Council of Chalcedon — in spite of the shortcomings of the Chalcedonian formula. This victory prevented the elimination of the Jesus-character of the Christ, in spite of later successful attempts in the East (Constantinople) to restate the decision of Chalcedon along the lines of Cyril. The authority of Chalcedon was too well established and the spirit of Chalcedon was too much in agreement with basic trends of Western piety — including later Protestant piety — for it to be defeated.

In the two great decisions of the early church, both the Christ-character and the Jesus-character of the event of Jesus as the Christ were preserved. And this happened in spite of the very inadequate conceptual tools. This is the judgment about the christological work of the church underlying the present christological exposition.

THE CHRISTOLOGICAL TASK OF PRESENT THEOLOGY

The general consequences which must be drawn from the preceding judgment are obvious but need concrete elaboration. Protestant theology must accept the "Catholic" tradition insofar as it is based on the substance of the two great decisions of the early church (Nicaea and Chalcedon).

Protestant theology must try to find new forms in which the christological substance of the past can be expressed. The preceding christological sections are an attempt to do so. They imply a critical attitude to both the orthodox and the liberal Christologies of the last centuries of Protestant theology. The development of Protestant orthodoxy, both in its classical period and in its later reformulations, showed the impossibility of an understandable solution to the christological problem in terms of the classical terminology. It was the merit of theological liberalism that it showed through historical-critical investigations, as, e.g., in Harnack's *History of the Dogmas* — the inescapable contradictions and absurdities into which all attempts to solve the christological problem in terms of the two-nature theory were driven. But liberalism itself did not contribute much to Christology in systematic terms. By saying that "Jesus does not belong within the gospel pronounced by Jesus," it eliminated the Christ-character of the event Jesus the Christ. Even historians like Albert Schweitzer, who emphasized the eschatological character of the message of Jesus and his self-interpretation as a central figure within the eschatological scheme, did not use this element for their Christology. They dismissed it as a complex of strange imagination and as a matter of apocalyptic ecstasy. The Christ-character of the event was drawn into the Jesus-character. It would be unfair, however, to identify liberal theology with Arianism. Its picture of Jesus is not that of a half-god. Rather, it is the picture of a man in whom God was manifest in a unique way. But it is not the picture of a man whose being was the New Being and who was able to conquer existential estrangement. Neither the orthodox nor the liberal methods of Protestant theology are adequate for the christological task which the Protestant church must now fulfill.

The early church was well aware that Christology is an existentially necessary, though not a theoretically interesting, work of the church. Its ultimate criterion, therefore, is existential itself. It is "soteriological," i.e., determined by the question of salvation. The greater the things we say about the Christ, the greater the salvation we can expect from him. This word of an Apostolic Father is valid for all christological thought. Differences, of course, arise if one tries to give a definition of what "great" means in relation to the Christ. For monophysitic thinking in its nuances from the early church up to today, great things are said about the Christ if his smallness, namely, his participation in finitude and tragedy, is swallowed up in his greatness, namely, his power of conquering existential estrangement. This emphasis on the "divine nature" is called a "high" Christology. But however high the divine predicates may be which are heaped in the Christ, the result is a Christology of low value, because it removes the paradox for the sake of a supranatural miracle. And salvation can be derived only from him who fully participated in man's existential predicament, not from a God walking on earth, "unequal to us in all respects." The Protestant principle, according to which God is near to the lowest as well as to the highest and according to which salvation is not the transference of man from the material to a so-called spiritual world, demands a "low Christology" — which actually is the truly high Christology.

By this criterion, the preceding christological attempt should be judged.

Reference has already been made to the concept of nature used in the terms "divine nature" and "human nature," and it has been indicated that the term "human nature" is ambiguous and the term "divine nature" is wholly inadequate. Human nature can mean man's essential or created nature; it can mean man's existential or estranged nature; and it can mean man's nature in the ambiguous unity of the two others. If we apply the term "human nature" to Jesus as the Christ, we must say that he has a complete human nature in the first sense of the word. Through creation, he is finite freedom, like every human being. With respect to the second meaning of "human nature," we must say that he has man's existential nature as a real possibility, but in such a way that temptation, which is the possibility, is always taken into the unity with God. From this it follows that, in the third sense, human nature must be attributed to Jesus insofar as he is involved in the tragic ambiguities of life. Under these circumstances it is imperative to dismiss altogether the term "human nature" in relation to the Christ and replace it by a description of the dynamics of his life — as we have tried to do. . . .

This analysis discloses that the term "divine nature" is questionable and that it cannot be applied to the Christ in any meaningful way; for the Christ (who is Jesus of Nazareth) is not beyond essence and existence. If he were, he could not be a personal life living in a limited period of time, having been born and having to die, being finite, tempted, and tragically involved in existence. The assertion that Jesus as the Christ is the personal unity of a divine and a human nature must be replaced by the assertion that in Jesus as the Christ the eternal unity of God and man has become historical reality. In his being, the New Being is real, and the New Being is the re-established unity between God and man. We replace the inadequate concept "divine nature" by the concepts "eternal God-man-unity" or "Eternal God-Manhood." Such concepts replace a static essence by a dynamic relation. The uniqueness of this relation is in no way reduced by its dynamic character; but, by eliminating the concept of "two natures," which lie beside each other like blocks and whose unity cannot be understood at all, we are open to relational concepts which make understandable the dynamic picture of Jesus as the Christ. . . .

Some traits of the christological position taken here are similar to Schleiermacher's Christology, as developed in his *Glaubenslehre*. He replaces the two-nature doctrine by a doctrine of a divine-human relation. He speaks of a God-consciousness in Jesus, the strength of which surpasses the God-consciousness of all other men. He describes Jesus as the *Urbild* ("original image") of what man essentially is and from which he has fallen. The similarity is obvious; but it is not identity.

Essential God-Manhood points to both sides of the relation and this in terms of eternity. It is an objective structure and not a state of man. The phrase "essential unity between God and man" has an ontological character; Schleiermacher's God-consciousness has an anthropological character. The term *Urbild* when used for Jesus as the Christ does not have the decisive implication of the term "New Being." In *Urbild* the idealistic transcendence of true humanity over human existence is clearly expressed, while in "New Being," the participation of him who is *also* the *Urbild* ("essential man") is decisive. The New Being is new not only over against existence but also over against essence, in so far as essence remains mere potentiality. The *Urbild* remains unmoved above existence; the New Being participates in existence and conquers it. Here again an ontological element makes the difference. But these differences, expressing variant presuppositions and consequences, should not hide the fact that similar problems and solutions arise when Protestant theology takes a path lying between classical and liberal Christology. This is our present situation. In the problems it puts before us, we must seek for solutions.

VI. EMIL BRUNNER*

The Biblical Understanding of Truth and Doctrine[8]

* Emil Brunner (1889–   ), Swiss dialectical theologian, taught at Zurich and at Princeton in the U.S. With Barth he protests against immanence in religion and all elements of mysticism in Christianity. Barth has taken him to task for admitting an element of truth in the Catholic position of analogy. Brunner maintains that besides the revelation of God through Jesus Christ, creation itself is a revelation of God.

[8] *Truth as Encounter* (Philadelphia: Westminster Press, 1964), pp. 153–157 *passim*.

WHY CHRIST

The Christian faith, most simply expressed, is *faith in Jesus Christ.*

The church would have done well if it had always withdrawn from involved doctrinal controversies to this simple confession of faith, the only one which is explicitly contained in the New Testament: Jesus Christ the Lord, Jesus Christ the Son of God, the Redeemer. For in this simple confession the nature of the Christian faith appears with complete clarity — it is trust in and obedience to the personally present Lord. Faith is not primarily faith in something true — not even in the truth "that" Jesus is the Son of God; but it is primarily trust in and obedience to this Lord and Redeemer himself, and on the ground of this trust, fellowship with him according to his Word: "Behold I am with you to the end of the world." Fellowship with the living Lord who is present with us: this is what faith in Christ in the New Testament preeminently means.

It is precisely this formulation which gives rise to the question: Why Christ after all? Why not simply God? How can we understand faith in a mediator as the expression of personal correspondence? Here, too, we can confidently expect to get a twofold elucidation of our thesis as well as of the New Testament testimony about Christ, because our thesis itself was obtained by using this testimony as starting point for our inquiry. To say that Jesus Christ is the content of faith, of truth, is a radical departure from the ordinary conception of truth. This is expressed in a decisive passage in the New Testament itself; in the Prologue to the Gospel of John we read: "But grace and truth came into being through Jesus Christ." Truth came into being! For one schooled in the Greek conception of truth this phrase is utterly perverse. Truth, after all, is precisely that which is timeless, the eternal which is not subject to change. For truth to *come into being* is a contradiction of terms. But truth that has come into being is the very core of the Biblical message. Truth is something that *happens,* that God *does.* Truth and grace can be spoken with the same breath: truth like grace is encounter between God and man; grace and truth came into being in Jesus Christ.

The presupposition of this tenet follows in the Prologue of the Fourth Gospel: "No man has seen God at any time." God, apart from his revelation in the form of a human being, is mystery. What we speculate about God is idolatrous interpretation of the divine mystery, of which we are all aware. The personal God can be known only in his personal revelation, and his personal revelation is the incarnation of the Word. The incarnation of the eternal Son of God is the unveiling of his quality of being person and hence at the same time his will to fellowship. For this is the Biblical conception of God's quality of being Person: love, self-communication — that love which through all eternity the Father has for the Son, and the Son for the Father. God's quality of being Person, revealed in Jesus Christ, is itself of such a nature that it establishes fellowship. Being person [*Person-sein*] and being in fellowship [*In-Gemein-schaft-sein*] are identical. Such is the Biblical concept of the personality of God. The revelation of himself as Person is therefore at the same time revelation of himself as Love; consequently truth and grace are the same. Not only are truth and grace manifested in Jesus Christ, but in him their real intentionality comes to realization. Jesus Christ not only reveals, he at once fulfills and realizes the will of God. Hence, "we saw in him the *doxa Theou,* the *gloria Dei,* the majesty of God." The incarnation of the Son is not only redemptive fact, but at the same time the realization of the divine world plan, the *oikonomia* that is to say, the divine realization of the eternal purpose to comprehend the universe in Christ as its head. We may not divide the nature from the will of God, as if they somehow were separable. His will is his nature; and his nature, his will. Hence, we may not talk about God without at the same time talking about his will, and what is meant by his will can be briefly stated: the Kingdom of God, revealed and grounded in the incarnate Son. The incarnation is not only our Lord's taking the form of a servant because of sin: at the same time it is majesty, because it is the realization of the divine world plan. It is the concretion of God's will to have a counterpart in whom his nature and his love are reflected and answer him. In Jesus Christ, God reveals himself as the God who approaches man, the God who because his nature is love wills that man answer him in love — in that love which he himself as Creator and Redeemer gives him. The event of the incarnation marks the coming into existence of truth and grace.

THE WORK OF THE REDEEMER

Nevertheless, I believe that the ancient Christian development of dogma did not quite remain on the track of the Biblical revelation. The incarnation as such is not the pivotal point of the Biblical revelation, but rather the *work* of the Redeemer. Jesus Christ did not come merely to come, but he came to redeem. To be sure, only the incarnate Lord — very God, very man — can be the Redeemer. But the Bible guides us to ponder less the secret of the person of Jesus than the mystery of his work. Let me reiterate once more that apparent commonplace: not the substantive but the verb is the chief word in Biblical language. The old Christian theology converted the Biblical verb-theology into a Greek substantive-theology. That is the Platonic, substantialist element in it. The Bible is never substantialist, but always actualistic. It is essentially historical; but the contemplation of the natures of Christ misleads to a certain naturalism.

I must correct at this point certain emphases in my own book *The Mediator.* It was indubitably an unconditional necessity for the church to defend the unity of God and man in Jesus Christ against all mythological, Gnostic, and moralistic-rationalistic attacks. But the church bogged (so to say) at that point. It gave the Christian faith a false orientation about the being instead of the work of Christ. In this way it imperiled the fundamental historical character of the evangelical message by means of a static Platonism. The Person of the Mediator must also be understood as an *act* of God, namely, as his coming to us in revelation and redemption. It must be understood as the divine act of turning himself toward and giving himself to man. In this sense Melanchthon's famous word, "To know his acts of kindness is to know Christ," signifies a decisive return to the Biblical understanding of Christ. We should compare with this statement the main Christological passages in the Pauline letters and we shall find it confirmed that predominant in the Biblical message is the movement, the coming down, the sending of the Son to us, his self-giving for us, his taking on himself the form of a servant, his taking on himself the sinful flesh, above all, his suffering, dying, and rising again, his obeying, his loving and revealing, his expiating and redeeming. Even the Person of the Mediator is comprehended with the verb, if I may so express it, not with the substantive. One could actually say: Jesus Christ, even and especially in his divine-human *being* as Person, is God's *act,* just as he is the *Word* of God. In him — not only through him — does God *do* something to us. In him, God reveals himself; in him, God reconciles the world unto himself; in him, God redeems us. Consequently, in this connection too, where we are considering the Person — the mystery of the Person of Christ — what is essential is not something as it is in itself [*Anischseiendes*], a divine-human Person as he is himself [*Person-an-sich*], but the relation of God, the dealing of God with the sinful and lost humanity, the revelatory and redemptive *act* of God.

THE NAME OF CHRIST

Perhaps we can understand this whole point of view best if we begin by discussing the *name of Christ* itself. The Mediator has a functional name — the Messiah, through whom God rules and who carries into effect God's will to Lordship. Think of the parable of the wicked husbandmen, which I have already mentioned in another connection: the disobedient tenants who have usurped the seignorial rights are to be led back to obedience by the messengers of the lord.

Finally he sends his own son with the same intention. The son is no messenger: he is the will of the lord himself, personally present. In him the lord stretches out his hands toward the property that has been wrested from him. Jesus Christ as the Messiah is restorer of the Lordship of God, the Kingship of God. *The office,* his function, gives him his name; God comes to us in his Son, in order to realize his Kingdom. Correspondingly, the first Christian creed apart from the Messianic name is the confession: He is the Lord. *Kyrios Christos.* In this Person the will to Lordship and the lordly power of God meet us. Jesus is the personified and incarnate kingly will of God; God's kingly will becomes a human person. To believe in him thus means primarily that one bows to his sovereign will as God's will and becomes obedient to him.

This becomes especially clear in the Johannine concept: Jesus is *the Word of God.* What God says to us in this Person. In him, God speaks to us his will, his intention, his decree, his world plan, his love. Unlike the prophets, he is not the conveyor of a word, a message — the prophet, after all, is nothing himself; not he, but his message is important. He himself is the message, his Person is God's revelatory doing. He himself, *in persona,* is the self-communication of God; consequently, we must always grasp the being and doing, the acts, words, and passion of the Lord as a totality. He himself therefore is the meeting with God (so to say); or, as the Old Testament believers expressed it, he himself is God's visitation to men, God's coming near, God coming to us, Immanuel. In him, God opens to us the mystery of himself. "Who sees me, sees the Father."

VII. JOHN A. T. ROBINSON*

The Man for Others[9]

* John A. T. Robinson (1919–   ), Bishop of Woolwich, England, is a contemporary controversial voice in Protestant theology. A New Testament scholar, he has written *The Body of Christ in Paul, Liturgy Coming to Life, The New Reformation?*

CHRISTMAS AND TRUTH

The doctrine of the Incarnation and Divinity of Christ is on any account central to the entire Christian message and crucial therefore for any reinterpretation of it. It is also the point where resistance to reinterpretation is likely to be at its maximum and where orthodoxy has its heaviest investment in traditional categories. This is true both at the level of technical theology, where any restatement must run the gauntlet of the Chalcedonian Definition and the Athanasian Creed, and at the popular level, where one will quickly be accused of destroying the Christmas story. But if it is necessary in our thinking about God to move to a position "beyond naturalism and supranaturalism," this is no less important in our thinking about Christ. Otherwise we shall be shut up, as we have been hitherto, to an increasingly sterile choice between two.

Traditional Christology has worked with a frankly supranatural scheme. Popular religion has expressed this mythologically, professional theology metaphysically. For this way of thinking, the Incarnation means that God the Son came down to earth, and was born, lived and died within this world as a man. From 'out there' there graciously entered into the human scene one who was not 'of it' and yet who lived genuinely and completely within it. As the God-man, he united in his person the supernatural and the natural: and the problem of Christology so stated is how Jesus can be fully God and fully man, and yet genuinely one person.

The orthodox "answer" to this problem, as formulated in the Definition of Chalcedon, is within its own terms unexceptionable — except that properly speaking it is not a solution but a statement of the problem. But as a correct statement, as "a signpost against all heresies," it had — and has — an irreplaceable value. "The Christological dogma saved the Church," says Tillich, "but with very inadequate conceptual tools."[10] To use an analogy, if one had to present the doctrine of the person of Christ as a union of oil and water, then it made the best possible attempt to do so. Or rather it made the only possible attempt, which was to insist against all efforts to "confuse the substance" that there were two distinct natures and against all temptation to break the unity that there was but one indivisible person. It is not surprising, however, that in popular Christianity the oil and water separated, and that one or the other came to the top.

In fact, popular supranaturalistic Christology has always been domi-

9 *Honest to God* (Philadelphia: Westminster Press, 1963), pp. 64–77.

10 *Systematic Theology*, Vol. II, p. 161.

nantly docetic. That is to say, Christ only appeared to be a man or looked like a man: "underneath" he was God.

John Wren-Lewis gives a vivid description of an extreme form of this in the working-class religion in which he was brought up.

I have heard it said again and again that the ordinary person sees Jesus as a good man and no more. Modernist clergy hold it up as a reason why doctrines like that of the Virgin Birth will not appeal widely, while Anglo-Catholic clergy urge that the ordinary man must be taught to recognize Jesus as *more* than a good man, but both agree in their estimate of where the ordinary man stands, and I am sure they are quite wrong, even today. Certainly up to the Second World War, the commonest vision of Jesus was not as a human being *at all*. He was a God in human form, full of supernatural knowledge and miraculous power, very much like the Olympian gods were supposed to be when they visited the earth in disguise.[11]

But even if such a view would be indignantly repudiated by orthodox Churchmen, and however much they would insist that Jesus was "perfect man" as well as "perfect God," still the traditional supranaturalistic way of describing the Incarnation almost inevitably suggests that Jesus was really God almighty walking about on earth, dressed up as a man. Jesus was not a man born and bred — he was God for a limited period taking part in a charade. He looked like a man, he talked like a man, he felt like a man, but underneath he was God dressed up — like Father Christmas. However guardedly it may be stated, the traditional view leaves the impression that God took a space-trip and arrived on this planet in the form of a man.

[11] *They Became Anglicans*, p. 165.

Jesus was not really one of us; but through the miracle of the Virgin Birth he contrived to be born so as to appear one of us. Really he came from outside.[12]

I am aware that this is a parody, and probably an offensive one, but I think it is perilously near the truth of what most people — and I would include myself — have been brought up to believe at Christmas time. Indeed, the very word "incarnation" (which, of course, is not a Biblical term) almost inevitably suggests it. It conjures up the idea of a divine substance being plunged in flesh and coated with it like chocolate or silver plating. And if this is a crude picture, substitute for it that of the Christmas collect, which speaks of the Son of God "taking our nature upon him," or that of Wesley's Christmas hymn, with its "veiled in flesh the Godhead see."

But my point is not to ask how far particular expressions, or the general trend of thought they present, verge on the limits of orthodoxy but to put the question whether the entire supranaturalistic frame of reference does not make anything but a Christological *tour de force* impossible. For as long as God and man are thought of as two "beings," each with distinct natures, one from "the other side" and one from "this side," then it is impossible to create out of them more than a God-man, a divine visitant from

[12] For a powerful protest, even within the supranaturalist scheme of thought, that Jesus belonged, through and through, to the stuff of humanity, cf. Nels F. S. Ferré, *Christ and the Christian* (1958), Ch. II. Cf. W. N. Pittenger, *Proclaiming Christ Today* (1962), p. 87. "There is no salvation in telling men that Jesus is an 'intruder' from another world, who has not really shared our condition because, as an alien, he is not in fact one of us."

"out there" who chooses in every respect to live like the natives. The supranaturalist's view of the Incarnation can never really rid itself of the idea of the prince who appears in the guise of a beggar. However genuinely destitute the beggar may be, he *is* a prince; and that in the end is what matters.

But suppose the whole notion of "a God" who "visits" the earth in the person of "his Son" is as mythical as the prince in the fairy story? Suppose there is no realm "out there" from which the "Man from heaven" arrives? Suppose the Christmas myth (the invasion of "this side" by "the other side") — as opposed to the Christmas history (the birth of the man Jesus of Nazareth) — has to go? Are we prepared for that? Or are we to cling here to this last vestige of the mythological or metaphysical world-view as the only garb in which to clothe story with power to touch the imagination? Cannot perhaps the supranaturalist scheme survive at least as part of the "magic" of Christmas?

Yes, indeed, it can survive — as myth. For myth has its perfectly legitimate, and indeed profoundly important, place. The myth is there to indicate the significance of the events, the divine depth of the history. And we shall be grievously impoverished if our ears cannot tune to the angels' song or our eyes are blind to the wise men's star. But we must be able to read the nativity story without assuming that its truth depends on there being a literal interruption of the natural by the supernatural, that Jesus can only be Emmanuel — God with us — if, as it were, he came through from another world. For, as supranaturalism becomes less and less credible, to tie the action of God to such a way of thinking is to banish it for increasing numbers into the preserve of the pagan myths and thereby to sever it from any real connection with history. As Christmas becomes a pretty story, naturalism — the attempt to explain Christ, like everything else, on humanistic presuppositions — is left in possession of the field as the only alternative with any claim to the allegiance of intelligent men.

Naturalism has on the whole been remarkably favorable to Christianity in the realm of Christology. Once the "dogma" of his deity has been put out of the way, the humanist picture of Jesus is noticeably sympathetic, especially when compared with the sharpness of its "antitheism." Indeed, the non-Christian secularist view of Jesus shades imperceptibly into the estimate of his person in Liberal Christianity. To do it justice, let us then take the naturalistic interpretation of Christ at its highest and most positive.

This has even been ready to use the epithet "divine" of Jesus — in the sense that he was the most God-like man that ever lived, that what he said and did was so beautiful and so true that he must have been a revelation, indeed, the supreme revelation, of God. According to this view, the divine is simply the human raised to the power of "x." As Kierkegaard put it in a devastating parody more than a hundred years ago, "If the thing is well said, the man is a genius — and if it is unusually well said, then God said it." And by this Jesus is put "on the same level as all those who have no authority, on the same level as geniuses, poets and the thinkers."[13]

---

[13] "Of the Difference between a Genius and an Apostle" (1847) in *The Present Age* (Eng. tr., 1940), p. 146 f.

He is one of them, albeit the highest of them.

Unfortunately this is clearly not what the New Testament is saying of Jesus. Nor does the naturalist interpretation of Christ side with Athanasius on what he recognized to be the crucial divide. To say that Jesus had a unique experience of God, that he displayed all the qualities of God, that he was like God or that God was like him — this can never add up to saying that he was "of one substance" with the Father. And on that line Athanasius was correct in seeing that the battle must be fought, however much one may legitimately deplore the categories in which that test of orthodoxy had to be framed.

Yet the Liberals were entirely justified in the courage with which they were prepared to abandon the supranaturalistic scaffolding by which hitherto the whole structure had been supported. That house had to collapse, and they had the faith to see that Christianity need not collapse with it. Moreover, however inadequate the Liberal theology may now appear to us, it undoubtedly helped many to hold on to their faith at a time when otherwise they might have thrown it up completely. As the supranaturalistic scheme of things became incredible, a naturalistic theology was all that stood between an entire generation and abandoning the spirit and power of Jesus altogether. And the spirit and power was able in many cases to prove itself greater than the theology. Yet equally the theology has not sufficed to commend the spirit and power. Modern humanistic naturalism has found less and less need to speak of Jesus as in any sense "divine." The belief that we are at this point and in this person in touch with

God has increasingly been left to the religious minority that can still accept the old mythology as physically or metaphysically true. This is a dangerous situation for the Christian faith, and in no way helps to answer Bonhoeffer's searching question: "How can Christ become the Lord even of those with no religion?"[14]

THE CLAIM OF THE NEW TESTAMENT

But before we ask, with Bonhoeffer, "What *is* Christ for us today?"[15] we should stop and pose the prior question of what it is we have to reinterpret, of what in fact the New Testament is saying. For I believe that the supranaturalist, like the naturalist, estimate of Christ, whatever its intention, tends to be a distortion of the Biblical truth. I do not say it necessarily is, since the mythological-metaphysical framework can obviously provide the setting, as it has in the past, for an entirely orthodox Christology. But in practice popular preaching and teaching presents a supranaturalistic view of Christ which cannot be substantiated from the New Testament. It says simply that Jesus *was* God, in such a way that the terms "Christ" and "God" are interchangeable. But nowhere in Biblical usage is this so. The New Testament says that Jesus was the Word of God, it says that God was in Christ, it says that Jesus is the Son of God; but it does not say that Jesus was God, simply like that.[16]

---

[14] Dietrich Bonhoeffer, *Prisoner for God* (New York: Macmillan, 1956), p. 122 f.

[15] *Op. cit.*, p. 122.

[16] Or, rather, not in any passages that certainly require to be interpreted in this way. Passages that *may* be so interpreted are Rom 9:5 and Heb 1:8. But see in each case the alternative translations in the Revised Standard Version or the New English Bible.

What it does say is defined as succinctly and accurately as it can be in the opening verse of St. John's Gospel. But we have to be equally careful about the translation. The Greek runs: *kai theos en ho logos.* The so-called Authorized Version has: "And the Word was God." This would indeed suggest the view that "Jesus" and "God" were identical and interchangeable. But in Greek this would most naturally be represented by "God" with the article, not *theos* but *ho theos.* But, equally, St. John is not saying that Jesus is a "divine" man, in the sense in which the ancient world was familiar or in the sense in which the Liberals spoke of him. That would be *theios.* The Greek expression steers carefully between the two. It is impossible to represent it in a single English word, but the New English Bible, I believe, gets the sense pretty exactly with its rendering, "And what God was, the Word was." In other words, if one looked at Jesus, one saw God — for "he who has seen me, has seen the Father."[17] He was the complete expression, the Word, of God. Through him, as through no one else, God spoke and God acted: when one met him one was met — and saved and judged — by God. And it was to this conviction that the Apostles bore their witness. In this man, in his life, death and resurrection they had experienced God at work; and in the language of their day they confessed, like the centurion at the Cross, "Truly this man was the Son of God."[18] Here was more than just a man: here was a window into God at work. For "God was in Christ reconciling the world to himself."[19]

[17] Jn 14:9.
[18] Mk 15:39.
[19] 2 Cor 5:19.

The essential difference comes out in the matter of Jesus' claims. We are often asked to accept Christ as divine because he claimed to be so — and the familiar argument is pressed: "A man who goes around claiming to be God must either be God — or else he is a madman or a charlatan (*aut deus aut malus homo.*)" And, of course, it is not easy to read the Gospel story and to dismiss Jesus as either mad or bad. Therefore, the conclusion runs, he must be God.

But I am not happy about this argument. None of the disciples in the Gospels acknowledged Jesus because he claimed to be God, and the Apostles never went out saying, "This man claimed to be God, therefore you must believe in him." In fact, Jesus himself said in so many words, "If I claim anything for myself, do not believe me." It is, indeed, an open question whether Jesus ever claimed to be the Son of God, let alone God.[20] He may have acknowledged it from the lips of others — but on his own he preferred "the Son of Man." In Mark 14:61 f., he is reported to reply to the question at his trial, "Are you the Christ, the Son of the Blessed?," with the simple words, "I am." But in the parallel passage in Matthew[21] he gives an equivocal answer: "The words are yours" (as he does in all the Gospels when questioned by Pilate) — and what conceivable interest would Matthew have in watering down Jesus' claim?[22] We

[20] Indeed, by implication he *denied* being God: "Why do you call me good? No one is good but God alone" (Mk 10:18).
[21] Mt 26:63 f.
[22] I believe that the original text in Mark was probably "You have said that I am," and that Matthew has shortened this to "You have said," while the answer in Mark has subsequently been abbreviated (and heightened) to "I am." See my book, *Jesus and His Coming* (1957), pp. 43–51.

cannot be sure what titles Jesus claimed, and we should be wise, like the Apostles, not to rest our faith on them. Their message was rather that "God has made him both Lord and Christ, this Jesus whom you crucified."[23] That is to say, through the Resurrection God vindicated and set his seal upon this man as the one through whom he spoke and acted in final and decisive fashion. He vested himself utterly and completely in the man Christ Jesus; in him all his fullness dwelt.[24] What God was, the Word was.

There is a paradox running through all Gospels that Jesus makes no claims for himself in his own right and at the same time makes the most tremendous claims about what God is doing through him and uniquely through him. Men's response to him *is* men's response to God: men's rejection of him *is* men's rejection of God. And the fourth Gospel merely highlights this paradox (it does not, as is usually said, present quite a different picture of the claims of Jesus) when it combines the saying that "the Son can do nothing of his own accord, but only what he sees the Father doing"[25] with the uncompromising assertion, "No one comes to the Father, but by me."[26] Jesus never claims to be God, personally: yet he always claims to bring God, completely.

This paradox[27] is the point from which our reinterpretation of Christology must start. As the summary of his ministry in the fourth Gospel, Jesus cries out and says, "He who believes in me, believes not in me but in him who sent me. And he who sees me sees him who sent me."[28] Jesus, that is to say, reveals God by being utterly transparent to him, precisely as he is nothing "in himself." And Tillich makes this the criterion of the whole Christian claim that Jesus is the final revelation of God:

The question of the final revelation is the question of a medium of revelation which overcomes its own finite conditions by sacrificing them, and itself with them. He who is the bearer of the final revelation must surrender his finitude — not only his life but also his finite power and knowledge and perfection. In doing so, he affirms that he is the bearer of final revelation (the "Son of God" in classical terms). He became completely transparent to the mystery he reveals. But, in order to be able to surrender himself completely, he must possess himself completely. And only he can possess — and therefore surrender — himself completely who is united with the ground of his being and meaning without separation and disruption. In the picture of Jesus as the Christ we have the picture of a man who possesses these qualities, a man who, therefore, can be called the medium of final revelation.[29]

And thus it comes about that it is only on the Cross that Jesus can be the bearer of the final revelation and the embodiment of God's decisive act: it is "Christ crucified" who is "the power of God and the wisdom of God."[30] For it is in this ultimate surrender of self, in love "to the uttermost,"[31] that Jesus is so completely united to the Ground of his being that he can say, "I and the Father are one. . . . The Father is in me and I am in the Father."[32]

It is in Jesus, and Jesus alone, that there is nothing of self to be seen,

---

[23] Acts 2:36.   [25] Jn 5:19.
[24] Col 1:19.   [26] Jn 14:6.
[27] Fastened on also by D. M. Bailie, *God Was in Christ* (1948), pp. 125–132.

[28] Jn 12:44 f.   [32] Jn 10:30, 38.
[29] *Systematic Theology*, Vol. I, p. 148.
[30] 1 Cor 1:23 f.
[31] Jn 13:1.

but solely the ultimate, unconditional love of God. It is as he emptied himself utterly of himself that he became the carrier of "the name which is above every name,"[33] the revealer of the Father's glory[34] — for that name and that glory is simply love. The "kenotic" theory of Christology, based on this conception of self-emptying, is, I am persuaded, the only one that offers much hope of relating at all satisfactorily the divine and the human in Christ.[35] Yet the fatal weakness of this theory as it is stated in supranaturalist terms is that it represents Christ as stripping himself precisely of those attributes of transcendence which make him the revelation of God.[36] The underlying assumption is that it is his omnipotence, his omniscience, and all that makes him "superhuman" that must be shed in order for him to become truly man. On the contrary, it is as he empties himself not of his Godhead but of himself, of any desire to focus attention on himself, of any craving to be "on an equality with God"[37] that he reveals God. For it is in making himself nothing, in his utter self-surrender to others in love, that he discloses and lays bare the Ground of man's being as Love.

WHAT IS CHRIST FOR US TODAY?

It was some such Christology, I believe, towards which Bonhoeffer was working and of which he left such tantalizing intimations behind him.

[33] Phil 2:5–11.
[34] Jn 17:4 f.
[35] Cf. in particular its superb elaboration in P. T. Forsyth, *The Person and Place of Jesus Christ* (1909), pp. 313–316.
[36] See the damaging criticism of D. M. Baillie, *op. cit.*, pp. 94–98, and A. M. Ramsey, *From Gore to Temple* (1960), 30–43.
[37] Phil 2:6.

Describing the process of increasing secularization, of man's coming of age without God, as a process which Christians must *welcome*, he says, in a passage which was quoted earlier:

God allows himself to be edged out of the world and on to the cross. God is weak and powerless in the world, and that is exactly the way, the only way, in which he can be with us and help us. Matthew 8:17 makes it crystal clear that it is not by his omnipotence that Christ helps us, but by his weakness and suffering. . . . Man's religiosity makes him look in his distress to the power of God in the world; he uses God as a *Deus ex Machina*. The Bible however directs him to the powerlessness and suffering of God; only a suffering God can help.[38]

And from this he proceeds to sketch out a Christology. All he has left us is a single pregnant paragraph of notes for the "outline for a book" he never lived to write:

What do we mean by "God"? Not in the first place an abstract belief in his omnipotence, etc. That is not a genuine experience of God, but a partial extension of the world. Encounter with Jesus Christ, implying a complete orientation of human being in the experience of Jesus as one whose only concern is for others. This concern of Jesus for others the experience of transcendence. This freedom from self, maintained to the point of death, the sole ground of his omnipotence, omniscience and ubiquity. Faith is participation in this Being of Jesus (incarnation, cross and resurrection). Our relation to God not a religious relationship to a supreme Being, absolute in power and goodness, which is a spurious conception of transcendence, but a new life for others, through participation in the Being of God. The transcendence consists not in tasks beyond our scope and power, but in the nearest Thou[39] at hand. God

[38] *Op. cit.*, p. 164.
[39] E. Bethge in *Chicago Theological Seminary Register*, Vol. LI; (Feb., 1961), p.

in human form, not, as in other religions, in animal form — the monstrous, chaotic, remote and terrifying — nor yet in abstract form — the absolute, metaphysical, infinite, etc. — nor yet in the Greek divine-human of autonomous man, but man existing for others, and hence the Crucified. A life based on the transcendent.[40]

Jesus is "the man for others," the one in whom Love has completely taken over, the one who is utterly open to, and united with, the Ground of his being. And this "life for others, through participation in the Being of God," is, transcendence. For at this point, of love "to the uttermost," we encounter *God*, the ultimate "depth" of our being, the unconditional in the conditioned. This is what the New Testament means by saying that "God was in Christ" and that "what God was the Word was." Because Christ was utterly and completely "the man for others," because he *was* love, he was "one with the Father," because "God is love." But for this very reason he was most entirely man, the son of man, the servant of the Lord. He was indeed "one of us"; and the symbol of the Virgin Birth can only legitimately mean what the fourth Gospel takes it to mean (if, indeed, its description of Christians reflects that of Christ[41]), namely, that the whole of his life is a life "born not of the will of the flesh, nor of the will of man but of God." He is indeed not "of this world" but "of love." The source and spring of his whole being is God: his is a life conceived and sustained utterly by the Holy Ghost. But he is for that reason only the more truly "the proper Man." In the man Christ Jesus stands revealed, exposed at the surface level of "flesh," the depth and ground of all our being as Love.[42] The life of God, the ultimate Word of Love in which all things cohere,[43] is bodied forth completely, unconditionally and without reserve in the life of a man — the man for others and the man for God. He is perfect man and perfect God — not as a mixture of oil and water, of natural and supernatural — but as the embodiment through obedience of "the beyond in our midst," of the transcendence of love.

---

according to St. John (1955), p. 137 f.: "The reading which refers explicitly to the birth of Jesus is to be rejected; but it remains probable that John was alluding to Jesus' birth, and declaring that the birth of Christians, being rooted in God's will alone, followed the pattern of the birth of Christ himself."

[42] Jn 1:14. Such I believe is what St. John is saying in the words *sarx egeneto*, not (as the later term 'incarnation' suggests) that something from outside comes into and is encased in 'flesh.' Indeed, unless it is read with supranaturalist spectacles, the Prologue requires as little 'demythologizing' as any part of the New Testament.

[43] Col 1:17.

32: "Terrible translation mistake (in E.T.): 'nearest thing.' "

[40] *Ibid.*, p. 179.

[41] Jn 1:13. The plural 'were born' should be preferred to the variant reading 'was born.' But see C. K. Barrett, *The Gospel*

CHAPTER 7. MODERN DEVELOPMENTS IN CATHOLIC THOUGHT

INTRODUCTION

I. KARL RAHNER*

Current Problems in Christology[1]

---

* Karl Rahner (1904–   ) taught in Austria and studied theology under the Jesuits in Holland. After finishing his studies and being ordained a Jesuit, he studied under Martin Heidegger at Freiburg. He was professor of dogmatic theology at Innsbruck and now teaches at the University of Munich. Concerned basically with the relation between God and man, Rahner unceasingly "inquires into the Word, the Revelation of the triune God embodied in the faith of the Church and become flesh in Jesus Christ." He has written *The Church and the Sacraments, Inspiration in the Bible,* a multivolume *Theological Investigations,* and numerous other works.

Once theologians and the ordinary magisterium of the Church have begun to pay attention to a reality and a truth revealed by God, the final result is always a precisely formulated statement. This is natural and inevitable. In no other way is it possible to mark the boundary of error and the misunderstanding of divine truth in such a way that this boundary will be observed in the day-to-day practice of religion. Yet while this formula is an end, an acquisition and a victory, which allows us to enjoy clarity and security as well as ease in instruction,

[1] *Theological Investigations* (Baltimore: Helicon Press, 1961), Vol. I, pp. 149–155, 165–200 *passim.*

179

if this victory is to be a true one the end must also be a beginning. It follows from the nature of human knowledge of truth and from the nature of divine truth itself, that any individual truth, above all one of God's truths, is beginning and emergence, not conclusion and end. In the last resort any individual human perception of truth only has meaning as beginning and promise of the knowledge of God. But whether the latter is conceived of as *visio beatifica* or otherwise, it can only be genuine, only make blessed, in the knowledge of his incomprehensibility: at that point, then, in which comprehension and the determining limits of what is known are jointly transcended in the Incomprehensible and the Unlimited. Because every truth of the God who reveals himself is given as an incitement and a way to the closest immediacy of communion with him, it is all the more an opening into the immeasurable, a beginning of the illimitable. The clearest formulations, the most sanctified formulas, the classic condensations of the centuries-long work of the Church in prayer, reflexion and struggle concerning God's mysteries: all these derive their life from the fact that they are not end but beginning, not goal but means, truths which open the way to the — ever greater — Truth. The fact that every formula transcends itself (not because it is false, but precisely because it is true) is not due just to the transcendence of the mind which apprehends it and, in apprehending it, is always off beyond it after the greater fullness of Reality and Truth itself. Nor is this self-transcendence due merely to the divine grace of faith, which always transforms the perception of a truth in propositional form into a movement of the mind towards the apprehension

of God's ontological truth in itself. This transcendence is at work precisely in the movement of the formula itself, in that it is itself surpassed with a view to another. This certainly does not mean that the first formula has to be given up or abolished in favor of another, as though it were antiquated or another could take its place. On the contrary: it preserves its significance, it remains precisely living, by being expounded. This is so true and so obvious, that whole books can and must be written about the principle of identity, that is to say, the simplest, clearest, most necessary and undeniable formula of all, because it cannot really be said with much confidence that someone who monotonously keeps on repeating it — dressed up with a few "clarificatory" phrases — has in fact understood it. Anyone who takes seriously the "historicity" of human truth (in which God's truth too has become incarnate in Revelation) must see that neither the abandonment of a formula nor its preservation in a petrified form does justice to human understanding. For history is precisely *not* an atomized beginning-ever-anew; it is rather (the more spiritual it is) a becoming-new which preserves the old, and preserves it all the more *as* old, the more spiritual this history is. But this preservation, which recognizes the true uniqueness of something which has taken place once for all, is only historical preservation when — the history goes on, and the movement of reflexion departs from the formula which has been reached in order to discover it (just this old formula itself) again.

This holds good of the Chalcedonian formulation of the mystery of Jesus too. For this formula is — a formula.

Thus we have not only the right but the duty to look at it as end *and* as beginning. We shall never stop trying to release ourselves from it, not so as to abandon it but to understand it, understand it with mind and heart, so that through it we might draw near to the ineffable, unapproachable, nameless God, whose will it was that we should find him in Jesus Christ and through Christ seek him. We shall never cease to return to this formula, because whenever it is necessary to say briefly what it is that we encounter in the ineffable truth which is our salvation, we shall always have recourse to the modest, sober clarity of the Chalcedonian formula. But we shall only really have recourse to it (and this is not at all the same thing as simply repeating it), if it is not only our end but also our beginning. We must say something here about this incompleteness which the formula does not resolve but in fact preserves.

Anyone who speaks of incompleteness in a matter like this must be prepared to be dismissed with contempt. This sort of language is hardly "scientific." It has to try to get a hearing without the help of the apparatus of learning; inevitably it sounds a little vague, rather like the cheap political programme which promises the emergence of a New Age, although the new Government is probably going to be just as bad as the old. It cannot by itself put into practice what it demands, and that is what is most questionable about it. or if someone says that this matter or that must be considered or investigated, or should be freshly analyzed and treated of more comprehensively and profoundly, and yet this does not come about immediately in reality, he speaks like a man who proposes a route by which he himself has never traveled. It may very well be that many of his wishes and conjectures do not touch upon the essential, that the really decisive point will be overlooked. Nevertheless preliminary reflexions of this conjectural and tentative kind are unavoidable, and can only be despised or rejected in principle by someone who thinks that as far as Christology proper is concerned we have already reached the end. But if we are always at the beginning, then the first step is always the uneasy feeling of a need to ask whether it might not be possible to give this or that matter closer attention and find a better solution.

The object which this anxious seeking for the question (it is nothing more) has in view is not of course simply the whole plenitude of the "objective Spirit"[2] of Revelation and theology in their long history. If we had clearly before us the plenitude of what was once perceived in faith and meditated upon in theology throughout its entire history, we should already in great part have found the question we are looking for and its answer too, for it is the bitter grief of theology and its blessed task too, always to have to seek (because it does not clearly have present to it at the time) what, in a true sense — in its historical memory — it has always known. The history of theology is by no means just the history of the progress of doctrine, but also a history of forgetting. That is the only reason why historical theology and history of doctrine have a real, irreplaceable and necessary task within dogmatic theology itself. What was once given in history and is ever made present anew does not primarily form a set of premises from which we

[2] In the Hegelian sense. —Tr.

can draw new conclusions which have never been thought of before. It is the object which, while it is always retained, must ever be acquired anew, by *us*, that is, we who are just such as no one else can ever be in all history. So that when in considerable uncertainty, we set about asking — and the question itself has to be found first — what it is that we must bring back to mind so as to be able to make our own what we believe, the starting-point of this attempt to ask questions cannot be the whole of Revelation and its history in theology. It is the *answer* which lies there. The starting-point can only be the generally accepted position in theology today (meaning here Christology), as it is found in modern textbooks, in the conception which everybody would agree is the ordinary one, in what appears really clearly in our ordinary theological consciousness today. Any attempt to describe this starting-point is inevitably going to give the impression of being ill-informed, of generalizing unjustly and of distorting current theology. For this "current theology" cannot easily be detached from its entire past; because along with the average it always offers — thank God — something deeper and closer to the sources of life; because when it is attacked and defends itself, it can always surpass itself and relate what it holds to the past and the future. And so it is impossible to avoid the danger of seeming to caricature current Christology when one attempts to describe what it finds clear and what would have to become still clearer to it in the future. Just because in theology everything is connected with everything else, it is always going to be the case that anyone who is sensitive to the reproach of not having examined this or that

question sufficiently or given it a satisfactory answer, can impatiently, but with a good conscience, hold that he has always really been aware of the question in point, and "basically" even discussed it and analyzed it sufficiently. One can only ask such a theologian why he has only discussed so briefly and casually what clearly deserves precise and detailed treatment, and whether he has not forgotten in other places what he — so he claims — regards as "obvious," and whether this does not show that after all what everybody knows and what has long since been cleared up doesn't perhaps count for much. One has only to consider how few really living and passionate controversies there are in Catholic Christology today which engage the existential concern of the faithful (is there a single one?). Unless someone is inclined to regard this fact simply as a mark of superiority, a proof of unruffled orthodoxy and crystal-clear theology, he will listen with patience and good will to the most modest attempt, undertaken with the most inadequate means, to depart from the Chalcedonian formula in order to find the way back to it in truth.

We should also observe the following point. The degree of theoretical precision and existential vitality with which man understands what he hears depends on the degree to which he comprehends it within the total content of his spiritual being. If this were not the case, there would never have been Councils of the Church with their definitions, because a new age would always have been able to live on in the old clarity; or we should have to suppose that the *only* reason for these Councils was the fact that there had been evil heretics who maliciously obscured what in itself had been said with quite sufficient clarity and what in itself would have been quite sufficient for later ages in spite of their unlikeness. If then the ordinary theology current today is to be asked why what it has told *us* is insufficiently clear, by "us" is meant we as we must be today; for man's unique standpoint in history is inescapably given him in advance and helps to determine the perspective within which we have to consider God's eternal truths too, if we are really going to let them become a reality of mind, heart and life in our personal existence. This is not to say that it is in general particularly profitable for theology to take as the explicit starting-point of a critical consideration of the average Christology current today, any characteristic features of just that spiritual situation which has been imposed upon us, insofar as they are apprehended *reflectively*. Such a method is seldom successful, if only because these reflexively apprehended characteristics of the time are probably signatures of a time which is on the way out; it is unlikely that we should discover from them postulates big with promise for the Christology of tomorrow. It is preferable simply to look at the facts, that is to say at Christology itself — always providing that one has the courage to ask questions, to be dissatisfied, to think with the mind and heart one actually has, and not with the mind and heart one is supposed to have. One can then be confident that after all something will perhaps emerge which we ought to be thinking today. For it is quite meaningless to want to be modern on purpose. The only thing one can do in this situation is not to suppose that it is necessary to deny who one is (out of anxiety or distrust or falsely under-

stood orthodoxy), but rather allow oneself honestly to have one's say, and really build on the fact that God can give his grace to this age of ours too, as he once gave it to sinners.

Let us then begin by going to the heart of the matter. This is primarily Biblical theology. There is no question here of practicing Biblical theology in its own right; our intention is much more modest. We propose to show by means of a kind of transcendental hermeneutics[3] starting from dogma that the Church's Christological dogma never claims to be an adequate condensation of Biblical teaching, and so that there does remain from the viewpoint of dogma a place for further Christological Biblical theology. It is only in this sense that we shall speak of Biblical theology in what follows. It should be the source of dogmatic theology and so also of Christology. Without it, according to *Humani Generis*,[4] dogmatic theology becomes sterile. And here we are already faced with a serious problem. How are we to pursue Biblical theology for Christological purposes, both generally speaking and in dogmatic theology in particular? Is it rash or unjust to say that among Catholic writers, the professional exegetes in this field do not practice Biblical theology, and that the dogmatic theologians know or make use of only those parts of the Scriptures which they require in order to prove Christological theses which have been laid down in advance in a canon already become traditional? Or, in case the first suggestion seems too hard, what noteworthy influence has

[3] An expression reminiscent of Kant, Dilthey, Heidegger. —Tr.

[4] Pius XII, *Litterae Encyclicae "Humani Generis"* (12 August 1950), AAS XLII (1950), pp. 568–569; Denz 3014.

modern Biblical theology had (so far as it is practiced) upon the structure and content of the traditional scholastic theology?[5] Of course the theses of this scholastic theology are true and important, so far as they are dogma. Of course these theses are the concise, condensed expression of the fundamental testimonies in Scripture concerning Jesus Christ, an expression achieved by the immense labor of an irreversible spiritual and cultural history under the guidance of the Spirit of God in the Church. But is it true that the Chalcedonian dogma, and what little else has been acquired for the theology of the schools in the history of dogma, is a condensation and summary of *everything*, without remainder, of which we hear in Scripture about Jesus the Christ and about the Son, or, again, of what we *might* hear if only we were to speak once more of what has still not entered into scholastic theology? Anyone who answers this question in the affirmative would deny that the Scriptures are the *inexhaustible* source of truth about Christ.[6] But is this conviction noticeable as an active force and a holy disquiet in the ordinary practice of Christology today? For example, let us take L. de Grandmaison's undoubtedly great work on Christ; after all its minute historical investigations, does it not, looked at *theologically*, simply arrive once again at the scholastic position in Christology? Is this to be explained merely by the fact that it has an apologetic end in view and not an immediately theological one?

---

[5] "Traditional" here refers to the actual practice of recent centuries, especially since the Enlightenment and the (fruitful and perilous) restoration of scholastic theology after the theology of the Enlightenment.

[6] "Humani Generis," AAS, p. 568; Denz 3014.

Let no one say that nothing more is really possible in this field any longer. Something is possible, because something *must* be possible, if it is a matter of the inexhaustible riches of God's presence with us and if we honestly admit that we often find traditional Christology difficult to understand (we shall return to this point later) and so have questions to put to its source, the Scriptures.

. . . Here we must remember that the world is something in which everything is related to everything else, and that consequently anyone who makes some portion of it into his own history, takes for himself the world as a whole for his personal environment. Consequently it is not pure fantasy (though the attempt must be made with caution) to conceive of the "evolution" of the world *toward Christ*, and to show how there is a gradual ascent which reaches a peak in him. Only we must reject the idea that this "evolution" could be a striving upward of what is below by its own powers. If Col 1:15 is true, and is not attenuated in a moralistic sense; if then in Christ the world as a whole, even in its "physical" reality, has really reached historically[7] through Christ that point in which God becomes all in all,[8] then an attempt like this cannot be false in principle. But if it is in fact possible to attempt something like this, we can make use of the general categories of the God-creature relation (distance-proximity;

---

[7] Though in a history which is at the same time essentially spirit, freedom, "moral."

[8] And this must be understood in an essentially Christological sense, not as something abstractly metaphysical, "permanently valid"; because God in Christ really *became* world, and so "All" in all.

image-concealment; time-eternity; dependence-independence) in their radical, sharply differentiated form in order to make fundamental statements about Christ, and regard all other realities in this field of what is distinct from God as deficient modes of this primary Christological relation.

The fact that classical Christology makes permanently valid statements about Christ which attribute to him an entitative determination[9] already (relatively) fixed and familiar (such as "He is man" — so that we must already know what "man" is) is no argument against this view. We may not say that it is illegitimate to try to take Christ as the starting-point in order to define these entitative determinations, and that consequently a "Christian" ontology must necessarily be false in principle. For it will be clear on reflexion that our presupposition is that statements about Christ himself (even though they are intended to serve as a point of departure for the more general statements of a theological ontology) are made with the help of a general doctrine of creation (and the ontology contained in it). Christology most certainly cannot and should not form an absolute point of departure for an ontology (and hence still less for an anthropology). Nevertheless the parallels in philosophical knowledge of God and the world show that a retrospective use can be made of Christology for ontological and anthropological assertions: God is known from the world,

and yet we can start from God in order to say what the world is.

. . . All we wish to suggest is that a Christology using categories appropriate to the description of consciousness need not be false a priori or impossible. If there is an ontic Christology, there can also be an existential[10] one (or however one may wish to describe statements about the way in which a spiritual being is present to itself). Thus we may confidently ask whether an absolutely exact understanding of our Lord's statements about his "spiritual" relationship to God (the Father) could not lead to statements which would be equivalent, as ontological (existential)[10] statements, to those of an ontic Christology. The fact that this existential[11] relationship of Christ as man to God is not immediately available in our own experience, thus where our concepts have their origin, does not absolutely forbid our making such statements. For the ontic relationship of his human nature is not immediately available to us either, and yet it can be stated in an analogical, indirect and asymptotic way. Otherwise there would be no Christology at all which could say something about what Christ really is. It is true that there have been attempts in this direction in modern Protestantism which, owing to hostility to the metaphysics in the "Greek" theology of the Fathers and Scholasticism and the use of philosophically inadequate instruments, have led to heresy, because they reduce the mystery of Christ to the level of our own religious experience and our own relationship to God; but this is still no proof that such attempts are impossible and false a priori. Sup-

---

[9] *Sachverhalt.* This can ordinarily be rendered "state of affairs." The word has however a technical philosophical usage, in which it means something like "the objective content of a proposition." "Entitative determination" is offered as a rough approximation. —Tr.

[10] *Existentielle.*
[11] *Existential.*

pose someone says:[12] "Jesus is the man whose life is one of absolutely unique self-surrender to God." He may very well have stated the truth about the very depths of what Christ really is, *provided* that he has understood (a) that this self-abandonment presupposes a communication of God to the man; (b) that an absolute self-surrender implies an absolute communication of God to the man, one which makes what is produced by it into the reality of the producer himself; and (c) that such an existential statement does not signify something "mental," a fiction, but is in the most radical way a statement about being. It may be objected that a Christological statement like this, bearing on Christ's mind, either remains outside the limits of Christological dogma and its ontic formulations (and thus is heretical), or must appeal to ontic formulations in order to characterize the uniqueness and specific otherness of this relationship to God in distinction from any religious experience of our own or of the prophets. The second alternative[13] may be granted, though it does not follow from this that such existential statements are superfluous. It is true that these statements (so far as we possess concepts for them) may perhaps[14] not be capable, without the help of formal ontic

concepts, of distinguishing precisely enough from other relationships a conscious existential relationship to God which is not available to our immediate experience. Yet they are extremely useful in filling out the formal emptiness of a *purely* ontic Christological statement, which would otherwise be in danger of being filled out in some other way, namely by interpretations of Christological formulas which are not indeed formulated explicitly, but which only too easily crystallize around the formulas without being noticed; these interpretations then make Christ out to be nothing but God clothed in a human form. If this danger is really avoided by asserting a conscious relationship of the man Jesus with respect to God, and by asserting it in such a way that the assertion of the distinctively unique character of this relationship is *eo ipso* an implicit or explicit assertion of the *unio hypostatica;* then the Scriptural accounts of Jesus' conscious dispositions to the Father would really be translated into theological Christology.

. . . At the beginning of this section it was said that our rough knowledge of what man is, when we used the formula of Chalcedon, was due to the fact that we daily learn what it is to be human by experience of each other and of ourselves. The slightest of discussions of the problems of this formula has shown that the attempt to advance our understanding of what this unity (unconfused and undivided) is which makes the human nature that of the Logos itself, would also further our understanding of who man is; we see that Christology is at once beginning and end of anthropology, and that for all eternity such an anthropology is really theo-logy. For God himself has become man. The less

---

[12] This example is not meant to anticipate the successful performance of an undertaking which has here only been postulated. It is only intended to illustrate, in a case which is clearly highly problematic and in need of cautious treatment, what the task proposed would in general involve.

[13] As something not wholly avoidable "*quoad nos.*"

[14] This question, which would lead us into general considerations belonging to the metaphysics of knowledge, cannot be treated of here, and must be allowed to remain open.

we merely think of this humanity as something added on to God, and the more we understand it as God's very presence in the world and hence (not, all the same) see it in a true, spontaneous vitality and freedom before God, the more intelligible does the abiding mystery of our faith become, and also an expression of our very own existence. . . .

A theological phenomenology of the religious attitude with regard to Christ is greatly to be desired. It cannot be denied that in the ordinary religious act of the Christian, when it is not referred precisely to the historical life of Jesus by way of meditation, Christ finds a place only as God. We see here the mysterious monophysite undercurrent in ordinary Christology and a tendency to let the creaturely be ovewhelmed in face of the Absolute, as though God were to become greater and more real by the devaluation and cancellation of the creature. Another sign of this is to be observed in the fact that Christ's humanity no longer has any part to play in the theology of the *visio beatifica*, as this is ordinarily presented. Theology is only concerned with the One who has become man insofar as he appeared at the historical time of his life on earth as Teacher, Founder, and Redeemer. There is hardly any developed doctrine of his abiding function as man; and correspondingly, the doctrine of the specific character of our abiding relationship to him as Man-for-all-eternity is extremely fragmentary. Something is said about the adoration which is due to him even as man. But no one seems to have much to say about the fact that our basic religious acts, which are continually effected through the mediation of Christ, have an "incarnational" struc-

ture. There is hardly any mention of Christ in the tractate *de Virtutibus Theologicis:* the discussion moves merely in the thin atmosphere of pure theological metaphysics. Reflexion on the permanence of Christ's humanity according to Chalcedon, which alone really brings God within the reach of our acts, has not yet penetrated as far as these tractates on the theological virtues or on *religio*.[15] The Council of Chalcedon has still to conquer here. The anti-Arian reaction, the special character of the Latin doctrine of the Trinity and the existential undercurrent of monophysite tendency in Christology, have all delayed this victory. But this very fact, that Christ more or less vanishes for an act momentarily directing itself to God, has led to a situation, for which there are other causes as well, in which the Incarnation appears to be almost a transient episode in God's activity in his world and is thus unreflexively felt to be a myth unworthy of faith. In view of this situation, a theological phenomenology of an "incarnational" piety, valid now and always, would not only have significance for the doctrine of the spiritual life; it would also be important as a means of removing the basic causes which have led to a demand for "demythologization."

. . . Dogmatic Christology might pay a little attention to the general history of religions. There is no intention here of proposing a "hunt for parallels" to the doctrine of the Incarnation in other religions, nor ultimately of showing that such parallels do not really exist. In the last resort

---

[15] Cf. K. Rahner, "Die ewige Bedeutung der Menschheit Jesu für unser Gottesverhältnis," *Geist und Leben* XXVI (1953), pp. 279–288 (which appears in Vol. III of the German edition of these studies).

the point of such a study would be to examine the history of religions from the standpoint of our knowledge of the historical Incarnation, and from this standpoint alone, the only one to offer a really illuminating interpretation of a history otherwise unintelligible in itself: and to examine this history with a view to seeing whether and how far man in fact shows himself in history for what he unquestionably is in the depth of his concrete nature: a being who in the course of his history looks out for the presence of God himself. When the early Fathers kept a lookout for such an activity of the Logos, the beginnings of his Incarnation as it were, in saving history before Christ (at least in the Old Testament), they were better advised than we are, for whom God rules there simply from heaven. It may in general be allowed that the history of religions[16] as a whole only escapes the mortal danger of infecting Christians with some sort of relativism when it is integrated (as Yes or No) in the single history of the dialogue between God and the world, a dialogue which flows into the Word become flesh, and when it is not interpreted merely as the product of a purely terrestrial religiosity of rationalism and as a human perversion. If this is true, it holds good also of the history of religions insofar as they were an unconscious Yes or No to the Word of God who was to come in human flesh.

Would it be a delusion to suppose that the abstract formalism of Chris-

[16] For the first time since the patristic era, this history is becoming a reality for the West again, in the perichoresis of all cultures and historical movements which is in fact taking place today. Cf. H. de Lubac, *La Rencontre du Bouddhisme et l'Occident*, Paris, 1952.

tology has also contributed to a decrease of interest in a theology of the mysteries of Christ's human life? There is still a lively theological (and not just pious) interest in the mysteries of the Life of Jesus in St. Thomas and even in Suarez. In the ordinary textbook-Christology current today, one has to keep a pretty close lookout to find anything about Christ's Ascension, as if this were a matter primarily for *theologia fundamentalis*. The Passion is treated of from an exceedingly formal viewpoint in soteriology, which seems very little interested in the concreteness of the Passion on the ground that some other moral deed of Christ's would have redeemed us "just as well" if God had so pleased. What do we hear of Christ's Circumcision, Baptism, his prayer, the Transfiguration, the Presentation in the Temple, the Mount of Olives, the abandonment by God on the Cross, the descent into the underworld, the Ascension into heaven and so on? Nothing or pretty well nothing.[17] All

[17] The Biblical exegetes proper often seem today to be intimidated by the dogmatic theologians and their true — and often presumed — office as censors. They take the utmost care to avoid going a single step beyond the letter of the text and getting down to the real theological issues involved. What really happened at the Transfiguration? What took place at the Ascension? What did eating involve for Christ after his Resurrection? What really happened when he descended into Hell? What is Mt 27:51 s. telling us about the saints who rose from the dead, and what is its theological significance? What took place when Jesus was tempted? What are we to think about his remaining behind in the Temple as a boy? How are the postulates of dogmatic theology capable of being harmonized with Jesus' wonderment, his "ignorance" and so on? It cannot be said that the exegetes have given much sign of theological heart for these questions and others like them.

this is left to piety, and it is rarely that we find anything more than applications of a moral and edifying kind here. The mysteries of Christ, which precisely in their once-for-all character and indissoluble historicity form the law of once-for-all world history, are all too easily misconceived as mere illustrations and examples, as "instances," in which general moral laws, which are just as clear even apart from Christ's life, are exemplified. Instead of a genuine theology of Christ's life, we find that the theology (not in itself unjustified) of certain abstract privileges enjoyed by Christ has forced itself into the foreground; and that this theology draws attention to certain features (in the field of knowledge, for instance, Christ's *visio* in the course of his life on earth, his infused knowledge and so on) which distinguish him from us, and even these features it does not always postulate for reasons which are really illuminating. This development is conditioned (if not perhaps with a very high degree of self-awareness) by that purely formal understanding of the unity of Christ as united, of which we have spoken above. In a conception like this an event in the field of Christ's humanity only has "interest" insofar as it is dignified by being adopted by Christ's person, and thus precisely not in itself; or again insofar as it possesses special features not to be found elsewhere among human beings. Once attention has been turned in these two directions, the only soteriology to be expected is of that single type which (perfectly correct in itself) we do in fact find even today. This still contains a section on certain permanent "*consectaria unionis hypostaticae*," but lacks any theological consideration of the history (which

is in itself theological in the highest degree) of the particular, once-for-all events of the life of Christ as man, born of a woman, subject to history, law and death. This human reality as human (not as something abstract, of course) in its "bare" humanity can only be of theological importance if it is as such (as just this) the manifestation of God in the world, not just as something joined on in a logically subsequent way; if, that is to say, it is one with the Logos in virtue of being the reality of the Logos itself, and not the reality of the Logos in virtue of being "one" (how?) with the Logos. If we are to have a true theology of the human life of Jesus (not merely a theology of the extraordinary in Jesus' life) we must recover that right view of things which does not (by "abstracting") overlook just that which cannot be really separated from what is human in Jesus: we must learn to see that what is human in Jesus is not something human (and as such uninteresting for us in the world) and "*in addition*" God's as well (and in this respect alone important, this special character however always merely hovering above the human and forming its exterior setting, as it were). On the contrary, in this view the everyday human reality of this life is God's Ek-sistence, in the sense cautiously determined above: it is human reality *and so* God's, and *vice versa*. Then it will no longer be necessary to ask the question: What is there exceptional about this life over and beyond ours as we are already familiar with it, whose heights we have already climbed and into whose depths we have already plunged, what is there about it (still strictly only as a plus-quantity) which could make it important for us too? But the question we must ask is: What does our life mean, this life which we ultimately fail to understand when we examine ourselves, however familiar with it we may be, what does it mean when it is first and last the life of God? It is because we need this ultimate interpretation of our lives, one which is not to be had elsewhere, that we must study the theology of Christ's life and death. Why does this happen so seldom in current Christology?

Thus we have reached the point of laying down requirements for *soteriology*, and have indicated why and how the average textbook-Christology leads to inadequacies or omissions in this field. The gravamen of our charge may be simply formulated as follows: as far as soteriology is concerned, the average theology current in our schools today is only interested in the formal value of Christ's redemptive act, not in its concrete content, the inner structure of the redemptive process in itself. Now the account usually given of the infinite worth of Christ's act as regards satisfaction and merit, on account of the infinite dignity of the Person, is a perfectly correct one. But it would be false to suppose that this accounts for all that is essential in soteriology. Yet this is in fact what is supposed. The simplest proof of this statement is found in the fact that the satisfaction theory in soteriology not only assumes tacitly but also explicitly maintains that Christ would equally have been able to redeem us by any other moral action, provided only that God had so willed it and had accepted this action as vicarious satisfaction. The inner content of the redemptive act (i.e., the Cross, death, obedience, abandonment by God, death due to the action of sinners themselves) thus only has signifi-

cance for the Redemption as such in its abstract moral quality, which as it were gives up its substratum and its matter for the value which this action acquires in virtue of the dignity of the divine Person; the precise content of the action makes no difference. Now we have no intention of denying that God would have been able to forgive us our sin in regard to any one of Christ's acts at all, and that this forgiveness would be "Redemption," and what is more Redemption on account of a *"satisfacio condigna."* But if the matter is so regarded, essential facts and problems of a really adequate soteriology are overlooked, in that a soteriology is bound to say how *we* were redeemed in concrete fact. . . . Anyone who wishes to proclaim the Incarnation as something worthy of faith, that is, who wishes to make it possible for modern man to assimilate this Truth of all truths, must find a place for it in his *single* historical world. But it is no longer a simple matter for modern man to accept as worthy of faith the position that the event of the Incarnation should have taken place just once. Why is there no Godmanhood in general? Or better: why does this exist in fact (as regards grace and eternal life) in such a way as precisely to "require"[18] that the *unio hypostatica* in the strict sense took place just once? How are we to understand the inner connection and unity of the cosmos as a whole, the nature of man and angel, in such a way as to make it comprehensible that the Logos became "only" man, and yet that as such he is Head and End

---

[18] It need hardly be said that the question is left open here as to how far this "requirement" signifies a pure *convenientia*, i.e., a genuine connection of meaning obtaining in objective reality, or a strict necessity.

of the whole cosmos (including the angels), and this not only in respect of a higher dignity (than that of the angels) but also in respect of a real function which he exercises with regard to the angels as well? We have to offer a picture of the world in which the *one* Christ, the one Christ as *man*, seems meaningful. This point is of kerygmatic importance today. A clearer and more explicit treatment of it would help to show (and this itself is important) that the classical Christology of the dogma is in no need of demythologization.

The same is true of the *time* of the Incarnation.

The Fathers took a more active interest in this question than the thinkers of later times. Today it has become important again: on account of the prolongation in time both of human history *before* Christ, as well as of possible history *after* Christ. Both are more extensive, stirred by more various movements, than the Middle Ages used to think. In the expectations of many men, the higher development of humanity seems only to reach its ultimately intended realization in a mastery of the material world, the unification of men in society and their planned, i.e., rationally ordered, life in common. It is of the first importance to show, with a sympathetic and yet critical regard for current patterns of thought, why this expectation does not contradict the fact of faith, that the finally decisive Event of history for all time to come has happened already: God's becoming man. To the stature of this Event all humanity can only asymptotically grow, in all its cosmic and moral dimensions, in the dimensions of grace and eschatology, whatever conceivable "evolution" it may un-

dergo. It can never surpass this Event, because the summit of all "evolution," the irruption of God into the world and the radical opening of the world to the free infinity of God in Christ, has already been realized for the whole world, however true it may be that what has already taken place definitively in this Event must still reveal itself within the world in the reflection and image of all history still to come, in an eschatological climax.[19]

It would be to the benefit of both Christology and other dogmatic tractates if both were more clearly aware of their unity. The fact of this unity has already been touched on more than once in the foregoing discussions. The division and structure of the tractates in the textbooks of dogmatic theology available today is a problem in its own right, and a much more serious and important problem than is generally recognized. Perspectives and existential allocations of attention are very nearly as important as the question, "Is what is said here correct?" We shall say nothing about these matters here. But even within the customary framework of a modern treatise of dogmatic theology more Christology could be studied in the other tractates than is actually the case; it would be highly beneficial for these tractates. We have already discussed the way in which the truth and richness of content both of a "protology"

---

[19] In such a theology of time in Christ, it would naturally also be necessary to discuss the question to what extent the grace of Christ, the communication of the Spirit, justification, could exist *before* Christ; and again, why, for example, there was no *visio beatifica* before Christ; and why, then, in the former case the *"post Christum"* became in the historical development of theology a *"propter Christum," "intuitu meritorum Christi futurorum,"* while this is not possible in the latter case.

as well as of an eschatology essentially depend on its becoming clear that man and his environment and his history are from the first devised with a view to Christ, and that the man Christ at the end of all history still retains his fundamental significance. The tractate *de Gratia* is commonly entitled *de Gratia Christi*. Commonly it contains little else about Christ. And yet we only have a Christian understanding of grace when it is conceived of not only in the most metaphysical way possible, as a divinization, but rather as assimilation to Christ. And the existential transposition of this is the following of Christ, something about which moral theology ought to say rather more, although it offers a schema less handy for casuistical purposes than the Ten Commandments or other schema of natural moral law. Furthermore, why is it only in Christology that Christ is said to have sanctifying grace in his soul? Why is it not stated conversely that grace is the unfolding within human nature of the union of the human with the Logos (in the sense mentioned above) and is therefore, and *arising thence*, something which can also be had in those who are not the ek-sistence of the Logos in time and history but do belong to his necessary environment? Sacramental theology is again becoming more Christological today, so too the theology of the Church as a doctrine of the "Mystical Body of Christ." A theology of history, and what is more a Christocentric one, is almost entirely lacking.

Would it not be fitting for someone to make a systematic study of the ways in which the real teaching of faith about Christ is unreflexively misconceived? This is not a question of the "official" heresies from the earliest days up to the liberalism of our time, or if these, only insofar as behind them a profound misconception of the real dogma is at work. It would rather be a matter of investigating with exactitude and system what sort of idea the average Christian and non-Christian really has of Christ, whether to "believe" this idea or reject it as not worthy of belief. It would probably emerge that the content of this idea by no means coincides with the real dogma, or at any rate renders the dogma with really serious, that is disastrous, distortions and omissions. We should then have to ask which misunderstood formulations of the dogma, either in solemn pronouncements or (what is of more practical importance) in the normal catechesis and preaching, have given rise and continue to give rise to such pre-theoretical and cryptogamic heresies in Christology. Such an investigation could be of use not only for apologetic and kerygmatic ends. It could make clear to academic theology that what are apparently very ticklish questions of theology could be of the highest missionary significance, provided that they were properly put and answered. For a true theology of proclamation is nothing else than the one theology, which takes its religious task so seriously with all the scientific means at its disposal, that it becomes at once more scientific and more kerygmatic.

II. KARL ADAM

The Approach to Christ of Religious Psychology[20]

The human mind by its very nature has a *disposition* toward the experience of what is holy. It is constructed in a manner that whenever it comes upon a genuine instance of holiness, it is permanently bound to it with absolute certainty. As Rudolf Otto explains in his classic work *The Idea of the Holy* (Eng. tr., rev. ed., London, 1936) this holiness is fundamentally a mystery, something utterly beyond our experience, something "altogether different." The feeling roused in us by holiness is something qualitatively completely different from the feeling evoked by subjective values within us. It is the feeling of being faced by something foreign to us, unknown, strange. The word "mysterious" clearly expresses the content of this emotional experience. We would never call a machine mysterious, even if we had no idea of its construction. Whatever it is, it belongs within our range of experience. But to our sensibilities, what is holy seems on the contrary to belong to a different sphere of existence, occult, transcendent, "numinous," which in its essence seems to be hidden from us. Thus the first mark of holiness is that it has upon us the effect of a mystery, an arcanum. More precisely, it has the effect of a *mysterium tremendum* — i.e., our first impression of it causes us to shrink away from it. A kind of hesitancy, a strange fear arises in us. And this fear too is qualitatively different from the fear we might have of a robber, or of any danger within ourselves. What we fear is this very thing so "altogether different," ineffable, numinous that we discern in holiness. It is not *metus*, but *stupor*. The same kind of shudder is there as in fear of ghosts. Otto maintains that fear of ghosts is nothing but a false offshoot of the true *stupor*, the hesitant fear roused in us at the sight of what is holy. But the same power in holiness that makes us recoil from it as a *mysterium tremendum* draws us to it. It shelters a hidden beauty, loveliness, and nobility which we are unable to utter in words, but which we nevertheless experience. Even as it keeps us at a distance, it draws us to it at the same time. We are compelled, as it were, to look back. A secret longing in us yearns after it. What is holy becomes for us a *mysterium fascinosum*. And this quality of fascination does not entice us after the manner of the beauty and loveliness of this world. It is the ineffable, unutterable, numinous quality that compels us. There is a sense of the awesome in our feeling for its loveliness. And it is this very sense of the awesome that binds us to it, and will not let us go. This tension of opposites, the polarity of these two effects, and the fact that each of these effects is accompanied by the impression of mystery, of the "altogether different" — this is the characteristic of what is holy.

Thus the human soul is organized to experience a value that is qualitatively distinct from all other earthly values. This means there is an organ in our soul sensitive to the super-

[20] *The Christ of Faith* (New York: Pantheon, 1957; London: Burns & Oates, 1957).

natural. This supernatural we grasp with our feelings in the experience of the *mysterium tremendum et fascinosum*. It is a peculiar experience, not to be derived from any other, utterly original, but on the other hand directed toward values and realities that cannot be found in the sphere of nature, and in structure utterly different. Everyone can verify this in his own experience. The human spirit is *a priori* possessed of the faculty of discerning the peculiarities of holiness wherever it is genuine and true — not when it occurs in distorted form, as in the appearance of ghosts, but when in fact it works upon us, repelling us, and attracting us as the *mysterium tremendum et fascinosum*, thus establishing itself as a genuine manifestation of holiness.

With reference to our problem of whether belief in Christ can be understood on a psychological basis, we can now say that if the figure of Christ were not a genuine manifestation of what is holy, mankind's sense of the numinous would long ago have wearied of him. Christ would not have been able to bind mankind to him for two thousand years, if our numinous sense had not discerned and experienced and gone on experiencing in his incarnate personality a true manifestation of holiness. Simon, Dositheus, Appollonius — all these mystery gods were able to compel the numinous sense of their followers only for a brief while, only for as long as they and their adherents were able to weave the halo of holiness about their heads by magic and suggestion. Once these means ceased — and they could not but cease the moment a critical sense of questioning and doubt arose among the faithful — once the faithful came to look for reasons to support their emotional experience, the devout found nothing more in them to nourish their numinous sense and bind them to their cult. They no longer experienced their Saviors as genuine manifestations of holiness.

Christianity is altogether different. No compulsion, no magic, no suggestion were needed to clothe Christ in the appearance of holiness. He came to his contemporaries as a poor carpenter. As we shall see later on, for a long time he deliberately held back his testimony to his mission. When at last he caused Peter to recognize him as the Christ, he did not work any stupendous miracle and rouse a spurious awe to support this affirmation, but spoke of his suffering soon to come. When he answered Caiaphas' question, "Art thou the Christ?" in the affirmative, he caused himself to be nailed to the cross. The heavenly light had hardly blazed across the darkness before he extinguished it himself. But it was not such lightning, such signs and wonders that led men to him to give him their faith, but, then as now, his mysterious essence, the *mysterium tremendum et fascinosum* of his person. From the moment Peter said, "Master, depart from me, I am a sinful man," for well or ill he was committed to him. From the moment the centurion affirmed, "I am not worthy for you to enter under my roof," he had become one of the faithful, committed to Jesus. This is the same process of flight from Jesus and commitment to him that it has been through the centuries. He will always be the awe-inspiring figure from which we shrink, and always the supremely lovable one toward whom we yearn. There will always be men who cry "*Crucifige*," and always men to kiss his feet and anoint them. And they will often be the same men. Such is the history of Christianity, the history of the *mysterium tremendum et fascinosum* revealed in the figure of God incarnate. We cannot escape this figure, neither by violence nor by destructive criticism. How rapidly we were able to deal with the mystery gods! The critical sense had only to prick its ears a little, and their shapes became ridiculous. But no critical sense can dissipate the figure of Christ. It will be able to erase or correct this or that historical account in the Gospels. Indeed, if it is bold and frivolous enough, it can condemn the entire Gospel account as a myth. It can accuse the Christian preachers, the Christian Church, the Catholic Church of being a farrago of stupidity and brutality, but it can never prevent men from experiencing the manifestation of holiness in Christ; it cannot prevent their most delicate sensibilities from affirming: He, he alone is the Holy One of God. In him alone truth and light have dawned. "Whither shall we go? Thou alone hast the word of eternal life."

So in the light of the history of the Christian faith, we can affirm this: Just as the belief in God incarnate did not arise merely historically, merely by means of written documents, not by "flesh and blood," but directly from the Father through an experience of Grace, so even today it does not come to us through human arguments, but by way of a direct *encounter in Grace with the Lord,* with the manifestation of holiness. Because this belief was not created by man, it cannot be threatened or destroyed by man either. Neither the sword of the Caesars nor the knife of the critics will ever probe as far as the innermost reaches, the true

home of our faith, as far as the *scintilla animae,* as the mystics put it, as far as the point where God and man come into contact, where the delicate sense of the divine dawns upon us, and causes us to testify before the figure of the Son of God: If the divine be anywhere, it is here in Christ Jesus. Certainly, Buddha and Mohammed also live on in the cult of the faithful. But we have already established at the beginning of our lectures that neither religious founder stands as Christ does at the heart of their faith. Not their persons but their messages are central to their religions. So we cannot speak of a numinous commitment to their persons, but only of a religious commitment to their messages. Even from the point of view of Christianity it is certainly possible that genuine numinous elements are to be found in these messages, working upon the faithful. But they lead only to legalized attitudes, confirmed by maxims and standards, and so always bear the stamp of the impersonal and factual. They lack the living, dynamic, inexhaustible, ever renewed spirit that is to be discerned in Christianity, in which faith is so eminently personal an act, the last surrender to the divine person whose infinite depths are the source of ever new energies and impulses of faith, and ever new possibilities of life and experience.

Having followed the psychological traces of Christ's mystery, we now turn back to the historical way of apprehending it. On this way, we have so far been able to assert the following: First, it is certain and historically demonstrable that the early Christian community in Jerusalem had already set Christ on the side of God and attributed divine properties to him.

They called him the "author of life," "the Lord and the Christ," "Judge of the living and of the dead." These articles of faith in the early Church are the more significant when we remember that it was made up of former Jews, who taught in strictly monotheistic terms.

Second, it is certain and historically demonstrable that on account of this monotheistic belief in the Jerusalem community there can be no question that the statements of Christ's divinity in the Gospels originated in the community itself.

Third, the essential difference between the pagan-Hellenistic Saviors and the Christian Savior — who, after all, was confirmed by the early Church's three hundred years of martyrdom — does not admit the possibility that the belief in the divinity of Christ could have arisen on Hellenistic ground. The only conclusion left is that this belief must go back to Christ's own testimony as to himself, to what he said himself about his divine nature. Without some such instigation from Christ himself, it would be incomprehensible how Jews and Hellenists alike could come upon the idea of ranging Jesus, who was crucified, at the side of God.

III. JEAN DANIÉLOU*

Christology and History[21]

* Jean Daniélou (1905–   ), among the most noted contemporary French Jesuit writers, studied at the Sorbonne, received his doctorate in theology from the Institut Catholique and his doctorate in philosophy from the University of Paris. His interests and writings are versatile, covering such subjects as the liturgy, history, mysticism, Scripture and existentialism. He has lectured in the U. S. and taught at the University of Notre Dame. He has published *The Advent of Salvation* and *God and the Ways of Knowing*, two studies in comparative religion, also *Origen, The Presence of God* and *The Holy Pagans of the Old Testament*. In the *Lord of History*, Daniélou depicts Christ as God entering history, becoming its center and norm.

In working out the two themes with which we have been engaged, the history of salvation can be traced through the Old Testament along two lines: on the one hand, it appears as a series of divine interventions, a narrative of the *gesta Dei*; on the other, as the story of successive human responses. The human aspect of this reciprocity has been shown as rather negative; though strictly there is another side to the picture; there is progress in the

21 *The Lord of History* (Chicago: Henry Regnery Co., 1958), pp. 183–196 *passim*.

Old Testament as well, as will appear later. But just as it was not our aim, when speaking of the wrath of God, to exhaust the tale of his visitations, so here we are concerned only to give instances.

It remains true to say that throughout the Old Testament the two lines of our exposition belong to two separate fields of thought and experience. At the end of each inquiry it was found that this dual history could only be fully apprehended, and only reached its own fulfillment, in the person of the incarnate Word. Here is the end of the chapter of the works of God, itself the most wonderful of all: here, too, the culmination of the progress of the people of God through the ascending scale of types. In this point of view, Christ is seen to be at once the key, and the central point, of history. The dogmatic definition of the two natures in Christ by the Council of Chalcedon illuminates the whole theology of history.

The Protestant theologian Jean-Louis Leuba, in a recent book (*L'institution et l'évènement*), has compared the New Testament doctrine of Christ with the Christological definitions of Chalcedon, criticizing the latter for having "suppressed one dimension of the gospel message, namely, time." He goes on to say:

The Council's formula shows the full development into Christological speculation of the theological doctrine of the Logos; it is instinct with the same notions of substance as characterize the whole philosophical movement from which it springs. The concepts employed are entirely static — essence, nature, person. In the New Testament, the unity of Christ exists and appears only in the unfolding story of the conception and birth of Jesus, his death, resurrection, ascension, kingdom and second coming. . . . This is not to say that the definitions of Chalcedon are false, but that they bear the same relation to New Testament Christology as the trace of a movement bears to the movement itself.

According to this account, the distinguishing mark of the doctrine of Chalcedon is anti-historicism. It is perhaps an over-simplification to say that the theologians of the fifth century no longer concerned themselves with the time-process: Jacques Liebaert, in his book on the Christological doctrine of St Cyril of Alexandria,

shows how important it was for him at least. But the period was, admittedly, one of recession in regard to those historical preoccupations which dominated much of the thinking of the earlier centuries, from Irenaeus to Augustine. The shift of emphasis can be traced in the evolution of Augustine's own work. It corresponds to a change in the situation of Christianity, which had at first to vindicate its own historical emergence upon the pagan and Jewish scene, but was now itself a part of history. A certain fading of eschatological prepossessions occurs even in the text of the Creed, where the words "in these last days," qualifying the article of the Incarnation — which was part of the primitive Kerygma, and is still found in the fourth century[22] — finally disappears. Consequently, the definition of the Council of Chalcedon is indeed designed rather to establish the intrinsic principles of Christology than to situate the person of Christ in the history of salvation.

But the definition is by no means irrelevant to the theology of history. On the contrary. This very preoccupation, at the time of Chalcedon, with the substantive principles of the Incarnation, means that the fundamental problems of eschatology were, in the last analysis, to be resolved along these lines. It is because of the union of the two natures that Christ can be understood as the fulfillment of the Old Testament, and as the end ($\tau \acute{\epsilon} \lambda o s$) of the whole plan of salvation; it is in the same way, finally, that his second coming can be shown to represent the consummation of this plan. The dogma of Chalcedon thus provides a basis for the theology

---

[22] Gal 4:4; 1 Pet 1:20; *Const. Apost.* VII: 41 (Funk, I:444).

of history, which, otherwise, is liable either to founder in a doctrine of endless Becoming, or to evaporate in a timeless Ideal. These aberrations are actually found in the first ages of Christianity, as Ebionism on the one hand and Gnosticism on the other; the last traces of them persist among Nestorians and Monophysites. The same errors reappear even now when thinkers disregard the precise terms of Chalcedon, and consequently abandon all real eschatology: for it is just this definition that gives a structure to time, and turns it into history.

As far as it concerns the theology of history, the essential contribution of the New Testament is the affirmation of Christ as the present reality of the prophetic predictions of the Old. It is not the purpose of the New Testament to proclaim the existence of a paradise to come — the Old Testament is full of that message, but in the New, paradise is here and now, with Christ: "This day thou shalt be with me in Paradise."[23] It is not the purpose of the New Testament to declare that a servant of God shall be sacrificed for the sins of the world, but that Christ is this lamb that was slain: "Look, this is the Lamb of God; look, this is he who takes away the sin of the world";[24] and that the immolation of this victim fulfills the destiny of mankind.[25] The New Testament is precisely the record of this present reality, this *Dasein*. The operative words are *hodie, ecce*. This is what makes the Gospel "news," as St. Irenaeus rightly saw: it "introduced an altogether new thing, bringing forth now him that had been foretold."[26]

With the coming of Christ, "the last days" of which the Old Testament speaks have arrived. The New Testament declares it in many passages. "In old days, God spoke to our fathers in many ways and by many means, through the prophets; now at last in these times he has spoken to us with a Son to speak for him."[27] These "last times" refer to the Incarnation: ". . . till the appointed time came. Then God sent out his Son."[28] Again, the reference is to the Passion and Resurrection: "he has been revealed once for all, at the moment when history reached its fulfillment, annulling our sin by his sacrifice";[29] "it was his loving design, centred in Christ, to give history its fulfillment by resuming everything in him."[30] . . . The two streams of prophecy remain radically distinct throughout the Old Testament: the coming of Jehovah in the last days to judge the world from his eternal habitation, and the coming of Messiah to set Israel free from her enemies and to inaugurate a new people, are envisaged in reality as two separate events, and give rise to two divergent literary traditions. From the first comes the idiom of transcendental eschatology, culminating in the apocalyptic books; from the second, temporal messianism, represented in the main by the prophetic books. In later Judaism, some efforts were made to harmonize these points of view, but for the most part only through introducing an order of succession between two phases: the earthly kingdom of Messiah, to be followed by the coming of Jehovah in the end of the world.

The essential doctrine of the New Testament is that these two things

---

[23] Lk 23:43.   [26] *Adv. haer.* IV: 34:1.
[24] Jn 1:29.
[25] Apoc 5:6–7; 1 Pet 1:19–20.

[27] Heb 1:1–2.   [29] Heb 9:26.
[28] Gal 4:4.   [30] Eph 1:9–10.

come together in Jesus. The evangelists attribute to him the fulfillment at once of the prophecies that foretold the coming of Jehovah, and those concerning the Messiah. They quote of him the words of Isaiah about the preparations for Jehovah in the desert,[31] and identify in him the new Moses leading the chosen people out into the desert in a new Exodus.[32] He is that new Israel, whose faithfulness is contrasted with the infidelity of the old;[33] he is also that God who sets up his dwelling in the midst of the new Israel.[34] He is at once God, giving the New Law from the Mountain,[35] and the Prophet foretold by Moses, making known to the people what is the will of God. His name is κύριος, Lord, the scriptural designation of divine sovereignty — and χρίστος, the messianic king.

Two kinds of history terminate in the one person of Christ. He appears within the historical framework of mankind, which he brings to its fulfillment — that is the significance of the genealogies of Christ at the beginning of Matthew and Luke. St Leo, using this argument against Eutyches, as proving the reality of human nature in Christ, brings out the force of the two-fold genealogy: "The evangelist Matthew, following the sequence of generations, shows how the promise made to Abraham was fulfilled in Christ, in whom all families of the earth shall be blessed. The evangelist Luke, starting from the birth of the Savior, traces back the series of his ancestors, to show that the ages before the Flood are included in this mystery, so that all generations from the beginning culminate in him that is

the salvation of all men."[36] And in another sermon, St. Leo emphasizes Christ's kinship in the seed of David.[37] Thus the three filiations of Christ, from David, from Abraham, and from Adam, are successively brought out into prominence.

But on the other hand, part of Christ's activity visibly continues the record of Jehovah's action in the Old Testament — the creation, the dwelling in a tabernacle made with hands, the making of a covenant, the destruction of death. These are works of God, in line with the wonders chronicled in the former narrative of divine interventions. Together with the genealogical continuity, linking Christ with the sons of Adam, we find a theological continuity: his work belongs to the historical framework of the *mirabilia Dei,* of which it is the last and supreme instance. How these two successions come together in one was the critical problem of primitive Christology. Christ himself indicated the terms of it when he asked the Pharisees: "David calls Christ his Master; how can he be also his son?"[38]

There was no doubt of the fact that Christ fulfills both types of prophecy: the question was as to the manner of this fusion of two things in one person. Some of the Biblical formulae were open to several interpretations. By attending too exclusively to the human filiation of Christ, and his prefiguration in the heroes of the Old Testament story, it was possible to fall into an adoptionist solution, in which the Savior is regarded simply as a man full of the presence of God. The Antiochene theologians ran this risk; Nestorius succumbed to it. Al-

---

[31] Mt 3:3.
[32] Mk 9:4.
[33] Mt 4:4.
[34] Jn 1:14.
[35] Mt 5:21.

[36] *Serm. X in Nat.* P.L. 54, 234.
[37] *Serm. IV in Nat.* P.L. 54, 204.
[38] Mt 22:45.

ternatively, when soteriology alone was taken into consideration, as by the school of Alexandria, and the Incarnation was seen as nothing else but the saving work of God, there might be a tendency to minimize the humanity of Christ, and the significance of his human genealogy for the seed of Abraham which he assumed and brings to perfection.

The dogma of Chalcedon, however, furnishes an unambiguous answer to the eschatological problem of Christianity. If Christ is "the last Adam" the mystery of his personality contains the truth about "the last things." Christological definition opens the way to a right judgment of the theological meaning of history. The formula for the union of the two natures in the incarnate Word, saving the perfect integrity of each and the unity of the person, was the key for interpreting much evidence that was otherwise indecisive. In the words of Dom Jean Leclercq epitomizing the thought of St. Leo: "Among the prophetic witnesses to the Messiah, some foretold him as God, others as man. The hypostatic union harmonizes the testimony."

Jesus Christ, God and man in the unity of one person, represents the last end, the τέλος of history, but not indeed the finish, πέρας. After this there is a period of waiting, while the work done by Christ is promulgated and takes effect throughout the human race. He is the culmination of the Old Testament, but also the First-born of the new creature: not only ἀρχή and τέλος, alpha and omega, but also, from another point of view, the τέλος-ἀρχή, the end of one world and beginning of another, the turning-point of history. This pattern is another of the distinguishing marks of the Christian theology of history. It is prefigured in the story of Noah, who represents both the judgment and destruction of the old world and the inauguration of a new.[39] It is finally worked out in the mystery of the passion and resurrection of Jesus Christ, when the old world came to an end and the new creation was brought into being, both alike in the one divine person. What is now awaited is the completion of the new creature in the gradual building up of the body of Christ.

What the Fathers had to say of the first advent is equally applicable to the Second Coming. The eschatological attitude essentially involves this duality.

Among those who conceive a direct relation between human history and the second coming of our Lord, various Fathers of the first three centuries, and Hippolytus in particular, devoted much effort to speculations upon the "weeks of years" in the book of Daniel, or upon the seven millennia, with a view to dating the end of the world. Others worked out a system based on the succession of empires. Eusebius founded the theology of history upon the providential coincidence of Christian monotheism and Constantinian monarchy. People are always elaborating such projects — Bossuet made the framework of his *Discours sur l'histoire universelle* to this pattern, and in our own generation, the idea of successive civilizations, as Toynbee, for instance, exhibits it, springs from the same source.

As early as the third century, however, the particular hypothesis of Hippolytus was already challenged by Origen, who declared for the radical independence of the Church's growth from the course of human history.

[39] Daniélou, *Sacr. fut.,* p. 61.

After him, Augustine inclined for a while toward the chiliastic doctrines prevalent among the Latin Doctors of the West, but eventually came round to the idea of a distinction and discontinuity between the history of the *civitas Dei* and the history of human empires. The point is well taken by Karl Löwith: "It is true that Augustine failed to relate the first cause, that is, God's providential plan, to the 'secondary causes' operative in the process as such. But it is precisely the absence of a detailed correlation between secular and sacred events which distinguishes Augustine's Christian apology from Bossuet's more elaborate theology of political history."[40] Reinhold Niebuhr's contemporary eliminating of any ideological notions of progress from the history of salvation is evidence of a similar reaction.

But neither of these two contrasting points of view can finally be held to the exclusion of the other: which brings us back once more to the definitions of Chalcedon, showing how the two theological positions involved are strictly complementary. Just as the dogma of the hypostatic union, illuminating the course of past history, enabled us to reconcile the two opposing tendencies of the Old Testament, reaching their single culmination in Christ, so the same doctrine, illuminating time to come, provides the definitive interpretation of world history in the period of waiting before the second advent.

On the one hand, the history of this time consists of the mighty works of God, the Sacramental activity of the Church, foreshadowing and preparing the eschatological events to come in the end of the world. In this aspect,

the history of salvation, from the creation to the last day, concerns one everlasting presence of God among men; its supreme moment is in Christ's Incarnation, as its termination will be in his Second Coming. This history has no other laws than the sovereign wisdom and liberty of God himself.

But it is also true to say of this period that it consists in a development of the Incarnation. The Word of God took flesh in the unbroken succession of human generations to ensure the completion of the series; and it is in the generations of men that he continues to bring about, by his grace, the deification of mankind, sharers in his Resurrection. This work is not solely a salvation of individual souls, for "the whole of nature, as we know, groans";[41] "creation is full of expectancy . . . waiting for the sons of God to be made known."[42] This long-awaited liberation is indeed an effect of the power of God alone, but all humanity is included in its scope. History thus takes on a new significance, as consisting of that which is to be set free. And mankind shares in the achievement, as well as in the gift, of this saving freedom: every one of Christ's members co-operates, "each limb receiving the active power it needs," so that the whole body "organized and unified by each contact with the source which supplies it, . . . achieves its natural growth, building itself up through charity";[43] and it depends on man to hasten the coming of the Lord's day.[44] Thus then, the union of the two natures in the person of Christ, the Head of the mystical body, is as it were projected in the life of that body, the Church. Every misconception about the the-

[40] *Meaning in History*, p. 172.

[41] Rom 8:22. [43] Eph 4:16.
[42] Rom 8:19. [44] 2 Pet 3:12.

ology of church history arises from some neglect of either the divine or the human element therein. To consider this history as a series of divine operations outside any context of institutional fact, as K. Barth does, is to ignore the human element, where the humanity of Christ lives on in the perfection of unity with God that continues from the hypostatic union. But equally, to regard the Second Coming as belonging to the evolution of mankind, and as marking the final achievement of human progress, is to ignore the divine element, the work of the creator himself in the history of his creation. The truth is that Christ will come again at the end of the world, and that the end of the world will be the coming again of Christ.

IV. ROMANO GUARDINI*

The Humanity of Christ[45]

* Romano Guardini (1885–   ) was born in Verona, Italy, but has spent most of his life in Germany. Appointed chaplain to Pope Pius XII in 1952, he had previously been professor of the philosophy of religion at the University of Berlin until its appropriation by the Nazis in 1939. He is now professor of philosophy at the University of Munich. He has written *Jesus Christus, Conscience, The Lord.*

PREFACE

I

. . . We view with mixed feelings the pre-eminence which the science of psychology claims in our day. The procedures of observation and analysis seem to intrude into every sphere of life. They choose above all to focus on the structure of personality, not excluding — indeed rather preferring — the structure of those personalities we call great. While the achievements, no doubt, merit attention, we must bear in mind that both the methods and the results of psychological research are determined, even more than are those of other sciences, by the motives which lie behind them. We have, therefore, every right to be skeptical, for these motives, whether acknowledged, half acknowledged, or unacknowledged, are multifarious and frequently quite unacceptable.

Psychological analysis may well be motivated by the desire to improve our understanding of the nature and destiny of some personality and to assess it more accurately — to give it, that is, the honor due to it. It may, however, just as well spring from the will to insert both personality and man as such in a merely natural context, thus confounding him with an order inferior to him. Were that effort to achieve its aim, the result would be a triumph at the cost of reverence.

Motives of both kinds have always exerted their influence and are doing so today. Those of the second kind, however, have been greatly strengthened by certain contemporary trends. Democracy of the truly radical sort

45 *The Humanity of Christ* (New York: Pantheon Books, 1964), pp. ix–xxiv.

will not tolerate graduations of rank among men. Positivism and materialism both deny any essential difference between the spiritual and the animal, between man and beast. According to totalitarianism the business of science is not to discover what actuality is, but to change it and make it what it should be. In practice this means placing men at the disposal of power. All this enables us to understand why those who care about human worth and dignity distrust psychology, especially in instances where what is at stake is the worth and dignity of a great man, and why they feel that some destructive force is at work, some technique of laying violent hands upon what has a claim to be reverenced.

Inestimably greater, then, are the misgivings bound to arise when the subject of a psychological enquiry is none other than that One who not only surpasses all the great men of history, but, indeed, completely transcends everything merely human — none other than Jesus Christ.

On the other hand, we must not forget that he called himself the Son of Man, a name which, all things considered, is much more than a mere term designating the Messiah, which he had taken over from the prophets. Jesus Christ is man, more unreservedly man than anyone else can ever be; for to realize human nature as he did was an achievement possible only for one who was more than mere man.

This point of view is in sharp contrast with the modern tendency to interpret man in terms of a lower order: to see in his present state a stage in an uninterrupted, steady ascent from the pre-human, and in his structure an admittedly more complex, but essentially identical, ordering of the same elements as in that of the animals. The contrary is true: man can be properly understood only in terms of what is above him. The final word on the meaning of the biblical text: "God created man in his own image" (Gen 1:27) was only spoken by "the Word made flesh" (Jn 1:14).

Seen in this light, the problem of a psychology of Jesus appears to be one of the most urgent tasks confronting theology.

II

Early Christology sought, as its first task, to establish, beyond any shadow of doubt, that Jesus of Nazareth was more, and other, than a mere creature. Our minds, dulled by everything said and written on the subject, can no longer comprehend the passion with which for centuries the early Christians fought out the issues of Christology — a passion which can, in spite of its many all too human features, yet be called holy. In the end, the declaration affirming Christ to be the eternal, consubstantial Son of the Father was established as a pillar of truth never again to be shaken.

The second phase came when the Christian mind saw clearly that this Son of God had truly become man in Christ. It was not that he had come merely to dwell *in* a man: he came as an actual member, indeed, as *the* crucial and all-important member, in the whole history of the human race. He was completely within human history, yet at the same time quite independent of it. Indeed, the very reason for the uniqueness, the redemptive force of his entry into human history, is to be sought in the fact that he came from the freedom of him who is above all history and above the whole world. This is what he meant when he said, as St. John reports: "I have power to lay down [my life], and I have power to take it up again" (Jn 10:18).

Thus the divine rigor of this true incarnation had to be purified from every notion which, while apparently affirming a maximum of incarnation, in fact destroyed its reality, because it substituted for a personal event one which, in spite of the appearance of sublimity, still remained at the natural level: namely, the confusion of the natures. A being in whom the human blended with the divine in a single, undifferentiated substance would be a myth. And so arose the concept of one person in two distinct natures, a concept which exceeds the capacity of the human mind, to be sure, but which guarantees the integrity of the God-Man.

The reality of the divine nature in Christ was now unassailable, his true humanity was likewise established, as was also the indissoluble unity of the two natures in the person of the Logos: a unity which constituted the basis for the historicity of Christianity, a unity which we may perhaps even say made God himself historical. In saying this, we mean, of course, something very different from the pantheistic processes of the Absolute. And so, we now have these truths before us in a form which is both sublime in purity and rich in content, both truth and mystery together: they have become dogma.

And then the spirit began to ask further: what was the place in history of the Son of God made man. This led to attempts to merge the unique historicity of Jesus in the universal historicity of human life; and this resulted in all those images of Christ which represented him as sheer man — even though a most extraordinary man — or, on the other hand, as an idea, a myth, the content of an experience.

We know that these ways are wrong. Alerted by the attitude of the Church, theology is able to ward off all such attempts. But this resistance — if I interpret it correctly — has remained essentially negative. It has told us what is not. Now a positive task must be undertaken. We have seen how the existence of Christ proceeds from an event which resists any attempt to identify it with universal historical concepts. We have seen also that we cannot penetrate the heart of his personality, not merely empirically, because we lack the necessary means for such an insight, but in principle. For, to achieve this, we would have to be able to reduce the absolute reality of the divine nature and the relative reality of human nature to a common denominator — which is impossible.

But something else is possible: the fact can be brought home to us that the existence of Christ was a real earthly existence, taking place within the framework of actual history. He had his own inward and outward experiences, his encounters with men and things, his decisions and actions to be constantly taken and performed, and so forth. All this took place within the realm of being and event, that is to say, it can be understood. Hence the questions what, how, why, wherefore, whence and whither, can properly be asked and answered; and so also can the psychological questions, but — and it is an important but — they must be asked with regard to a fact which prescribes both an attitude and a method. This fact is the one already mentioned: the incomprehensibility for us of both the origin and the heart of Christ's personality.

So this psychology is going to be of a peculiar kind. If the word means, as it generally does, an analysis of personality and individual circumstance, then there can be no such thing as a psychology of Christ. The eternal decree that he was to become man, no less than the existence of the Logos in human flesh, resists any attempt to induce it to a psychological concept — or to an historical one, for that matter. On the other hand, the decision of the Logos to become man embraces everything that is essential to human nature, including the possibility of being understood. All the circumstances which determine human existence — body, soul, mind, society — attain their fulfillment in the being and life of Christ. Basing ourselves on these circumstances, we can, it is true, come to an understanding or, in other words, a psychology, but we are going to find that, owing to its inherent limitations, this psychology will be baffled at each line of approach toward precisely these circumstances which we try out. And, it must be repeated again, this defeat results not from any lack of material, from any dullness of insight or deficiency of method, but from the very nature of the object being investigated. The more complete the material, the more penetrating our insight, the more thorough our method, the clearer and more decisive becomes the impasse in the conviction forced upon us that our undertaking simply opens out onto the incomprehensibility of God incarnate.

Finally, we must go into the question of method, for this sums up the whole difficulty. In view of the confusing variety of images of Christ current today, we must ask the further question: Which Christ have we in mind?

If we answer: The one who brought us the fullness of revelation and revealed himself therein, then another question must be posed: Where is he to be found? There is only one answer to this: In the New Testament. But this means, in the complete New Testament, in all its books, and from their first to their last sentence, and this brings us to the heart of the theological problem.

The reality of Christ has been made known to us by means of the words, i.e., the recollections of the apostles, of all the apostles from Mark to John. But this does not mean that the genuineness of the figure Christ diminishes the further the witness is removed in time. The interval in time between Luke and Mark does not mean that the theologian must be wary of the later Gospel. It is even likely that the passage of time will have allowed the writer to gain a fresh insight into the nature of Christ. As a result of discipleship, prayer and meditation on his sayings and acts, a new experience of his reality will have been gained, so that when he proclaims Christ's message he will be able to say things which before were impossible or untimely.

When research comes back from St. John's Gospel to an examination of the earlier ones, this does not mean that it discovers forthwith more authentic strata of the reality of Christ, but only ones that were perceived earlier. On the other hand, if, as we proceed from the earliest to the later statements about him, we find the emergence of strata in the picture of Christ which show evidence of riper reflection, greater metaphysical comprehension, and a more concrete appreciation in terms of contemporary problems, the message proclaimed does not become less genuine; but factors do emerge and impose themselves precisely because of the general situation and the stage reached in the progressive unfolding of the message.

Were we in a position to disregard all such accounts and gain an immediate impression of Jesus Christ as he was on earth, we would not be confronted by a "simple" historical Jesus, but by a figure of devastating greatness and incomprehensibility. Progress in the representation of the portrait of Christ does not mean that something was being added to what was proclaimed; it means that we are witnessing the unfolding step by step of that which "was from the beginning," on the supposition, of course — and this is fundamental — that as God willed the revelation of the redeeming truth of his eternal "Word" in Christ, so he also willed and brought it about that this truth should, in fact, be handed on to later generations;[46] and handed on in such a way that it could be included in the simplicity of the act of faith, and need no specialized knowledge to extract it from the text of the Gospel message.

We have said that the source for our knowledge about Christ is the memory of the apostles, of all the apostles and throughout the whole time that they were proclaiming the divine message right up to their death; that is, from the day of Pentecost until the death of John. These were no mere individual reporters, each one of whom would be credited only to the extent of his personal abilities. They spoke as apostles, that is, as "pillars" and members of the Church. The Church, that is, the sum total of local communities, their faith, liturgical life, prayer, etc., is not something existing alongside or apart from them, so that it would be legitimate to make a distinction between a valid original witness and a secondary "theology of the community." The apostles are themselves the Church. They are the Church in her earliest kerygmatic phase, when she derives her commission and authority directly from Christ and the Pentecostal enlightenment.

---

[46] It passes understanding how any study of the biblical texts which does not take into account this supposition, but treats them like any other historical source, can merit the name of theology. Such an approach presupposes a vagueness about basic principles which is quite inadmissible in the realm of scientific thought. We have to do here, however, with a perversion of the idea of science which can be observed in other domains also. Science is the study of a subject by means of the method required by this subject, not by means of some generally applicable method which undermines its specific character.

Theology can be called a science precisely because it uses, not the methods of general history or psychology, but the method demanded by the nature of the object being investigated, which in this case is revelation. This nature is not something purely personal which the student subjectively attributes to his subject, and which then has to be discarded as soon as the investigation becomes scientific. Theology is rigorously scientific only when it accepts the nature of revelation as the determining factor in its choice of method. It is obvious that this consideration recognizes in the phenomenon a special complication, and that the processes of research require a special competence in the student's eye to enable him to identify unerringly his object, and in the dialectic which will serve him in its conceptual elaboration. Only to the extent in which theology fulfills these conditions can it be regarded as truly scientific.

This phase, as we have said, extends from the author of the first logion to the writer of the Apocalypse.

It is obviously pertinent to ask what kind of picture of Jesus they painted in the various historical stages of their preaching. A particular interest attaches to the question of the picture found in the very earliest preaching. The search for these strata, however, must not be dominated by a suspicion as to the validity of that preaching which would tend to assume that it became less and less reliable as the first century wore on. Our aim must not be to "get behind" the apostolic preaching in order to reach the authentic Jesus, thus freeing ourselves from too close a dependence on the "temporal limitations" of the apostolic message. The authentic Jesus is revealed to us by the apostles, by them alone, and by all of them together.

The attitude we are criticizing would be, not "scientific," but agnostic. It would amount to a volatilizing of the only specific object of theological investigation, and, consequently, of the whole scientific character of theology. The different ways in which Paul, as compared with Mark, and John contrasted with Matthew, recount the Gospel message are an element of their apostolic mission. The fact that they were impelled (or enabled) to fulfill their task by the changed circumstances of the later period in which they lived and worked is due just as much to the Spirit of Christ as was their enlightenment at Pentecost. So the picture of Christ which is transmitted by the later preaching of the apostles is as authoritative for the reality of Christ and as much an object of faith as is the content of the earliest preaching. By the same title, it constitutes, as readily as the former, the valid object of theology as a science.

The attitude described earlier also closes its eyes to the full reality of Christ in terms of method. It begins with the assumption that the first, "historical" Jesus was the "simple," unmetaphysical, purely human individual, and that his true greatness lay in his human genius, the depth of his religious experience, and the power of his teaching. Thereafter, it is affirmed, this primitive reality was metaphysically inflated in the course of the first century, was assimilated to the mythical category of the "Savior" and adapted to suit the religious needs of the communities which felt the need of a cult figure. To admit this is to abandon at the outset everything that could merit the name of "revelation" in the true sense of the term, namely, the communication of a reality not conditioned by man, but sent to him from God in order to judge and redeem all mankind. At the same time, it abandons at once everything which the passage of time, the increasing remoteness from the original event, the development in historical circumstances, and the tradition that welds all that together, can contribute to a disclosure of the "beginning" of that Reality which is the foundation of redemption and the controlling force of history. To repeat: the contrary of that premise is true. If we could get back to the "original," that is, if we could work our way back to the picture of Christ as it existed before it had been turned over in the apostles' minds or elaborated by their preaching, before it had been assimilated by the corporate life of the faithful, we could find a figure of Christ even more colossal and incomprehensible than any conveyed by even the most daring statements of St. Paul or St. John.

The Christ who interests the scholarly theologian and the faithful Christian alike is the figure which comes to us from the whole of the apostolic preaching. And this is so, not because that preaching is concerned with the "Christ of faith" as distinct from the "Christ of history," for that would mean that the Christ of faith existed only by virtue of a religious attitude toward him and was not existent and real by himself. Later accounts would then be nothing more than idealized versions of the various experiences of Christ; evidence of the various ways in which the apostles and their hearers had seen him in the course of the first century, preliminary drafts for the way in which the faithful of later generations would view him.

To make sense we must see things the other way around. The Christ whom serious believers believe in is the original reality. The statements of the apostles are guides to him which never quite do justice to the fullness of his divine-human nature. The apostles never state more about the historical Jesus than he actually was; it is always less. Consequently, everyone who reads the New Testament aright feels that every sentence is pregnant with meaning regarding a reality which surpasses all that is said about it.

As opposed to the rationalist approach, true biblical theology must now accomplish a kind of "Copernican revolution." Its scientific purpose must not be to isolate from supposedly over-emphasizing representations, as likewise supposedly simple original reality; its object must be to bring out clearly all the elemental greatness of the original, on the basis of a whole series of representations, all of which are valid, but all of which, in spite of a gradual deepening of perception somehow fall short.

It is this elemental greatness of the original which has been at work in history, has built up the Church, and has furnished the irrepressible impulse toward activity and transformation, which is a matter of past as well as present experience. This is what "is, and was, and shall be." This is the only source of salvation.

This is the Jesus Christ we intend to study in this work. The psychology of which we are speaking here is no kind of analysis of a merely human personality who was an initiator, for there never was such an individual. Rather does it try to understand the figure which emerges from the whole apostolic preaching of the first century and which in each phase of its proclamation points back to an original reality which towers above them all.

We are perfectly aware that both the object and the method of our undertaking will be called "dogmatic," in a derogatory sense, by that theology which calls itself "critical"; that this school considers such a subject matter to be chimerical and its method unscientific. In fact, however, the attitude of this school is based upon a false premise, namely, that the person of Jesus and its historical witness must be treated in exactly the same way as any other historical phenomenon.

True theology must open its eyes to that peculiar taboo of recent times, the spirit or principle of "scientism," which claims to be universally applicable, but in fact belongs to the spheres of the natural sciences and history, and which, even in those spheres, has assumed a purely positive and quantitative character. There has been a widespread inclination for theology to accept this limitation, and as a result much harm has been done. It is high time theology freed itself from this influence and appealed to standards consistent with its own nature. We need hardly add that this does not mean that we are underestimating or ruling out any of the exacting demands of philology or history.

V. E. SCHILLEBEECKX*

Christ the Primordial Sacrament[47]

---

* E. Schillebeeckx (1914–), Dominican theologian, was born in Antwerp and is now professor of dogmatic theology at the University of Nijmegen, after having taught theology for many years at Louvain.

The purpose of his *Christ the Sacrament of the Encounter with God* is basically to arrive at the insight that the sacraments are the properly human mode of encounter with God.

---

1. ENCOUNTER WITH THE EARTHLY CHRIST AS SACRAMENT OF THE ENCOUNTER WITH GOD

The dogmatic definition of Chalcedon, according to which Christ is "one person in two natures," implies that one and the same person, the Son of God, also took on a visible human form. Even in his humanity Christ is the Son of God. The second person of the most holy Trinity is personally man; and this man is personally God.[48] Therefore Christ is God

[47] *Christ the Sacrament of the Encounter with God* (New York: Sheed and Ward, 1963), pp. 14–19.

[48] St. Thomas expresses himself strongly. "Ipsum Verbum . . . personaliter . . . est homo" – the Word himself is personally man – (*De Unione Verbi Incarnati*, q.un., a. 1); and more strongly yet: "In quo [Christo] humana natura assumpta est ad hoc quod sit persona filii Dei" – in whom (Christ) human nature was assumed in order that it might be the person of the Son of God. (*S.T.*, III, q. 2, a. 10.) Unjustifiably, the Leonine edition "corrects" the manuscripts, which all, with one exception, have *persona* and not *personae* as the Leonine would have it. This latter weakens the text, where St. Thomas wishes to say that the humanity of Jesus is in reality a manner of being of God the Son himself.

in a human way, and man in a divine way. As a man he acts out his divine life in and according to his human existence. Everything he does as man is an act of the Son of God, a divine act in human form; an interpretation and transposition of a divine activity into a human activity. His human love is the human embodiment of the redeeming love of God.

The humanity of Jesus is concretely intended by God as the fulfillment of his promise of salvation; it is a messianic reality. This messianic and redemptive purpose of the incarnation implies that the encounter between Jesus and his contemporaries was always on his part an offering of grace in a human form. For the love of the man Jesus is the human incarnation of the redeeming love of God: an advent of God's love in visible form. Precisely because these human deeds of Jesus are divine deeds, personal acts of the Son of God, divine acts in visible human form, they possess of their nature a divine saving power, and consequently they bring salvation; they are "the cause of grace." Although this is true of every specifically human act of Christ,[49] it is nevertheless especially true of those actions which, though enacted in human form, are according to their nature exclusively acts of God: the miracles and the redemption. Considered against the background of the whole earthly life of Jesus, this truth is realized in a most particular way in the great mysteries of his life: his passion, death, resurrection and exaltation to the side of the Father.[50]

That is not all. Because the saving acts of the man Jesus are performed by a divine person, they have a divine power to save, but because this divine power to save appears to us in visible form, the saving activity of Jesus is *sacramental*. For a sacrament is a divine bestowal of salvation in an outwardly perceptible form which makes the bestowal manifest; a bestowal of salvation in historical visibility. The Son of God really did become true man — become, that is to say, a human spirit which through its own proper bodiliness dwelt visibly in our world. The incarnation of the divine life therefore involves bodily aspects. Together with this we must remember that every human exchange, or the intercourse of men one with another, proceeds in and through man's bodiliness. When a man exerts spiritual influence on another, encounters through the body are necessarily involved. The inward man manifests itself as a reality that is in this world through the body. It is in his body and through his body that man is open to the "outside," and that he makes himself present to his fellow men. Human

encounter proceeds through the visible obviousness of the body, which is a sign that reveals and at the same time veils the human interiority.

Consequently if the human love and all the human acts of Jesus possess a divine saving power, then the realization in human shape of this saving power necessarily includes as one of its aspects the manifestation of salvation: includes, in other words, sacramentality. The man Jesus, as the personal visible realization of the divine grace of redemption, is *the* sacrament, the primordial sacrament, because this man, the Son of God himself, is intended by the Father to be in his humanity the only way to the actuality of redemption. "For there is one God, and one mediator of God and men, the man Christ Jesus."[51] Personally to be approached by the man Jesus was, for his contemporaries, an invitation to a personal encounter with the life-giving God, because personally that man was the Son of God. Human encounter with Jesus is therefore the sacrament of the encounter with God, or of the religious life as a theologal attitude of existence toward God.[52] Jesus' human redeem-

---

[49] See, for example, St. Thomas, *S.T.*, III, q. 48, a. 6; q. 8, a. 1, ad 1; q. 78, a. 4. Here St. Thomas is relying above all on Greek patrology.

[50] Cf. *S.T.*, III, q. 48, a. 6; q. 50, a. 6; q. 56, a. 1, ad 3; q. 57, a. 6, ad 1.

[51] 1 Tim 2:5.

[52] By "theological attitude of existence" we mean a vital human activity of which God himself is the object and the motive, and in the perfecting of which God is co-active: namely, the life of grace in faith, hope and love, the only virtues which of their nature bring about a personal relationship with God.

(Need we make an apology for resurrecting the word "theologal" in this work? Current today in its Dutch, French, and German equivalents, and indicating existential God-centeredness as distinct from the abstract-analytic nuance of "theological," it was employed in this same sense in English in the sixteenth and seventeenth centuries, but has since fallen into disuse. Cf. the *Oxford English Dictionary*. Tr.)

ing acts are therefore a "sign and cause of grace." "Sign" and "cause" of salvation are not brought together here as two elements fortuitously conjoined. Human bodiliness is human interiority itself in visible form.

Now because the inward power of Jesus' will to redeem and of his human love is God's own saving power realized in human form, the human saving acts of Jesus are the divine bestowal of grace itself realized in visible form; that is to say they cause what they signify, they are sacraments.

2. THE ACTIONS OF JESUS' LIFE AS MANIFESTATIONS OF DIVINE LOVE FOR MAN AND HUMAN LOVE FOR GOD: BESTOWAL OF GRACE AND RELIGIOUS WORSHIP

"As the Father has sent me, I also send you. When he had said this, he breathed on them and he said to them: Receive the Holy Spirit; whose sins you shall forgive, they are forgiven them."[53] Thus it is as a revelation of God's merciful redeeming love that we are to understand the sending of the Son on earth. By the incarnation of the Son God intended to divinize man by redeeming him; but being saved from sin man is brought into a personal communion of grace and love with God. This implies two things. First, the fullness of grace which properly belongs to the man Jesus in virtue of his existence as God was intended by God to be a source of grace for others; from him all were to receive. Christ's love for man thus manifests God's love for men by actually bestowing it; it is the redeeming mercy of God himself coming to meet us from a human heart. But as well as this movement down from above, coming to us from God's love by way

[53] Jn 20:21–23.

of Jesus' human heart, there is in the man Jesus also a movement up from below, from the human heart of Jesus, the Son, to the Father.

The human actions of Jesus' life as they come from above show us their character as acts of redemption of his fellow men; these acts, in the mode of a human love, are the merciful redeeming love of God himself. As coming from below they show their character as acts of worship; these acts are a true adoration and acknowledgment of God's divine existence; they are a service of praise or cult, religion, prayer — in a word, they are the man Jesus' love of God. Thus Jesus is not only the revelation of the redeeming God; he is also the supreme worshipper of the Father, the supreme realization of all religion. Jesus became the Redeemer in actual fact by freely living his human life in religious worship of and attachment to the Father. In Christ not only were God and his love for men revealed, but God also showed us in him what it is for a man to commit himself unconditionally to God the invisible Father. In this way God revealed to us the embodiment of religion, the countenance of a truly religious man. The living and personal relation of Jesus to the Father reveals to us what is meant by the majesty and mercy of God. In and through the religious service of Jesus, God has revealed himself.

If we now consider that this humanity of Jesus represents us all, then it also becomes clear that the movement up from below is a movement to the Father ascending, by way of Jesus' humanity, from the whole of mankind. Therefore Jesus is not only the offer of divine love to man made visible but, at the same time, as prototype (or primordial model) he is the supreme realization of the response of human love to this divine offer: "in our place" and "in the name of us all," as Scripture repeatedly says. Whatever Christ does as a free man is not only a realization in human form of God's activity for our salvation; it is also at the same time the positive human acceptance, representative for all of us, of this redeeming offer from God. The man Jesus is personally a dialogue with God the Father; the supreme realization and therefore the norm and the source of every encounter with God. As a reality religion can only be understood in the context of the incarnation of God the Son. For since redeemed existence means that through the intervention of God mankind itself is once more turned toward God in close communion of life with him, then the whole of mankind is already truly redeemed objectively in the man Jesus, as in its Head.

The foundation of all this is the incarnation. But this incarnation of God the Son is a reality which grows. It is not complete in a matter of a moment; for example, at Jesus' conception in Mary's womb or at his birth. The incarnation is not merely a Christmas event. To be man is a process of becoming man; Jesus' manhood grew throughout his earthly life, finding its completion in the supreme moments of the incarnation, his death, resurrection and exaltation. Only then is the incarnation fulfilled to the very end. And so we must say that the incarnation in the Son itself redeems us. This mystery of Christ or of redemption we can call, in its totality, a mystery of saving worship; a mystery of praise (the upward movement) and of salvation (the downward movement).

This ascending and descending dynamism pervades the whole human life of Jesus. For although Jesus in his earthly life was always the humiliated "Servant of God," he remained even in his humiliation the Son of God, the grace-abounding revelation of God.[54] And although in his glorification Christ can bestow grace in full measure, there too he remains a man who, in religious and filial[55] service, adores and honors the Father from whom he must receive all. Nonetheless we can trace a development in the course of the saving history of the mystery of Christ. By the fact that he became man, the Son of God is fundamentally already the Christ. But we must also realize that it was only upon his rising from the dead that, because of the love and obedience of his life, the Father *established* him absolutely as the Christ. We must look closely into this growth toward the fullness of redemption, for in it we are confronted with the mystery of Christ's life, which is this: The man Jesus, as "Servant of God," by his life of obedience and love on earth, even unto death, earned for us that grace of salvation which he, in glory with the Father, can himself as Lord and Christ, bestow upon us in abundance. This saving reality calls for the closest consideration, for in it we find the key to the sense of the sacramentality of the Church in its relation to the *Kyrios,* the risen and glorified Lord, and so also to the Holy Spirit.

[54] Therefore St. Thomas says repeatedly: ". . . thus by the power of his divinity his [Jesus'] actions bring salvation for us, seeing that they cause grace in us, both by merit and by a certain efficient causality." (S.T., III, q. 8, a. 1, ad 2.)

[55] There is no exact English translation of the word *Kinderlijk,* which for this author sums up what he has said of Christ's relation to his Father in his risen humanity, with all this implies. (Tr.)

VI. PIERRE TEILHARD DE CHARDIN*

The Universal Christ and the Great Communion[56]

* Teilhard de Chardin (1881–1955), French Jesuit, taught geology at the Institut Catholique in Paris, directed the National Geologic Survey of China and was director of the National Research Center of France. Teilhard, who called himself "a pilgrim of the future," has outlined in his *Phenomenon of Man* and his *Divine Milieu* a breathtaking conception of the process of evolution in which he offers a unified, synthesized view of all reality recapitulated in Christ.

The essence of Christianity consists in asking oneself that question, and in answering: "The Word Incarnate, Our Lord Jesus Christ."

Let us examine step by step how we can justify to ourselves this prodigious identification of the Son of Man and the divine milieu.

A first step, unquestionably, is to see the divine omnipresence in which we find ourselves plunged as *an omnipresence of action*. God enfolds us and penetrates us by creating and preserving us.

Now let us go a little further. Under what form, and with what end in view, has the Creator given us, and still preserves in us, the gift of participated being? Under the form of an essential aspiration toward Him — and with a view to the unhoped-for cleaving which is to make us one and the same complex thing with Him. The action by which God maintains us in the field of His presence is *a unitive transformation*.

Let us go further still. What is the supreme and complex reality for which the divine operation molds us? It is revealed to us by St. Paul and St. John. It is the quantitative repletion and the qualitative consummation of all things: it is the mysterious Pleroma,

in which the substantial *One* and the created *many* fuse without confusion in a *whole* which, without adding anything essential to God, will nevertheless be a sort of triumph and generalization of being.

At last we are nearing our goal. What is the active center, the living link, the organizing soul of the Pleroma? St. Paul, again, proclaims it with all his resounding voice: it is He in whom everything is reunited, and in whom all things are consummated — through whom the whole created edifice receives its consistency — Christ dead and risen *qui replet omnia, in quo omnia constant.*

And now let us link the first and last terms of this long series of identities. We shall then see with a wave of joy that *the divine omnipresence* translates itself within our universe by the network of the organizing forces of the total Christ. God exerts pressure, in us and upon us — through the intermediary of all the powers of heaven, earth and hell — only in the act of forming and consummating Christ who saves and suranimates the world. And since, in the course of this operation, Christ Himself does not act as a dead or passive point of convergence, but as a center of radiation for the energies which lead the universe back to God through His humanity,

[56] *The Divine Milieu* (New York: Harper and Row, 1960), pp. 99–104.

the layers of divine action finally come to us impregnated with His organic energies.

The divine milieu henceforward assumes for us the savor and the specific features which we desire. In it we recognise an omnipresence which acts upon us by assimilating us in it, *in unitate corporis Christi.* As a consequence of the Incarnation, the divine immensity has transformed itself for us into *the omnipresence of christification.* All the good that I can do *opus et operatio* is physically gathered in, by something of itself, into the reality of the consummated Christ. Everything I endure, with faith and love, by way of diminishment or death, makes me a little more closely an integral part of His mystical body. Quite specifically it is *Christ whom we make or whom we undergo in all things.* Not only *diligentibus omnia convertuntur in bonum* but, more clearly still, *convertuntur in Deum* and, quite explicitly, *convertuntur in Christum.*

Christ the Fulfillment of Natural Evolution[57]

To the Christian humanist — faithful in this to the most sure theology of the Incarnation — there is neither separation nor discordance, but coherent subordination, between the genesis of mankind in the world and the genesis of Christ in mankind through His Church. The two processes are inevitably linked in their structure, the second requiring the first as the matter upon which it descends in order to super-animate it. This view entirely respects the progressive effective concentration of human thought in an increasingly acute consciousness of its unitary destiny. But instead of the vague center of convergence envisaged as the ultimate end of this process of evolution, the personal and defined reality of the Word Incarnate, in which everything acquires substance, appears and takes its place.

Life for Man. Man for Christ. Christ for God.

*And to ensure the psychic continuity, at every phase, of this vast develop-*ment embracing myriads of elements strewn throughout the immensity of time, there is a single mechanism — education.

All the lines join together, complete themselves and merge. Everything becomes one whole.

Which brings us to this final summing up, wherein is revealed the gravity and unity, but also the complexity, of the seemingly humble task of the Christian educator:

a It is primarily through education that the process of biological heredity, which from the beginning has caused the world to rise to higher zones of consciousness, is furthered in a reflective form and in its social dimensions. The educator, as an instrument of Creation, should derive respect and ardor for his efforts from a profound, communicative sense of the developments already achieved or awaited by Nature. Every lesson he gives should express love for, and cause to be loved, all that is most irresistible and definitive in the conquests of Life.

b It is through education, by the progressive spread of common viewpoints and attitudes, that the slow

[57] T. de Chardin, *The Future of Man* (New York: Harper and Row, 1964), pp. 34–36, 304–305,

convergence of minds and hearts is proceeding, without which there seems to be no outlet ahead of us for the impulse of Life. Directly charged with the task of achieving this unanimity of mankind, the educator, whether his subject be literature, history, science or philosophy, must constantly live with it and consciously strive for its realization. A passionate faith in the purpose and splendor of human aspirations must be the flame that illuminates his teaching.

c Finally, it is through the medium of education that there ensues, directly and indirectly, the gradual incorporation of the World in the Word Incarnate: indirectly, in the degree in which the heart of a collective mankind increasingly turned inward upon itself is made ready for this high transformation; directly, to the extent that the tide of grace historically released by Jesus Christ is propagated only by being borne on a living tradition. But the teacher who seeks to be wholly effective in transmitting these two influences, the humanizing and the Divine, must be as it were overwhelmed by the evidence of their inseparable, structural relation. To have experienced and understood, in order to teach others to experience and understand, that all human enrichment is but dross except inasmuch as it becomes the most precious and incorruptible of all things by adding itself to an immortal center of love: such is the supreme knowledge and the ultimate lesson to be imparted by the Christian educator.

These three propositions complete a logical structure whose perfect harmony proclaims its truth. . . .

Incapable of being mingled or confounded with the participating being whom He sustains, inspires and links with Himself, God is at the birth, the growth and the ultimate end of all things. . . .

The unique business of the world is the physical incorporation of the faithful in Christ, who is of God. This major task is pursued with *the rigor and harmony of a natural process of evolution.* . . .

At its inception an operation of a transcendent order was required, grafting — in accordance with mysterious but physically regulated conditions — the Person of a Deity onto the Human Cosmos. . . .

Et Verbum caro factum est. That was the Incarnation. By this first and fundamental contact of God with our kind, by virtue of the penetration of the Divine into our nature, a new life was born, an unexpected enlargement and "obediential" prolongation of our natural capacities: Grace. Grace is the unique sap passing from a single trunk into the branches, blood flowing into the veins from the pumping of a single heart, nervous impulses reaching the limbs at the bidding of a single head; and the radiant Head, the powerful Heart, the fruitful Trunk, these are inevitably Christ. . . .

The Incarnation is a renewal and a restoration of all the forces and powers of the universe; Christ is the instrument, the center, the end of all animate and material Creation; by Him all things are created, sanctified, made alive. This is the constant and customary teaching of St. John and St. Paul (the most "cosmic" of the sacred writers), the teaching conveyed by the most solemn sentences of the Liturgy . . . but which we repeat, and which future generations will repeat to the end, though they cannot master or measure its mysterious and profound significance: it is bound up with the comprehension of the Universe.

From the commencement of things an advent of ploughing and harvesting began, in the course of which, gently and lovingly, the determinists reached out and moved toward the growing of a fruit that was beyond hope and yet awaited. So harmoniously adapted and arranged that the Supreme Transcendent might seem to be engendered wholly of their immanence, the energies and substances of the world concentrated and purified themselves in the stem of Jesse, composing of their distilled and accumulated riches the sparkling jewel of Matter, the pearl of the Cosmos and its link with the personal, incarnate Absolute: the blessed Virgin Mary, Queen and Mother of all things, the true Demeter. And when the day of the Virgin dawned, the profound and gratuitous finality of the Universe was suddenly revealed: from the day when the first breath of individualization, passing over the burgeoning supreme lower Center, caused the first monads within it to smile, everything moved toward the Child born of the Woman.

And since the time when Jesus was born, when He finished growing and died and rose again, *everything has continued to move because Christ has not yet completed His own forming.* He has not yet gathered in to Himself the last folds of the Garment of flesh and love which His disciples are making for him. *The mystical Christ has not yet attained His full growth.* In the Pursuance of this engendering is situated the ultimate spring of all created activity. . . . Christ is the Fulfillment even of the natural evolution of beings.

BIBLIOGRAPHY

GENERAL

Abbott, W. M., ed., *The Documents of Vatican II* (New York: America Press, 1966).

Altaner, Berthold, *Patrology* (New York: Herder and Herder, 1960).

Ante-Nicene Fathers, 24 vols. (Buffalo: Christian Literature, 1885–1896).

Barr, Robert R., *Main Currents in Early Christian Thought* (Glen Rock, N. J.: Paulist Press, 1966).

Bettenson, H., ed., *Documents of the Christian Church* (New York: Oxford University Press, 1963).

—— *The Early Christian Fathers* (New York: Oxford University Press, 1956).

Bindley, T. and F. Green, eds. *The Oecumenical Documents of the Faith* (London: Methuen and Co., Ltd., 1950).

Bouyer, Louis, *Dictionary of Theology* (New York: Desclée Co., 1965).

—— *The Spirituality of the New Testament and the Fathers* (New York: Desclée Co., 1963).

Clarkson, J., et al., *The Church Teaches: Documents of the Church in English Translation* (St. Louis: B. Herder Book Co., 1955).

Cozens, M. L., *A Handbook of Heresies* (New York: Sheed and Ward, 1959).

Denziger, H. J. D., *The Sources of Catholic Dogma* (St. Louis: B. Herder Book Co., 1957).

Dirksen, Aloys, *Elementary Patrology* (St. Louis: B. Herder Book Co., 1959).

Dorner, J. A., *History of the Development of the Doctrine of the Person of Christ* (Edinburgh: T. and T. Clark, 1862).

Eberhardt, Newman C., *A Summary of Catholic History* (St. Louis: B. Herder Book Co., 1959).

The Fathers of the Church, 72 vols., (New York: Christian Heritage, 1959).

Grillmeier, Aloys, *Christ in Christian Tradition* (New York: Sheed and Ward, 1965).

Hamman, H., *Early Christian Prayers* (Chicago: Henry Regnery Co., 1961).

A Handbook of Christian Theology (New York: Meridian Press, 1958).

Horden, William, *A Layman's Guide to Protestant Theology* (New York: Macmillan Co., 1955).

Henry, A. M., ed., *The Historical and Mystical Christ* (Chicago: Fides Publishers, 1958).

Kelly, J., *Early Christian Doctrine* (New York: Harper and Row, 1960).

Komroff, Manuel, *Jesus Through the Centuries* (New York, 1953).

Library of Christian Classics, 26 vols. (Philadelphia: Westminster Press).

MacKintosh, H. R., *Types of Modern Theology* (New York: Scribner and Sons, 1937).

McPhail, David, ed., *A Basic Bibliography for Ministers* (New York: Union Theological Seminary, 1960).

Nicene and Post-Nicene Fathers, 1st Series, 14 vols. (Buffalo: Christian Literature, 1886–1892; 2nd Series, 13 vols. (Buffalo: Christian Literature, 1890–1898).

Oxford Dictionary of the Christian Church (New York: Oxford University Press, 1957).

Peerman, D. G. and M. E. Marty, eds., *A Handbook of Christian Theologians* (New York: World Publishing Co., 1965).

Pohle-Preuss, *Christology* (St. Louis: B. Herder Book Co., 1922).

—— *Soteriology* (St. Louis: B. Herder Book Co., 1914).

Quasten, Johannes, *Patrology*, 3 vols. (Westminster, Md.: Newman Press, 1960).

Rahner, Karl, and Herbert Vorgrimler, *Theological Dictionary* (New York: Herder and Herder, 1965).

Reinisch, L., ed., *Theologians of our Time* (South Bend: University of Notre Dame Press, 1964).

Schaff, P., *Creeds of Christendom*, 3 vols.

(New York: Harper and Bros., 1931).

Toal, M. R., ed., *The Sunday Sermons of The Great Fathers* (Chicago: Henry Regnery Co., 1960).

van der Meer, F., *Atlas of the Early Christian World* (London: Nelson and Sons).

SELECTED

Adam, Karl, *The Christ of Faith* (New York: Pantheon, 1957; reprinted in a paperback edition, New York: Mentor Omega, 1962).

—— *The Son of God* (New York, 1940).

Anderson, H., *Jesus and Christian Origins* (New York, 1964).

Anselm, St., *Cur Deus Homo?* S. N. Deane, tr. (Chicago: The Open Court Publishing Co., 1939).

Athanasius, St., *The Incarnation of the Word of God* (New York: Macmillan Co., 1946).

Augustine, St., *St. Augustine: Letters*, W. Parsons, tr. (New York: Fathers of the Church, Inc., 1953).

—— *St. Augustine: The City of God*, 2 vols. (New York: Fathers of the Church, Inc., 1953).

—— *The Trinity*, S. McKenna, tr., (Washington: C.U.A. Press, 1963).

Baillie, D. M., *God Was in Christ* (New York: Scribner and Sons, 1848).

Barth, Karl, *Church Dogmatics* (New York: Scribner and Sons, 1936–1959).

—— *The Humanity of God* (Richmond, Va.: John Knox Press, 1960).

—— *Protestant Thought from Rousseau to Ritschl* (New York: Harper and Row, 1959).

Basil, St., *Letters*, 2 vols. (New York: Fathers of the Church, Inc., 1955).

Boethius, *The Theological Tractates*, Stewart and Rand, tr., (Cambridge: Harvard University Press, 1918).

Bonaventure, St., *Breviloquium*, E. E. Nemmers, tr. (St. Louis: B. Herder Book Co., 1946).

Bonnefoy, J.-F., *Christ and the Cosmos* (Paterson, N. J.: St. Anthony Guild Press, 1965).

Bowman, D., *The Word Made Flesh* (Englewood Cliffs, N. J.: Prentice-Hall, 1963).

Brunner, Emil, *Truth as Encounter* (Philadelphia: Westminster Press, 1964).

—— *Dogmatics* (Philadelphia: Westminster Press, 1950–1953).

Bultmann, Rudolph, *Kerygma and Myth* (New York: Harper and Brothers, 1961).

—— *Theology of the New Testament*, 2 vols. (London: S.C.M. Press, 1952).

—— *Jesus and the Word* (New York, 1934).

Calvin, John, *A Compendium of the Institutes of the Christian Religion*, H. T. Kerr, tr. ed., (Philadelphia: Westminster Press, 1938).

—— *Institutes*, J. Allen, tr. (Philadelphia: Westminster Press, 1960).

Carmody, J. and Clarke, T., *Christ and his Mission* (Westminster, Md.: Newman Press, 1966).

—— *Word and Redeemer* (Glen Rock, N. J.: Paulist Press, 1966).

Concilium, Vol. XI, *Who is Jesus of Nazareth?* (Glen Rock, N. J.: Paulist Press, 1966).

Cullmann, Oscar, *Christ and Time* (Philadelphia: Westminster Press, 1949).

—— *The Christology of the New Testament* (Philadelphia: Westminster Press, 1959).

Daniélou, Jean, *Christ and Us* (New York, 1962).

—— *The Lord of History* (Chicago: Henry Regnery Co., 1958).

De La Taille, M., *The Hypostatic Union and Created Actuation by Uncreated Act* (West Baden Springs, Ind., 1952).

Dewan, W. F., *The Person of Christ* (New York, 1962).

Durrwell, F. X. *The Resurrection: A Biblical Study* (New York, 1960).

Feiner, J., *et al.*, *Theology Today* (Milwaukee: The Bruce Publishing Co., 1964).

Fromm, Erich, *The Dogma of Christ* (New York: Holt, Rinehart and Winston, 1963).

Fuchs, E., *Studies of the Historical Jesus* (Naperville, Ill., 1964).

Fuller, Reginald H., *The Foundations of New Testament Christology* (New York: Charles Scribner's Sons, 1965).

Garrigou-Lagrange, R., *Christ the Savior* (St. Louis: B. Herder Book Co., 1950).

Glimm, et al., *The Apostolic Fathers* (New York: Cima Publishing Co., 1947).

Goguel, Maurice, *Jesus and the Origins of Christianity*, 2 vols. (New York: Harper Torchbooks, 1960).

Graham, Aelred, *The Christ of Catholicism* (New York, 1957).

Guardini, Romano, *The Humanity of Christ* (New York: Pantheon Books, 1964).

——— *The Lord* (Chicago: Henry Regnery Co., 1954).

Harnack, Adolf, *What is Christianity?* T. B. Saunders, tr. (New York: Harper Torchbooks, 1965).

Harvey, Van, *The Historian and the Believer* (New York: Macmillan, 1966).

Hegel, Friedrich, *On Christianity* (New York: Harper Torchbooks, 1948).

Henderson, Ian, *Paul Tillich* (Richmond, Va.: John Knox Press, 1966).

——— *Rudolph Bultmann* (Richmond, Va.: John Knox Press, 1966).

Herbert, A. G., *The Christ of Faith and the Jesus of History* (London, 1962).

Hitchcock, F. R. M., *Irenaeus: Against the Heresies* (London: S.P.C.K., 1916).

Kelly, J. N. D., *Early Christian Doctrines* (2nd ed.: London, 1960).

Knox, John, *Christ the Lord* (New York, 1958).

——— *The Church and the Reality of Christ* (New York, 1965).

Kopp, Joseph V., *Teilhard de Chardin: A New Synthesis of Evolution* (Glen Rock, N. J.: Paulist Press, 1964).

Kraft, H., *Early Christian Thinkers* (New York: Association Press, 1964).

Kramm, H. H., *The Theology of Martin Luther* (London: James Clarke, 1947).

Latourelle, René, *The Theology of Revelation* (Staten Island, N. Y.: Alba House Press, 1966).

Leclercq, J., *Christ and the Modern Conscience* (New York, 1961).

Luther, Martin, *Luther: Early Theological Works*, J. R. McCallom, tr. (Oxford: Basil Blackwell, 1948).

Luther, Martin, *Works of Martin Luther,* 6 vols. (Philadelphia: Muhlenberg Press, 1943).

McGiffert, A. C., *Protestant Thought before Kant* (New York: Harper and Brothers, 1961).

Mersch, E., *The Whole Christ* (Milwaukee: The Bruce Publishing Co., 1938).

Mouroux, Jean, *The Mystery of Time* (New York: Desclée Co., 1964).

Niebuhr, Reinhold, *Christ and Culture* (New York, 1951).

——— *The Nature and Destiny of Man* (New York: Charles Scribner's Sons, 1959).

Ogden, S. M., *Christ Without Myth* (New York, 1961).

Pius XI, Pope, *The Light of Truth: Encylical Letter Lux Veritatis* (Washington, D. C.: N.C.W.C., 1932).

——— *On Devotion to the Sacred Heart: Encyclical Letter Haurietis Aquas* (Washington, D. C.: N.C.W.C., 1956).

Pius XII, Pope, *Christ the Eternal King: Encyclical Letter Sempiternus Rex* (Washington, D. C.: N.C.W.C., 1951).

Rahner, Karl, *Theological Investigations I* (Baltimore: Helicon Press, 1961).

Riviere, J., *The Doctrine of the Atonement*, 2 vols. (B. Herder Book Co., 1909).

Robinson, John A. T., *Honest to God* (Philadelphia: Westminster Press, 1963).

Schillebeeckx, E., *Christ the Sacrament of the Encounter with God* (New York: Sheed and Ward, 1963).

Schleiermacher, Friedrich, *The Christian Faith* (Edinburgh: T. and T. Clark, 1960).

Sloyan, G. S., *Christ the Lord* (New York: Herder and Herder, 1962).

Strauss, David Friedrich, *Life of Christ* (London, 1846).

Teilhard de Chardin, Pierre, *The Divine Milieu* (New York: Harper and Row, 1960).

——— *The Future of Man* (New York: Harper and Row, 1964).

——— *The Phenomenon of Man* (New York: Harper Torchbooks, 1959).

Tertullian, *Tertullian: Apologetical Works* R. Arbesmann, *et. al.*, tr. (New York: Fathers of the Church, Inc., 1950).

Thomas Aquinas, St., *Summa Contra Gentiles: On the Truth of the Catholic Faith*, 5 vols. (Garden City, N. Y.: Hanover House, 1957).

——— *Summa Theologiae* (New York: McGraw Hill Book Co., 1963).

Tillich, Paul, *Systematic Theology*, 3 vols. (Chicago: University of Chicago Press, 1951–1957).

Tower, Bernard, *Teilhard de Chardin* (Richmond, Va.: John Knox Press, 1966).

Welch, Claude, ed., *God and Incarnation in Mid-nineteenth Century German Theology* (New York: Oxford University Press, 1965).

INDEX

221